CW00501765

Strange Power of Speech

Strange Power of Speech

Wordsworth, Coleridge, and Literary Possession

SUSAN EILENBERG

New York Oxford
OXFORD UNIVERSITY PRESS
1992

Oxford University Press

Oxford New York Toronto
Delhi Bombay Calcutta Madras Karachi
Petaling Jaya Singapore Hong Kong Tokyo
Nairobi Dar es Salaam Cape Town
Melbourne Auckland

and associated companies in
Berlin Ibadan

Published by Oxford University Press, Inc.
200 Madison Avenue, New York, New York 10016

Library of Congress Cataloging-in-Publication Data
Eilenberg, Susan, 1956–
Strange power of speech : Wordsworth, Coleridge, and literary possession / Susan Eilenberg.
p. cm. Includes bibliographical references and index.
ISBN 0-19-506856-4
1. Wordsworth, William, 1770–1850—Authorship. 2. Coleridge, Samuel Taylor, 1772–1834—Authorship. 3. Coleridge, Samuel Taylor, 1772–1834. Biographia literaria. 4. Wordsworth, William, 1770–1850. Lyrical ballads. 5. Authorship—Collaboration—History—19th century. 6. Copyright—Great Britain—History—19th century. I. Title.
PR5886.E45 1992 821'.709—dc20 91-25497

9 8 7 6 5 4 3 2 1

Printed in the United States of America
on acid-free paper

I am grateful to several publishers and editors for permission to quote from copyrighted works:

Samuel Taylor Coleridge, *Biographia Literaria*, edited by James Engell and Walter Jackson Bate. Copyright 1983 by Princeton University Press.

Samuel Taylor Coleridge, *Poetical Works*, edited by Ernest Hartley Coleridge. Copyright 1979 by Oxford University Press.

Collected Letters of Samuel Taylor Coleridge, edited by Earl Leslie Griggs. Copyright 1956 and 1959 by Oxford University Press.

Letters of William and Dorothy Wordsworth, edited by Ernest De Selincourt, revised by Chester L. Shaver, Mary Moorman, and Alan G. Hill. 2nd edition. Copyright 1967–1982 by Oxford University Press.

Lyrical Ballads (1798), edited by W.J.B. Owen. 2nd edition. Copyright 1969 by Oxford University Press.

Lyrical Ballads: The Text of the 1798 Edition with the Additional 1800 Poems and the Prefaces, edited by R. L. Brett and A. R. Jones. Copyright 1963 by Routledge.

The Poetical Works of William Wordsworth, edited by Ernest De Selincourt and Helen Darbishire. Copyright 1940–1947 by Oxford University Press.

The Prose Works of William Wordsworth, edited by W. J. B. Owen and Jane Worthington Smyser. Copyright 1974 by Oxford University Press.

F.W.J. Schelling, *System of Transcendental Idealism (1800)*, translated by Peter Heath. Copyright 1978 University Press of Virginia.

For my parents

Preface

The subject of this book is the relationship between tropes of literary property and signification in the writings and literary politics of Wordsworth and Coleridge. I argue that a complex of ideas about property, propriety, and possession informs the images of literary authority, textual identity, and poetic figuration to be found in much of the two writers' major work. During the period of their closest collaboration as well as at points later in their careers, Wordsworth and Coleridge took as their primary material the images of property and propriety upon which definitions of meaning and figuration have traditionally depended, grounding these images in writings about landed and spiritual property, material and intellectual theft, dispossession by creditors and possession by demons. The writings and the politics generated by the literalization of such images can be read as allegorical of the structures and processes of signification. Each such gesture, each such trope, addresses in some way the fundamental question, Who owns language? or, Who controls meaning? What follows is an attempt to understand what was at stake in the analogy between the literary and the material or the verbal and the economic.

Neither Wordsworth nor Coleridge owned the meaning even of the terms that intrigued them. What Wordsworth treated as a matter of real property, the ownership of tangible or tangibly valued goods, Coleridge interpreted as a matter of spiritual possession, the usurpation of one identity by another. When Wordsworth talked about land, Coleridge talked about ventriloquism; when Wordsworth talked about contracts, Coleridge talked about psychic possession. Wordsworth treated Coleridge's writings like unappropriated properties; Coleridge treated Wordsworth's like possessing demons. Neither poet could leave the other's material alone. Each revised, refigured, and reinterpreted the other's primary images in terms of his own. Their attempts at mutual appropriation and possession dramatized the complex meanings of the terms the poets sought to control, generating two competing versions of literary history and intertextuality, each interpreting the status of its own body of writings and reflecting upon its relation to the other.

The two languages (dialects, really) reflect the characters with which we are so familiar: Wordsworth the self-possessed realist, proud of his writings and eager to establish their value in their world; Coleridge the self-doubting parasite, writing, as he lives, in the margins of other men's texts and other men's lives. What Wordsworth believes in—the naturalness, expressiveness, and substantiality of words—Coleridge doubts; where Wordsworth's words take their place in the world of material objects and matters of fact whose indubitable integrity and self-presence they seem to share, Coleridge's words live a ghostly existence in exile from both stable subjects and stable objects, unsure of their relation to things in themselves and liable to semiotic subversion and invasion.

And yet, despite their differences, these two languages inhabit and describe what is acknowledged to be a common body of poetry. Both poetic dialects seem to confess their part in this greater common text to which neither one can lay undisputed claim. Wordsworth's talk of poetry as property suggests not only the power of his writing to incorporate into itself alien material, to appropriate a site, or *topos,* not originally its own, but also its liability to be thus incorporated or compromised itself, to be made vulnerable to alienation or loss. And though Coleridge's hints about the demonic nature of language suggest principally his sense of the uncanniness of writing, they suggest as well his awareness, akin to Wordsworth's, of the more disturbing aspects of poetic incorporation. As different as they seem to be, the two languages can thus be seen to derive from shared concerns about the meaning of the poets' collaboration and the significance of the textual boundaries their poetry surveyed and transgressed.

Taking each vocabulary to be motivated by aggressive designs upon the other and upon the reader, I am hesitant to accept either entirely at its word and grant it interpretive authority over the joint work. So although Wordsworth's writing, with its appeal to historical and material realities, would seem to call for a materialist or new historical reading, and Coleridge's work, with its evocation of demonic possession, might seem to require a psychoanalytic or even perhaps a theological interpretation, neither approach by itself (even supposing that a text has the authority to dictate the method of its own interpretation) is entirely suited to read the poems in their most immediate context: the structure and composition of the *Lyrical Ballads*. Moreover, if I am right in supposing that both Wordsworth's "property" and Coleridge's "possession" figure the same primarily literary problem, then to privilege either the historicist or the psychoanalytic approach would be to mistake the nature of the poems' significance and implicitly to grant primacy to one set of tropes or the other.

What makes it difficult to adhere to such a principle is that the texts themselves, enacting what they narrate, tend to blur the distinction between the merely literary and the real. These writings deny their own fictionality and realize their own tropes. When a text commits a theft, or colludes in its own dispossession, or even proclaims itself a material commodity and fetches a real price, it becomes foolhardy to persist in one's conviction that its talk of economics can be understood apart from the economics of the world around it. But it is equally dangerous to forget that what that text's worldly behavior amounts to is self-interpretation at the level of the signifier: its economics, practical or compelling as it may be, is a way of talking about the status of language in the material world and the constitution of the poem in its intertextual relations. It is a literary allegory and not a social explanation.

Individual aspects of the Wordsworth-Coleridge relationship and the problems it generates have long been under study. Stephen Parrish, Thomas McFarland, Lucy Newlyn, and Paul Magnuson have done the most, perhaps, to piece together the details of the poets' collaboration on a common body of poetry.[1] Paul Magnuson has recently described this corpus as a conversation or a lyric dialogue, making a strong case for the necessity of seeking significance in context. "Reading only Coleridge's poetry or only Wordsworth's is somewhat like listening to half a telephone conversation," Magnuson observes. "One gets the general drift of what is being said but misses the particular references and the subtleties of the dialogue."[2] Quite so. And yet, though Magnuson acknowledges the variety and intricacy of forms this dialogue could take, the conversational analogy fails to evoke the sheer strangeness of the vocal phenomenon the two poets somehow generated. For as often as not the poets speak not in rational alternation, or even in irrational alternation, but at once, even through one another's words; so that, listening to them, we cannot always be sure how many voices we are hearing. Thomas McFarland's symbiotic model of the relationship between the two poets—a symbiosis evident not just in their literary but also in their personal relations—may seem to come closer, in principle if not in practice, to accounting for the intensity of the two poets' mutual vocal dependence. But Magnuson is wary of the psychologizing McFarland's model requires. And perhaps his caution is well-founded. The collaboration we all study is, of course, shaped by the social and psychological cirumstances of two individual men, but the dynamic itself is in some sense independent of either of them, as we see when we look at the work they produced once their collaboration had ended. Wordsworth continued to regard his writings in terms of property, and Coleridge continued to regard his writings in terms of possession. Each positions himself in relation to an Other whose place a Wordsworth or a Coleridge may temporarily occupy, but the Other remains after the old friend and colleague is gone, an abstract possibility inherent in writing itself.

I am grateful for the work of those who have so thoroughly and scrupulously mapped the course of the poets' mutual borrowings. I find myself returning even more often, however, to a different sort of scholarship. The influence of Harold Bloom's conceptions of internalization and intertextuality should be everywhere evident.[3] Equally important to me are a number of works devoted to an analysis of the nostalgia, mourning, envy, and resentment romantic language exhibits towards the material world. These writings have formed my understanding of what is at stake in the analogy between literature and the objects of its reference. I am thinking particularly of Paul de Man's "Intentional Structure of the Romantic Image," "The Rhetoric of Temporality," and "Autobiography as De-Facement,"[4] as well as Geoffrey Hartman's work on what one of his titles calls "The Unremarkable Wordsworth": the matter-of-fact poet with a "touching compulsion" to inscribe his words on the material landscape and thus bind the apocalyptic power of imagination to nature.[5] Thomas Weiskel's remarks on Wordsworth's resistance to reading, Frances Ferguson's analysis of the *Essays upon Epitaphs,* and Cynthia Chase's work on Wordsworthian literalness represent valuable developments in the way we understand the phenomena de Man and Hartman opened to study.[6] Most of this work has to do primarily with Wordsworth; comparable studies of Coleridge, for whom other men's writings represented what nature (or what was so denominated) represented for Wordsworth, have been somewhat fewer but no less fine. Chief among these is Jerome Christensen's brilliant study of Coleridge's prose, which uses Coleridge's fascination with associationism to make sense of his "marginal method" and to connect the plagiarisms with his ambivalence towards the place of language in the material world. To Christensen's unpacking of the unstable synonymy of property and propriety I am particularly indebted.[7]

For me as for most of these critics, materiality—the materiality romantic poems may at times seem to emulate—figures as a symptom of literary self-consciousness, a trope rather than an autonomous fact. It is this sense that literature is fundamentally divided from the material world that distinguishes my project from that of others whose work may look in some ways similar to mine. Jerome McGann, David Simpson, and Marjorie Levinson work from the assumption that the production and interpretation of literature are determined by social forces whose existence the poetry and many of its readers deny. Alan Liu's massive new study of Wordsworth, an interpretation of the displacement of history by landscape and the mechanisms by which Wordsworth converted theft and ruin to poetic gifts and riches, traces provocatively the "stain" of material referentiality in a poetry uneasy about its own denials.[8] Like deconstructive and psychoanalytic critics, the new historicists speak of displacement and repression, and they regard their task as that of recovering the objects of this repression. For the new historicists, this means recovering not only social and economic relations but also the purpose and mechanisms of their repression; for the psychoanalysts and deconstructionists, it means recovering not only supplements and repressed ideas but also the structure of their deferral or forgetting. What the materialists deplore as an effect of ideology, a social flaw with a social solution, the deconstructionists and psychoanalysts regard as a manifestation of allegory or consciousness and as irremediable because constitutive of language and the speaking subject.

It is impossible not to admire much that the materialist critics have accomplished and not to appreciate the freshness and light they have brought to their analyses of romantic poetry. I cannot, however, bring myself to share their convictions about the fundamentally social or economic constitution of meaning. For the purposes of this study, tropes, even economic ones, are only tropes and matter by virtue of their tropical interplay. My concern to preserve this emphasis upon the formalist means that my obligations to the methods and criticism of the materialists are outweighed by my obligations to the work of such men as Marc Shell and Kurt Heinzelman, who have written about economics as a formal analogue to language rather than its ultimate meaning.[9] In economics, a system regulating the commensurability of the incommensurable, any value can be expressed in terms of any other value and all terms are equally tropical: monetary transactions take the form of metalepsis; barter takes the form of metaphor. It is not surprising, then, that as Shell and Heinzelman have shown, representations of economic themes or structures within a literary work express that work's consciousness of its own condition.

This book makes no attempt at exhaustive historical or canonical coverage. It omits far more than it covers, and the intertextual connections it develops are only incidentally causal or even chronological. What I study I study for the sake of its power to illuminate with especial vividness the imaginative structures that underlay Wordsworth's and Coleridge's writings both during the period of actual collaboration and afterwards.

The first and larger part of the book is devoted to readings of poems written originally for the first two editions of the *Lyrical Ballads*. The collection, the most complex of the poets' completed collaborative projects, matters to my study not just because of its remarkable contents but because of its formal and thematic self-consciousness. Given the poems' striking preoccupation with issues of property both common and enclosed, the fact of their publication precisely as a collection, their sharing (and resistance to sharing) of a common bounded textual space, shows in the light of a formal statement. The poems' mutual refigurations and reconfigurations and the revision and reappropriation of the first edition by the second provide wonderful examples of the ways in which the poets' editorial politics reflected their changing and divergent attitudes toward authority, naming, and signification.

The second part of the book is concerned with showing the development of these attitudes later in the poets' lives, after their friendship and collaboration had ended. The subjects of this section, Coleridge's *Biographia Literaria* and Wordsworth's involvement in the politics of copyright reform, reflect a continuing, troublesome, but still fruitful anxiety about the problem I see as central to the earlier *Lyrical Ballads:* what it means to claim a property in writing.

Chapter 1 provides an introduction to the problems posed by the relationship between the first two editions of the *Lyrical Ballads,* first published anonymously as a single volume in 1798, then in two volumes under Wordsworth's name in 1800. A reading of the title pages and their implications opens a discussion of the two poets' conceptions of literary property and literary propriety, concepts whose ancient and paradoxical associations determine the development of rhetorical theory and influence the poetics of the *Lyrical Ballads.*

Chapter 2 takes as its focus *The Rime of the Ancient Mariner,* that poem whose composition gave rise to the collaborative project that was to become the *Lyrical Ballads.* I read the *Rime* as an allegory of its own anonymity and an explication of the impropriety of its relations to language and voice. Its self-quoting, self-propagating structure, the formal counterpart to its obsessive thematic concerns with ventriloquy and possession, reflects an uneasiness about its nearest sources, failed collaborative projects themselves embarrassed by narrative improprieties. The *Rime,* I argue, is the first major text in which Coleridge confronts the uncanny autonomy of the imagination.

Wordsworth's response to the *Rime* and the threat it posed came two years later in the form of the second volume to the *Lyrical Ballads.* The new volume, marked with Wordsworth's name, manifests a new interest in appropriation, particularly literary appropriation. Property, which had been a subtheme of many of the 1798 poems, is here a dominant theme. The composition of the volume makes it clear that, having begun to think of his poems as properties, Wordsworth had begun too to think of property as an embodiment of poetic voice. Chapter 3 discusses the "Poems on the Naming of Places" as a series of attempts to work through the implications of this identification. While the place-naming poems make a show of naming previously unappropriated lands for the poet's friends, it becomes apparent that the poet is more deeply interested in the imaginative appropriation implicit in the act of naming. Chapter 4 analyzes the implications of Wordsworth's decision to remove Coleridge's "Christabel," written originally to stand at the end of the new second volume, and replace it with his own "Michael." I argue that "Michael"'s interest in property and dispossession reflects upon its relationship to the poem whose place in the volume and whose subject matter—vocal and spiritual possession—Wordsworth's composition appropriates for its own.

The subject of Chapter 5 is Wordsworth's involvement in the "Lucy" poems with a typically Coleridgean phenomenon: the usurpation of voice by its own unacknowledged tropes. Mourning the death of his beloved, the poet finds himself in elegiac competition with an uncanny image or voice, a mirror-figure or proleptic echo that doubles both himself and Lucy. The poet's efforts to mourn drive him to compose poem after poem, a group that resists grouping and enacts in its internal relations the same strategies of amnesia and displacement that structure each of the individual poems.

The next two chapters discuss the paradoxes of Coleridge's *Biographia Literaria,* an autobiography usurped upon by the alien voices of those Coleridge plagiarized and admired. Chapter 6 discusses the plagiarisms in the context of Coleridge's borrowed argument about the relationship between the I AM and the IT IS and considers what it can mean that a man should write his autobiography using another man's voice. Chapter 7 analyzes Coleridge's analysis of the principles behind poetic language generally and Wordsworth's poetry in particular, arguing that Coleridge's criticisms of the poetry he identified as supremely imaginative suggest his understanding of the uncanniness not just of Wordsworth's poetry but of imagination itself.

The final chapter takes as its subject Wordsworth's fascination with copyright as a system of laws that realized in legal terms his own desire to ground poetry in property, the figurative in the literal, and words in things.

At various stages along the way, many people—friends, colleagues, and teachers—have given me aid of several kinds. For their encouragement and their apt admonishment, for their patience and their impatience, I would like to thank Anne Badger, Leslie Brisman, Jill Campbell, Wai-chee Dimock, Margie Ferguson, Steve Fleischer, Jonathan Freedman, Paul Fry, Geoffrey Hartman, John Hollander, Margaret Homans, Stacy Hubbard, Sam Kassow, Jim McKusick, Stuart Moulthrop, Fred See, and Gordon Turnbull. I am grateful too to Paul Magnuson, who gave the manuscript a generous reading and offered valuable suggestions for revision. A Whiting Foundation Fellowship gave me time to think at an early stage in the project, and a grant from the Research Development Foundation of the State of New York helped me keep up with the price of books and photocopying later on.

Parts of Chapter 4 appeared in *Essays in Literature,* volume 15, no. 1 (Spring, 1988), and in *Criticism,* volume 30 (1988). Chapter 8 was published originally in *ELH,* volume 56 (1989). I am grateful for permission to reprint these essays here.

Buffalo, New York S. E.
May, 1991

Contents

Frequently Cited Texts

BL	*Biographia Literaria, Or Biographical Sketches of My Literary Life and Opinions*. Edited by James Engell and Walter Jackson Bate. Princeton: Princeton University Press, 1983.
CPW	*The Poetical Works of Samuel Taylor Coleridge*. Edited by Ernest Hartley Coleridge. 2 vols. 1912; rpt. Oxford: Clarendon Press, 1979.
EY	*The Letters of William and Dorothy Wordsworth: The Early Years, 1787–1805*. Edited by Ernest De Selincourt, revised by Chester Shaver. Oxford: Clarendon Press, 1967.
LY	*The Letters of William and Dorothy Wordsworth: The Later Years. Part I, 1821–1828; Part II, 1829–1834; Part III, 1835–1839*. Edited by Ernest De Selincourt, revised by Alan G. Hill. Oxford: Clarendon Press, 1976–1982.
MY	*The Letters of William and Dorothy Wordsworth: The Middle Years. Part I, 1801–1811*. Edited by Ernest De Selincourt, revised by Mary Moorman. *Part II, 1812–1820*. Edited by Ernest De Selincourt, revised by Mary Moorman and Alan G. Hill. Oxford: Clarendon Press, 1969, 1970.
Prose Works	*The Prose Works of William Wordsworth*. Edited by W.J.B. Owen and Jane Worthington Smyser. 3 vols. Oxford: Clarendon Press, 1974.
STCL	*Collected Letters of Samuel Taylor Coleridge*. Edited by Earl Leslie Griggs. 6 vols. Oxford: Clarendon Press, 1956–1971.

STCN — *The Notebooks of Samuel Taylor Coleridge*. Edited by Kathleen Coburn. 3 vols. Princeton: Princeton University Press, 1957–1973.

WPW — *The Poetical Works of William Wordsworth*. Edited by Ernest De Selincourt and Helen Darbishire. 5 vols. 1940–1949; rpt. Oxford: Clarendon Press, 1952–1959.

I

The *Lyrical Ballads*: Imagination's Entitlement

1

The Propriety of the *Lyrical Ballads*

My subject is what happens when a poet opens his mouth and somebody else's voice comes out. Sometimes we call this inspiration, but the effect is more ambiguous than that term suggests. Both Wordsworth and Coleridge suffered attacks of ventriloquism, or possession by apparently alien voices. Their endurance of these vocal visitations led to some of their greatest and, paradoxically, most characteristic work.

The phenomenon raises serious questions about the source of poetic voice and the meaning of authorship. Others have described the problem variously in terms of irony and influence, but I am interested in an approach that will show irony and influence to be aspects of a single more broadly defined problem. Because of the diversity of its manifestations—stylistic incongruity, reductive literalness, plagiarism, uncontrollable reiteration—it is hard to know what to call it, but it answers most readily to questions phrased in terms of property and possession. Does voice originate in the poet who speaks it? If poetic voice is property, what rights of ownership does a poet have? What does it mean when a poet treats his voice as if it belonged to someone else, or to no one at all?

Such questions would have occurred immediately to anyone who happened to pick up a copy of the *Lyrical Ballads* when it first appeared—anonymously—in 1798. Whose poems were these? The appearance of Wordsworth's name on the two-volume second edition two years later would have addressed that innocent and pressing question, but the contents of the new second volume might have suggested that the poet had been thinking harder about the matter than its apparent simplicity would seem to warrant. For the volume was filled with poems about naming and property and the power of names to create property. But while the presence of Wordsworth's name on the title page seemed to indicate that the poems belonged to him, the preface admitted that the name on the title page was not an undisputed title of ownership: someone whom Wordsworth would not name had a competing stake in the volume.

By 1800 the cooperative venture between Wordsworth and Coleridge that had generated the first *Lyrical Ballads* had become a source of anxiety and an occasion of rivalry. The new edition was not so much a collaboration between the two poets as a somewhat anxious celebration of the appropriative power of Wordsworth's voice. In the course of this celebration Coleridge—who had been writing what Wordsworth regarded as unsuitable poems, and writing too few even of those—was dispossessed of his property in the volume. The disturbingly anonymous *Ancient Mariner,* which had appeared at the head of the 1798 volume, was removed to a position of disgrace toward the rear of the first volume and tagged with Wordsworth's official disclaimer. "Christabel," a poem in which one figure steals another figure's voice, was suddenly and inexplicably dropped from the second volume. A Wordsworth poem about property and dispossession took its place.

Wordsworth explained his growing reservations about the collaborative effort and his attempts to remove Coleridge's poems from the *Lyrical Ballads* by saying their poems were too different and did not belong in the same work. It is indeed a continuing surprise to remember that *The Rime of the Ancient Mariner* was published in the same volume with "Expostulation and Reply," and Coleridge's later description of the division of labor that went into the *Lyrical Ballads* does indeed suggest an attempt to rationalize a project founded upon irreconcilable differences.[1] But was the problem really that their styles and aims were too different? Or was it rather that they were too alike—that each gave the other away?

The collaboration had failed partly because it really *had* failed but partly also because it had succeeded. Together, Wordsworth and Coleridge had achieved the creation of a voice, audible not just in the *Lyrical Ballads* but in the conversation poems, parts of the *Prelude,* and the great odes, that belonged properly to neither of them and to both. One effect of the collaboration was thus to undermine the propriety of poetic voice, that which creates an illusion of a single stable human identity behind the voice issuing from its mouth and guarantees the creator of that voice an exclusive property in it. On some level both poets recognized this. But while Coleridge embraced the implications of what they had done, Wordsworth fought them.

The 1800 *Lyrical Ballads,* together with its Coleridgean exclusions, can be read as an extended argument about propriety, a concept whose meanings and values the two poets—like that famous couple, Jack Sprat and his wife—divided between them. Its division produced two sets of images and tropes. One, which Wordsworth claimed, had to do with the integrity of human character and the solidity and significance of the material world. Its subjects were property and minor matters of fact, and its style was, at least apparently, as literal as possible. The other half of the set, Coleridge's lot, had to do with the artificiality and instability of character and language. Its subjects were demonic possession and dispossession, and its style was ostensibly allegorical.[2]

This imperfect division determined not just the character of the poems each poet would write but also the nature of their intertextual relations. Wordsworth's poems of property express a consciousness of writing as an act of appropriation;[3] Coleridge's poems of demonic possession (which haunt the property Wordsworth wished to claim) express an apprehension of imagination as usurpation or loss of identity. Each body of writing thus aggressively allegorizes the other. Wordsworth seeks to prove that Coleridge's "possession" really means "property"; Coleridge, to prove that Wordsworth's "property" really means "possession." Wordsworth demystifies the Coleridgean uncanny; Coleridge deconstructs the Wordsworthian matter-of-fact.[4] The *Lyrical Ballads* enact within and upon themselves the processes of possession and dispossession that they discuss.

The edition of 1800 was not merely an expansion of the edition of 1798; it was also, in part, a retraction or repression of that edition and a Wordsworthian reappropriation of what had been.

assumed to be the common conceptual and poetic ground it stood upon.[5] Much of the new second volume can be read in terms of the containment, domestication, or denial of what seem now to be the troubling implications of the blank spot on the original title page—for that blank spot provoked questions about authorship and ownership that reference to matters of biographical or legal fact did not suffice to answer and that Wordsworth especially had begun to find threatening. The addition of his name to the title page of the 1800 edition was at best an imperfect response to the problem the 1798 edition had come to represent: in naming himself as author of the *Lyrical Ballads,* Wordsworth emphasized the connection between the anonymity he had originally chosen and the taint of an impropriety from which he now wanted to dissociate himself; in keeping Coleridge's name obscure, he maintained the anonymity of the most profoundly and, to Wordsworth, objectionably anonymous pages in the entire work. His act of self-nomination, compulsively elaborated in the structure and contents of the new edition, had the effect of explicating the decision it was meant to annul.

The anonymity of the original volume of the *Lyrical Ballads* would be no issue for us if Wordsworth had not made it one. Though not as prevalent as it had been in earlier periods,[6] anonymous publication was no uncommon thing in 1798. Sometimes, as when political, satirical, or theological works were in question, the decision to publish anonymously was a matter of simple expediency. But pragmatic considerations do little to explain the "peculiar fascination"[7] of the phenomenon, which could bestow upon otherwise unremarkable works an authority both enigmatic and oracular. Whatever the "peculiar fascination" consisted of, it was sufficiently powerful to block authorial acknowledgement of some extremely popular works.[8]

What motivated Wordsworth and Coleridge to publish the *Lyrical Ballads* anonymously is unclear. Their own explanations sound a little disingenuous. They plead their love of "privacy and quiet"[9] and they resolve to acknowledge nothing but their major works;[10] they represent themselves as too obscure or too notorious to find favor with the reading public. So Coleridge wrote to Joseph Cottle:

> As to anonymous Publications, depend on it, you are deceived.—Wordsworth's name is nothing—to a large number of persons[11] mine *stinks*—The Essay on Man, Darwin's Botanic Garden, the Pleasures of memory, & many other most popular works were published anonymously.[12]

Coleridge professed to fear that politically conservative readers would refuse to buy the book if they knew that he and Wordsworth, known Jacobins, were behind it.[13] But he had a hard time convincing the publishers,[14] who seem to have been skeptical about these dangers and doubtful of the necessity of such secrecy. It is easy to see the reasons for their doubt: both Wordsworth and Coleridge had published under their own names before, both of them safely and Coleridge with gratifying results. Indeed, as H. W. Garrod argues, what success the *Lyrical Ballads* enjoyed may have been due to the public's belief that the volume was Coleridge's.[15] For a time even Wordsworth seems to have taken some such view of the matter. "Take no pains to contradict the story that the L. B. are entirely yours," he wrote at the end of 1799. "Such a rumour is the best thing that can befall them."[16]

The poets abandoned their attachment to the idea of anonymity only in September of 1800, when they discovered that the poet Perdita Robinson was planning to publish with Longman (Wordsworth and Coleridge's own publisher) a work to be entitled *Lyrical Tales*. The similarity of this title to their own and the thought of the possibilities for confusion disturbed them. Dorothy Wordsworth reports that for a time her brother intended to drop both their title and his anonymity and present the poems simply as *Poems by W. Wordsworth.*[17] This suggests that by 1800 Wordsworth, at least, may not have valued highly either his own anonymity or the original title; he could, after all, have considered keeping the title but adding his name and Coleridge's to the title page. It suggests too that although Wordsworth was willing to leave his own name off the poems, he had no intention of letting his readers credit them to someone else. Anonymity was one thing, false attribution another: to allow the public to believe the achievement was another poet's would be to sacrifice not only his proprietary interest in the volume but also his ambition to speak in the voice of the people, the voice of the lyrically impersonal *ballad.* At any rate, by this time there seems to have been no question of printing the poems under Coleridge's name, even to protect them from Perdita Robinson's.

Despite the collaborative origins of the project and Coleridge's ongoing efforts to help get the poems published, it had become clear that the volumes were now Wordsworth's property and that his poetics would determine the character of the work. Dorothy of course had always spoken of the *Lyrical Ballads* as "William's poems." By the time the matter of the title page had been decided, Coleridge had begun to speak of the volumes in the same way. He allowed Wordsworth to treat his poetic contributions as so much verbal lumber, matter worth no more than to be apologized for, censured, thrust into the dim corners of the collection, or even thrown out of the volumes altogether.

The remarkable feature of all this is not that Coleridge should have given way before the energy of Wordsworth's imperialistic design but that Wordsworth should have allowed Coleridge to retain even a minor and uneasy place in it. But Wordsworth was not yet ready to launch upon the world a volume of *Poems by W. Wordsworth;* he required Coleridge as both prop and scapegoat to his endeavor. If collaboration produced much of what is best in the first volume, rivalry and repression produced much of what is most valuable in the second. The 1800 edition of *Lyrical Ballads* simultaneously draws upon and repudiates Coleridge and the fruitful relationship he represented; it can be read both as an acknowledgment of debt and as a proclamation of autonomy.

Wordsworth seems to have suspected that what enabled him to inscribe his name on the title page—his relationship with Coleridge—may have undermined the integrity of his signature.[18] In the preface to the 1800 edition he admits rather uneasily that not everything in the *Lyrical Ballads* is his own. The reasons he gives for including the poems from which he so carefully dissociates himself suggest a reluctance to confront the real differences that lay between him and his friend:

> For the sake of variety and from a consciousness of my own weakness I was induced to request the assistance of a Friend, who furnished me

> with the Poems of the ANCIENT MARINER, the FOSTER-MOTHER'S TALE, the NIGHTINGALE, the DUNGEON, and the Poem entitled LOVE. I should not, however, have requested this assistance, had I not believed that the poems of my Friend would in a great measure have the same tendency as my own, and that, though there would be found a difference, there would be found no discordance in the colours of our style; as our opinions on the subject of poetry do almost entirely coincide.[19]

This paragraph graciously reinterprets the origins of the *Lyrical Ballads* and continues the simplification or streamlining of poetic intent that the 1798 "Advertisement" began. What was in reality an almost accidental conjugation of poems becomes a program of poetry; what was in reality a communal inception becomes an individual one. According to this version, the "Friend" did not work with Wordsworth as an equal partner but was invited to assist in a limited way, and his conceptions about poetry did not help shape Wordsworth's but followed in the direction of Wordsworth's lead.

Both in the preface and in his adjustments to the contents of the new edition, what Wordsworth stresses is decorum—poetic propriety. Propriety dictates his principal editorial decisions about the volumes, even those, such as his handling of *The Ancient Mariner,* that may strike us as most improper. When Wordsworth engineered the disgrace of *The Rime of the Ancient Mariner* or the ouster of "Christabel," he was principally motivated neither by malice nor by financial pragmatism; his treatment of Coleridge's materials bespeaks instead concern to preserve harmony among the pieces in the collection. Such, at least, was Coleridge's explanation of the matter. This is what he wrote to Humphry Davy a few days after the decision to exclude his poem:

> The Christabel was running up to 1300 lines—and was so much admired by Wordsworth, that he thought it indelicate to print two Volumes with *his name* in which so much of another man's was included—& which was of more consequence—the poem was in direct opposition to the very purpose for which the *Lyrical Ballads* were published—viz—an experiment to see how far those passions which alone give any value to extraordinary Incidents, were capable of interesting, in & for themselves, in the incidents of common life.[20]

But these remarks explain less than they pretend to do. If Wordsworth felt squeamish at the thought of printing another man's poems under his own name, his delicacy might have been more delicately soothed by the addition of Coleridge's name to the title page. The purpose of the anonymity was in any case destroyed by this time; people had been guessing that Coleridge was involved in the first edition, and if they had not already guessed that Wordsworth was involved too, they would know now. We may mistrust as well Coleridge's explanation about "Christabel"'s supposed violation of the principles of the *Lyrical Ballads*. Had those principles been binding, the *Rime,* that poem which in convenient hindsight appeared to both poets to have been the germ of what became the *Lyrical Ballads,* would have been expelled along with "Christabel."

What is really at stake is more clearly revealed in Wordsworth's own explanation to his publisher: "A Poem of Mr Coleridge's was to have concluded the Volumes; but upon mature deliberation, I found that the Style of this Poem was so discordant from my own that it could not be printed along with my poems with any propriety."[21] We know from remarks he made elsewhere that Wordsworth's aversion to stylistic discord was very real. In the preface to the *Lyrical Ballads* he takes care to assure the reader that he has not yoked together incongruities. He announces and reiterates his desire to avoid any "incongruity which would shock the intelligent Reader"[22] by mixing an artificial poetic style with the realer language of men. He will shock the reader instead with genuine propriety, with poems written in real language and according to real passions. And although incongruity is an evil, variety and mixture are delightful, for among the chief aesthetic pleasures is "the pleasure which the mind derives from the perception of similitude in dissimilitude." Hence the *Lyrical Ballads* are really *Lyrical Ballads with a Few Other Poems.* Why then could "Christabel" not be counted among the "Few Other Poems"? What in the name of "propriety" does its exclusion signify?

In appealing to "propriety," Wordsworth seems to have been thinking about the two senses of the concept whose recent "desynonimization" Coleridge was fond of remarking: propriety as decorum and propriety as property.[23] He was appealing to an entire complex—or chaos, perhaps—of ideas having to do with truth, aesthetics, representation, and power, a few of whose chief points the critic John Hughes had summarized a century earlier:

> Propriety of Thoughts is two-fold; the first is when the Thoughts are proper in themselves, and so it is opposed to Nonsense; and the other is when they are proper to the Occasion, and so it is opposed to Impertinence. Propriety of Words, the first Qualification of a good Style, is when the Words do justly and exactly represent, or signify, the Thoughts which they stand for.[24]

This propriety of words, Hughes goes on to say, is to be sought not in etymological researches but in "the conversation of People of Fashion, that speak well and without Affectation." It is, alas, a circular definition: propriety is, like fashion, something one will find in those who are known to possess it. We recognize it by its effect upon us, by the very sense of acknowledgment it creates.

From the beginning propriety had to do, like the rest of rhetorical theory, with plausibility rather than truth. It worked by disguising artifice as nature. An orator would strive for propriety in his speeches in order to persuade his audience, who might know little about the facts of whatever subject was being discussed, that he spoke from authority and that his recommendations could be trusted. The achievement of propriety, dependent upon the substitution of character for proof, was at bottom a means of creating a persuasive persona (or *prosopon*) or, in the case of poetry or drama, a believable character. The propriety of a speaker's words would be judged according to how well they expressed the matter under discussion and according to what was proper (likely or fitting) for him to say. Aristotle remarks,

> This aptness of language [*oikeia lexis*] is one thing that makes people believe in the truth of your story; their minds draw the false conclusion that you are to be trusted from the fact that others behave as you do when things are as you describe them; and therefore they take your story to be true, whether it is so or not.[25]

A speaker's language should thus seem to express naturally not only the emotions he ought to be feeling but also his character—not in any modern psychological sense, but in the classical sense that had persisted into the eighteenth century, that of a human class or type.[26] A king should speak like a king, a shepherd like a shepherd. To borrow the language of another is to forfeit not merely credibility but intelligibility. Propriety underwrites the legibility of identity itself.

Though the creation through dramatic propriety of a plausible persona might originally have been intended as a means by which to lend arguments power, the propriety of the persona came eventually to be considered more important than the propriety of words strictly considered—the calling of things by their proper or original names.[27] Tropes and figures of speech might very well, as George Puttenham said, be "abuses or rather trespasses in speach,"[28] thoroughly improper and unnatural, working "a kinde of dissimulation."[29] But there were circumstances in which their impropriety might be redeemed by the requirements of dramatic propriety. The wrong words could sometimes be the right ones.[30] Passion, for instance, could justify even the most improper figures, for men naturally make metaphors, especially when they are excited. "We forgive an angry man," says Aristotle,

> for talking about a wrong as "heaven-high" or "colossal"; and we excuse such language when the speaker has his hearers already in his hands and has stirred them deeply either by praise or blame or anger or affection. . . . Men do speak in this strain when they are deeply stirred, and so, once the audience is in a like state of feeling, approval of course follows. This is why such language is fitting in poetry, which is an inspired thing.[31]

The preservation of a persona might require that a writer resort to misnaming.

But the character for the sake of whose representation the names of things could expect to be abused might itself suffer a loss of propriety, and that in the name of propriety.[32] For propriety required a partial sacrifice of the proper—of the private or the individual—to the common. Social authority meant talking and behaving the way the rest of the community talked and behaved. Propriety in this sense was an expression and a precondition of shared values. John Locke defined "the Rule of Propriety" as "*common use*" or convention;[33] Adam Smith discussed it in terms of what enabled men to understand and sympathize with one another.[34] One's language had to achieve the same balance. Aristotle's terms, *to oikeion, to prepon,* and *to kurion,* suggest that for him propriety was usually a matter of familiarity, clarity, and authority. Words could be like neighbors, speaking a language we understand, enjoying the rights of citizens, and wielding the power of their acknowledged social position. Quintilian warned against using provincial or foreign expressions, lest they mark the speaker as an outsider: "If possible, our voice and all our words should be such as to reveal the native of this city, so that our speech may seem to be of genuine Roman origin, and not merely to have been presented with Roman citizenship."[35] The authority of a man's speech reflected his place in the social system; a foreign accent could mark him as one lacking a vote—or a voice—in civil affairs. Hugh Blair's demand for English "purity," diction "strictly English, without Scoticisms or Gallicisms," and cleansed of "vulgarisms or low expressions,"[36] expresses a less fully conscious perception of the same social reality. In short, propriety was the mark of a man's eligibility to participate in public discourse, his claim to a sympathetic hearing, his being one of "us" rather than one of "them." Propriety was what made it possible for an audience to identify with a character and his cause.

Aristotle and Quintilian knew that because style was supposed to express the speaker's social position, it could also be used to create an illusory or artificial authority. Propriety, particularly propriety of speech, implied a certain relation to place and property—indeed, the first organized use of rhetoric is said to have been the construction of legal pleas for the return of property unjustly confiscated by a tyrant.[37] As James Turner points out, property and place are different expressions of the same idea.

> "Land" and "place" are equivalent to "propriety"—meaning in seventeenth-century English both *property* and *knowing one's place.* The order of the universe, like the structure of society, was supposed to depend on a hierarchy of places from lowest to highest. Place is identity. Things out of place are not properly themselves, and move as living forces towards their natural home.[38]

Place is identity; property is identity.[39] According to Turner, property signifies, even justifies, the way things naturally are and properly ought to be.

But unless one took property itself to be a fact of nature, one had to account for its institution somehow. Puttenham accounted for it by means of a suggestive retelling of the myths of Amphion and Orpheus. He linked the origins of poetry with the origins of society and its earliest forms of property:

> It is written, that Poesie was th'originall cause and occasion of [men's] first assemblies, when before the people remained in the woods and mountains, vagarant and dispersed like the wild beasts, lawlesse and naked, or verie ill clad, and of all good and necessarie prouision for harbour or sustenance vtterly vnfurnished: so as they litle diffred for their maner of life, from the very brute beasts of the field. Whereupon it is fayned that *Amphion* and *Orpheus,* two Poets of the first ages, one of them, to wit *Amphion,* builded vp cities, and reared walles with the stones that came in heapes to the sound of his harpe, figuring thereby the mollifying of hard and stonie hearts by his sweete and eloquent perswasion. And *Orpheus* assembled the wilde beasts to come in heards to harken to his musicke, and by that means made them tame, implying thereby, how by his discreete and wholsome lesons vttered in harmonie and with melodious instruments, he brought the rude and sauage people to a more ciuill and orderly life.[40]

Puttenham's allegory represents poetic propriety as the ground of civil society; poets build the walls that mark the boundaries of the earliest common properties. He considers as well the theory that the first poems came into being at that moment in culture when shepherds "kept their cattell and heards in the common fields and forests" and practiced "the first art of lawfull acquisition or purchase," "quick cattel being the first property of any forreine possession."[41] According to this version of history, pastoral poetry reflects the ancient and innocent conversion of common into private property. But how innocent is the conversion? For all its charm, the story Puttenham tells is at bottom a sinister—even Coleridgean—sort of fable. It suggests that to sing is to take possession of one's audience and one's auditorium. It suggests too that to listen is to risk becoming the property of the poets, a member of the tame "heards" or part of the wall of entranced stones, transformed by poetry into sign or substance of another's possession.

Although Puttenham rejects the pastoral poetic theory of property's origin on the ground that the pastoral poets were not the same people as the shepherds who appeared in their poems, it is easy to see why the theory would have caught his attention. It seems to explain the inconsistency that lies at the heart of all accounts of propriety: the fact that propriety is allied simultaneously with public property and private, with that which a community possesses in common and that which the individual appropriates for himself.

For Wordsworth and Coleridge, bred in a rhetorical tradition founded, as we have seen, upon unstable, even paradoxical relations among unstable, even paradoxical concepts of language, character, and property, questions of literary property were still intricately bound up with questions of propriety and matters of style bound up with matters of ownership. Given the near alliance of property with propriety, it is hardly to be wondered at that the poets seemed occasionally to confuse the one with the other, treating them as literal and conceptual synonyms: thus the letter Wordsworth wrote to his publisher declaring his decision to remove "Christabel" from the *Lyrical Ballads* could suggest at once a sincere desire to preserve decorum in publication and a rather less noble anxiety to consolidate control over his property in the work. Even considering the potential for confusion between private and common properties latent in the rhetorical tradition, however, one may still wonder at Wordsworth's decision to treat the *Lyrical Ballads* as his private property—his and not Coleridge's. The decision marks a shift in his practice.

During the gestation of the *Lyrical Ballads* and to some extent even later, the poets' ideas about what constituted literary property were in flux. Indeed, it is not entirely clear that they regarded their early work in terms of property—in terms at least of *exclusive* property—at all. The two poets and their friends seemed largely indifferent to matters of literary paternity and showed an impressive but not limitless willingness to share literary property. Occasionally they made gifts of poems to other poets.[42] More frequently, and to the lasting confusion of scholars, they shared their writings with one another. Under the pressure of journalistic obligations and a natural tendency to value other men's creations because they were not his own, Coleridge borrowed entire verses, stanzas, paragraphs, and poems from Wordsworth's prose and poetry; moved by admiration and a taste for experimentation, Wordsworth borrowed images, styles, and poetic forms from Coleridge;

each, seeing what the other had made of borrowed materials, borrowed the borrowings back; and both made use of materials Dorothy Wordsworth had collected for her journals.[43]

The result is the notorious difficulty of establishing the authorship of materials that came out of the Wordsworth-Coleridge circle. Stephen Parrish notes that sometimes "the more quintessentially Wordsworthian a passage is, in its vocabulary, tone, and style, the greater the likelihood that Coleridge wrote it!"[44] Paul Magnuson observes that "When [Wordsworth] seems to be the most personal and individual, he comes close to ventriloquizing Coleridge's voice and appropriating his texts."[45] As these critics and others have shown,[46] much of the poetry written during this period can be regarded more as the product of conscious or unconscious collaboration between the poets than as the work of that particular individual who happened to have written it down.[47] The poets shared their ideas so freely that in many cases the decision to call some image or structure Coleridgean or Wordsworthian must be arbitrary.

The poets shared and took, but not altogether without self-consciousness; even Dorothy's words were not quite free for the taking. Wordsworth had to struggle sometimes to make his sister's materials his own: "After tea I read to William that account of the little boy belonging to the tall woman, and an unlucky thing it was," wrote Dorothy, "for he could not escape from those very words, and so he could not write the poem. He left it unfinished, and went tired to bed."[48] And if there were problems appropriating Dorothy's voice, the problems were even greater between the two poets. Although another's words could provide the germ for one's own writing, there was always the danger that they might prove threateningly, intractably other; they might refuse to be assimilated. The differentiation of voice that Mary Jacobus has called "the most important effect of their partnership"[49] did not come about naturally or without anxiety, nor can it be said ever to have been completed.[50]

The poets' habits of relative informality toward matters of property applied only within the boundaries of the immediate literary community. The group made a clear distinction between what belonged to themselves and what belonged to outsiders, and they defended their communal property vigorously against thoughtless or malicious trespass. When Peter Bayley published a volume of poems in which he poked fun at "The Idiot Boy," plagiarized heavily from the *Lyrical Ballads* and other poets' volumes, and insulted Wordsworth as "that most simple of all simple Poets,"[51] Wordsworth and his friends were indignant. Coleridge was to expose the plagiarisms not only from Wordsworth but from Akenside, Cowper, Bowles, and others. What hurt him, Wordsworth insisted, was not the fact of the robbery itself—for he insisted upon regarding plagiarism as fundamentally nothing more than an expression of love for the stolen material and its author. Nor was it the magnitude of the robbery that distressed him, the "pillaging . . . in a style of Plagiarism, I believe unexampled in the history of modern Literature." What disturbed him was the "complicated baseness . . . that anybody could combine (as this man in some way or other must have done) an admiration and love of those poems, with moral feeling so detestable"[52]—the fact that Bayley made fun of what he stole.

Friendly plagiarism, as the case of Sir Walter Scott shows, was another matter altogether. When the Wordsworths learned that Scott had apparently plagiarized from Coleridge's "Christabel" during the composition of *The Lay of the Last Minstrel,* they regretted the matter but sympathized with Scott for what they felt must have been an amiable mistake. Coleridge's words, they thought, had seduced Scott into repeating them. Dorothy wrote:

> For my part I do not think the Imitations are of so much importance, Coleridge's poem bearing upon its face so bold a character of origi[nality], and I cannot but add being so much superior to the other, but my Brother and Sister think that the Lay being published first, it will tarnish the freshness of Christabel, and considerably injure the first effect of it. At any rate this circumstance shows how cautious Poets ought to be in lending their manuscripts, or even *reading* them to Authors. If they came refreshed out of the Imitator's brain, it would not be so grievous, but they are in general like faded impressions, or as the wrong side of a Tapestry to the right.[53]

Wordsworth did not confront Scott on the resemblance between the two poems, feeling at first that to mention the problem to Scott, then a stranger, would be impolite, and later lacking the resolution to speak.

The situation might have been different had it been one of Wordsworth's own poems that Scott copied, but then perhaps it might not. Coleridge himself, with more at stake, reacted even more casually than the Wordsworths to the rumors of Scott's plagiarism.[54] He refused to approach another poet's works with the presumption "that all Thoughts are traditional, and that not only the Alphabet was revealed to Adam but all that was ever written in it that was worth writing."[55] He refused to accept the individual "parallelisms" between his poem and Scott's as evidence "of plagiarism or even of intentional imitation." Such "parallelisms" might be accidental. In any case a real plagiarist would have altered the lines enough to disguise them. A real plagiarist would have undertaken "to alter every one of these Lines or Couplets, without the least injury to the context, to retain the same meaning in words equally poetical & suitable, & yet entirely remove all the *appearance* of Likeness.—And this, Sir! is what an intentional Plagiarist would have done—He would have *translated,* not transcribed."[56] Thus to appropriate the contents of another writer's writings is to be guilty of plagiarism, but in plagiarizing successfully, a plagiarist transcends his crime. Though Coleridge would like to blame the plagiarist for the impropriety of the work he produces, he ends up conceding that a borrowing successfully absorbed into the borrower's poem is no plagiarism:

> He who can catch the Spirit of an original, has it already. It will not [be] by Dates, that Posterity will judge of the originality of a Poem; but by the original spirit itself. This is to be found neither in a Tale however interesting, which is but the Canvass, no nor yet in the Fancy or the Imagery—which are but Forms & Colors—it is a subtle Spirit, all in each part, reconciling & unifying all—. Passion and Imagination are it's [sic] *most* appropriate names; but even these say little—for it must be not merely Passion but poetic Passion, poetic Imagination.[57]

A good poem owns its contents, no matter where they come from; if the poetic imagination provides a good foster home for what it takes over, earlier origins cease to matter.

Wordsworth and Coleridge both, then, seem to have been concerned less with the integrity of the author's property in his writings than with the integrity of the work itself. In this their attitude resembled that of Sir Joshua Reynolds, great promoter of judicious imitation, who tended to regard plagiarism as a matter of an aesthetic rather than an ethical lapse. In his "Sixth Discourse" he pronounces plagiarism an evil only when committed so clumsily as to create an obvious incongruity or heterogeneity of materials or styles. Imitation of the ancients is not only proper but recommended; the classics are public property. However,

> It must be acknowledged that the works of the moderns are more the property of their authors; he, who borrows an idea from an antient, or even from a modern artist not his contemporary, and so accommodates it to his own work, that it makes a part of it, with no seam or joining appearing, can hardly be charged with plagiarism; poets practise this kind of borrowing, without reserve. But an artist should not be contented with this only; he should enter into a competition with his original, and endeavour to improve what he is appropriating to his own work. Such imitation is so far from having anything in it of the servility of plagiarism, that is a perpetual exercise of the mind, a constant invention. Borrowing or stealing with such art and caution, will have a right to the same lenity as was used by the Lacedaemonians; who did not punish theft, but the want of artifice to conceal it.[58]

If a writer works hard enough and with sufficient genius, he can absorb what he imitates so completely that it seems to become original. Part of the praiseworthiness of such diligent imitation lies in this exacting of creative labor, but part lies in its domestication of foreign material. A "seam" would be evidence of unassimilated foreignness, literary impropriety; too obviously the derivative author would have failed to assert control over his work, and his stolen material would have an unruly life of its own within the textual body of the host. The effect Wordsworth, Coleridge, and Reynolds all professed to deplore was the haunting of a later work by an earlier one it had too visibly wronged and too ineffectually repressed. To put it in terms both more general and more modern, they deplore the uncanny, a possession that threatens and disputes propriety—and property—in a radically disturbing way.

When in the 1800 preface Wordsworth addressed himself to the denunciation of "idle and extravagant stories in verse" and the "degrading thirst after outrageous stimulation,"[59] it is hard to feel certain he did not have in mind—at least in part—Coleridge's productions, with their zombies, spirits, curses, ghost ships, ventriloquists, and demonic maidens.[60] "Christabel" and *The Rime of the Ancient Mariner* overthrow the relation between character and self-expression prescribed by every pamphlet on rhetoric ever written. In these works, poetic voice shatters the character it is supposed to represent. The poems' inclusion in the *Lyrical Ballads* constituted a challenge to the propriety of the volumes as grave as that which their fictions portrayed.

Wordsworth's defense against this Coleridgean challenge involved a resolute natural homeliness of style and matter. To *ta xenika* Wordsworth would oppose *ta oikeia;* against the *unheimlich* he would set the *heimlich;* across from possession he would set property. But it had not been so very long since Wordsworth himself had indulged a genuine and unrestrained fondness for the Gothic, and something in him must have responded to the claptrap with an emotion more unruly than that of mere disapproval. Watching Coleridge in the midst of his improprieties, he must have felt a tug of identification that complicated his response.

It is a satisfying irony that what Wordsworth used to defend himself from the Coleridgean challenge, the language and forms he used to keep the Coleridgean uncanny at bay and to declare his freedom from improper literary obligation, came from Coleridge himself. It was from Coleridge, particularly from Coleridge as author of the so-called conversation poems, that Wordsworth learned how to use the homely, flexible, quasi-conversational style of "a man speaking to men," the style in which integrity, identity, and propriety find, it would seem, their natural expression. The conversational style was not, however, a simple gift from one poet to another; perhaps no literary influence can ever be that. What enabled Wordsworth to learn such a thing from another poet? What predisposed Coleridge to teach it?

Wordsworth's quick appreciation of the original conversation poems and their author in the early days of their association suggests something like recognition—the greeting one might give some long-lost friend or a seemingly impossible object of conjecture. When Wordsworth and Coleridge met—first, briefly, in 1795 and then in 1797—they did so as writers busy with works that can be seen to articulate different versions of what is essentially the same fantasy of sympathetic (sometimes involuntarily sympathetic) relations between a poet and his audience. At least in retrospect, these works, including Coleridge's new poems "The Eolian Harp" and "This Lime-tree Bower my Prison" and Wordsworth's still-evolving play *The Borderers,* appear to have established the terms of their collaboration and predicted the form of the relationship that would develop between the two poets.[61]

In *The Borderers* the outlines of this prophetic fantasy are clear and horrific: a man recreates his own guilty past in the experience of his credulous auditor; he converts another into his unhappy double, his second self, by telling him a story. Or as Reeve Parker describes it,

> Its intricate tragic structure develops through [Wordsworth's] elaboration of three interrelated premises: that character is engendered and shaped in passionate response to affecting narrative; that the person whose character is so engendered in effect reenacts the material of the narrative and at the same time becomes the image of the teller; and that through their passions in such reenactment and repetition the persons of the drama become bound to the purposes that embody their characters and in that bondage become tragically vulnerable.[62]

Because the story the villainous narrator tells is a conscious and malevolent fiction whose consequences are precisely calculated, what we have here is a drama of manipulation along the lines of *Othello* rather than an allegory of such influence as Wordsworth and Coleridge were to exercise over one another in the next few months and years, when innocent telling would beget telling and the roles of teller and auditor would be in constant exchange. Wordsworth would not have been inclined to see either himself or Coleridge in the role of either Rivers or Mortimer. Nevertheless, the play suggests the strength of Wordsworth's fascination with the power of narrative structures and roles to reproduce themselves in the actions and utterances of their auditors and interpreters.[63]

A properly susceptible Mortimer to this recitation, Coleridge would recreate the mimetic nightmare of *The Borderers* in his own writings. That the relationship between Rivers and Mortimer foreshadows that of the Ancient Mariner to the Wedding Guest and that of Geraldine to Christabel should be apparent. That it resembles the already well-developed relationship between the Coleridgean conversation poet and his audience may be less obvious.

The conversation poems were, of course, not conversations at all; though the poet speaks as if there were someone who might respond to his voice, no one ever answers Coleridge in these pieces.[64] The closest thing to a conversational response one gets here is Sara's frown at her husband's heretical speculations in "The Eolian Harp," or perhaps the music of the birds in "The Nightingale," which "answer and provoke each other's song" but from whose exchanges Coleridge himself is excluded. It is perhaps a little unfair to hold the poems to a standard of generic sociability supported only by the critical liberties we ourselves have taken in generalizing from the subtitle of the poem Coleridge called "The Nightingale: A Conversation Poem." Still, though it is critics who have invented the plural form of the conversation poem, there is something about the language of the poems that seems to license the category and acknowledge the incongruity between the style and the situation. For each of the conversation poems is based on the thwarted desire for response; the conversational aspect of their diction and address suggests a version of prosopopoeia, which, as Paul de Man describes it, is "the fiction of an apostrophe to an absent, deceased, or voiceless entity, which posits the possibility of the latter's reply and confers upon it the power of speech."[65] Coleridge invokes a bird, an absent friend, a sleeping baby, a film of ash fluttering on a grate—none of them in a position to reply in any audible or intelligible fashion—but he does so in such a way as to create images of natural, passionate, and intellectual responsiveness. So in "The Eolian Harp" the ruling analogy between animated nature and a world of "organic Harps diversely fram'd, / That tremble into thought, as o'er them sweeps / Plastic and vast, one intellectual breeze, / At Once the Soul of each, and God of all,"[66] works precisely to create the fiction of a cosmic counterpart to his own voice. Even in his idealizing imagination, however, where it acts as the figure of unmediated responsiveness indistinguishable from pure expression, the voice of the cosmic Eolian harp responds to something other than his own calling. Similarly, in "Frost at Midnight" Coleridge wishes that his infant son may grow up to "see and hear / The lovely shapes and sounds intelligible / Of that eternal language, which thy God / Utters," Who "shall mould / Thy spirit, and by giving make it ask." His blessing upon his son gives his son a voice to be used, in this fantasy, not in speech with his father but in communion with God.

This is the general pattern of the conversation poems: Coleridge uses the power of his voice to invoke a second voice or consciousness who will enjoy and express that vital wholeness or holiness of conversation and communion, blessings from which Coleridge is always mysteriously or accidentally excluded.[67] Through this other being the unfortunate Coleridge—lamed by hot milk or the wrong sort of upbringing, disqualified for happiness by philosophy or awkward circumstances—vicariously experiences goodness, love, wisdom, truth, and, indeed, immunity to all the ills and failings of mortality. This other being may sometimes seem to be someone special: the poet's baby, or his friend, or his beloved. But finally, as for instance the shifting of "Dejection"'s addressees suggests, it hardly seems to matter who or what occupies the position of vicar, so long as it *is* occupied. The person is irrelevant; the poetic double, the guarantor of the poet's voice and experience to whom is entrusted Coleridge's imaginative salvation, is an abstract functional necessity. It is the structure of projection and prosopopoeia that is essential, not the individual who may happen to become its object, as Charles Lamb was irritated to discover. For the Coleridgean conversation poem conjures an answering voice that, answering (in the poet's fond fantasy) some other and more potent voice, testifies metaleptically to the poet's own vocal power.

Despite our suspicion that the poet's self-sacrifices may function symbolically as acts of self-preservation, even self-exaltation, it is impossible not to be moved by the gentleness and generosity of Coleridge's conversation poems. Unlike Wordsworth's dramatic storyteller Rivers, Coleridge the conversationalist treats his second selves lovingly. When Wordsworth adapted the form in "Tintern Abbey" (and when he adapted it further in the *Prelude* and the "Intimations" ode, which follow from his achievements in "Tintern Abbey"), he retained Coleridge's gentleness but lost the generosity.

Wordsworth's conversation poetry reveals more starkly than Coleridge's the impersonality of the conversational form and the implications of its logic, which works to identify the poet with his silent auditor, the poetic persona with the conjured *prosopon.* Wordsworth's *prosopa* are turned to receive his voice and no one else's; their ears become his urns. Coleridge's imagination had liberated his son into a happy future of "wander[ing] like a breeze / By lakes and sandy shores, beneath the crags / Of ancient mountain, and beneath the clouds, / Which image in their bulk both lakes and shores / And mountain crags," but he did not stay to wish that his son might miss him or mourn him. Wordsworth's imagination of his sister's future is more obviously self-interested. She is to live on in order to keep his "genial spirits" from "decay"; she is to live on, not herself wandering like a breeze but, rather unpleasantly like the Old Cumberland Beggar, suffering "the misty mountain winds [to] be free / To blow against" her, preserving, museum- or mausoleum-like, the image of her brother.

That is, of course, a somewhat unfair characterization, as Dorothy herself would have felt; there is no lack of affection here, and in the office of keeper and restorer of his memory William offers his sister no less than what she would have wanted for herself. But when Coleridge heard the *Prelude,* that tremendous elaboration of "Tintern Abbey" which Wordsworth and his sister called "the poem to Coleridge," he found the experience of being so addressed—of being in the Dorothy-position—annihilating:

> even as Life returns upon the drowned,
> Life's joy rekindling roused a throng of pains—
> . . . .
> Sense of past Youth, and Manhood come in vain,
> And Genius given, and Knowledge won in vain;
> And all which I had called in wood-walks wild,
> And all which patient toil had reared, and all,
> Commune with thee had opened out—but flowers
> Strewed on my corse, and borne upon my bier
> In the same coffin, for the self-same grave!
> ["To William Wordsworth," 63–64, 69–75]

To occupy the place of Wordsworth's conversational object, of his second self, is to be emptied out and left voiceless. Nowhere does this appear more clearly than in the "Intimations" ode, where the position of vicar or second self is reduced to its most abstract and most nakedly elegiac form.[68] As Wordsworth moved to repudiate most nakedly elegiac form.[68] As Wordsworth moved to repudiate his dependence on Coleridge, this is the form the conversational guarantor of poetic voice and vitality assumed:

> those obstinate questionings
> Of sense and outward things,
> Fallings from us, vanishings;
> Blank misgivings of a Creature
> Moving about in worlds not realised,
> High instincts before which our mortal Nature
> Did tremble like a guilty Thing surprised:
> ["Ode: Intimations of Immortality," 142–48]

Ultimately, the cherished other self who guarantees our being reveals itself to be no individual, however young or generous, but abstract loss itself, or, in other words, the incongruity of our being in a world where matters of fact, the sheer otherness of things, can make claims upon us.

For Wordsworth as well as Coleridge, imaginative survival and salvation were matters not of persons but of relative positions of address, the availability of an auditor susceptible of being made into a second self. For some time each poet saw the other as just such a second self—the perfect auditor, perfectly sympathetic, capable of providing a home in his own voice and his own imagination for the words of the other. But even in the affectionate context of the conversation poems, conversation meant something other than address and full response; one voice, one consciousness, seemed always to have to empty itself out for the sake of another: uncomfortably enough, conversation implied something close to impersonality or even anonymity on one side or the other. And the poets' ideas about the gains and obligations of conversation were not, as we have seen, entirely symmetrical. Moreover, though one took a second self for comfort, for love, and for restoration, that other self could come to seem accusing, threatening, usurping, blank, an embodiment of loss, a figure rather of one's mortality than of one's immortality. It is not always heartening to see one's image mirrored or to hear one's voice echoed. Having lent one's voice or story to another for the sake of its perpetuation, one might eventually want it back. But then how to reclaim it? How to reassert one's own originality?

One of the means Wordsworth chose lay on the far side of the conversation poems. He ranged beyond conversational colloquialism to outright prosiness. Among the stubborn stumps, swollen ankles, and actual facts too blank for anyone to have bothered making up, Wordsworth finds an echoless, unresonant poetic space. Here there is no confirming or competing vocal response—not even a silent Dorothy, not even an absent Coleridge. The poetry of the matter-of-fact extrapolates from the implied vacancy or anonymity of the conversation poems into the realm of the voiceless, the blankly and helplessly insignificant.

The blankness of this poetry has sometimes drawn an answering blankness of readerly response. Not all of Wordsworth's contemporaries, not even all the members of the poet's circle, appreciated the apparent prosiness of his poems. Thus, Dorothy felt impelled to scold Sara Hutchinson for criticizing an early version of "Resolution and Independence":

> When you happen to be displeased with what you suppose to be the tendency or moral of any poem which William writes, ask yourself whether you have hit upon the real tendency and true moral, and above all never think that he writes for no reason but merely because a thing happened—and when you feel any poem of his to be tedious, ask yourself in what spirit it was written—whether merely to tell the tale and be through with it, or to illustrate a particular character or truth etc etc.[69]

But if Dorothy wanted the reader to look beyond the matter-of-factness, her brother sometimes refused to let the reader look at anything else. His notes to the poems insist upon calling the reader's attention to the factual bases of the stories he tells and to his externally derived authority for saying what he says; he almost ostentatiously refuses poetic license.

There is a critical tradition holding that Wordsworth's matter-of-factness demonstrates the poet's genuine attachment to the material world, whose very ineloquence bespeaks the self-evidence of truth. Thus John Jones sees the function of Wordsworthian "literalness" to be "self-guaranteeing"; things are what they are, and Wordsworth's literal presentation of them best conveys the strength and the significance of their reality.[70] F. W. Bateson agrees, suggesting that the "bathetic" voice is necessary as a ground or a "guarantee" of the authenticity of the more elevated voice.[71] "The very presence of the object," writes Frederick Garber, "stimulates intellectual activity while simultaneously guaranteeing, through its stability, that the activity is in some sense coherent and therefore has an element of truth within it."[72]

But Wordsworth's very matter-of-factness renders the status of the material world problematic. Events, people, and things are so opaque we cannot see them. One can argue just as plausibly for the imaginative hubris as for the realistic humility of the style, and read in Wordsworth's matters of fact an absolute contempt for the exterior world. Emile Legouis argues that Wordsworth's commonplaces are there not to offer a basis for transcendence but to be discarded along with other literary furniture:

> One by one Wordsworth discards, or rather rejects with contempt, all the peculiar privileges which from time immemorial the poet has enjoyed. He denies himself the marvelous; he will have none of either fiction or fable; scarcely even will he admit the need of a subject. . . . But Wordsworth renounces the extraordinary features of reality, no less than those of fiction. The mountains which occupy so large a place in his work appear in it only by accident.[73]

The strongest statement of this position comes from Hazlitt, who sees Wordsworth's literalism as evidence of an almost Mosaic or even divine strength:

> He chooses to have his subject a foil to his invention, to owe nothing but to himself. He gathers manna in the wilderness, he strikes the barren rock for the gushing moisture. He elevates the mean by the strength of his own aspirations; he clothes the naked with beauty and grandeur from the store of his own recollections.[74]

To this sublime end Wordsworth sacrifices not only traditional poetic diction but also story: "He takes a story merely as pegs or loops to hang thought and feeling on; the incidents are trifling, in proportion to his contempt for imposing appearances; the reflections are profound according to the gravity and the aspiring pretensions of his mind."[75] Anonymous, inanimate, and ineloquent "Fallings from us, vanishings" testify to the poet's imaginative power. If, voiceless in their own right, they nevertheless speak to us, it is because he does. Their significance can have no other source.

Wordsworth's matter-of-factness, his refusal of the sensational and the outer world, may look at first like loyalty to the natural, the familiar, the communally sanctioned—in short, to the bases of propriety. It looks like a certain means of defense against the uncanny he saw and feared in Coleridge. So does the logical consequence of this refusal, his decision to seek the sources of passion in their natural home, the human heart. But the resultant program, by which "the feeling developed gives importance to the action and situation, and not the action and situation from the feeling," renders his work liable to what Freud calls the "infantile element" in the uncanny, "the over-accentuation of psychical reality in comparison with material reality—a feature closely allied to the belief in the omnipotence of thoughts."[76] The effect, writes Freud, "is often and easily produced when the distinction between imagination and reality is effaced, as when something that we have hitherto regarded as imaginary appears before us in reality, or when a symbol takes over the full functions of the thing it symbolizes, and so on."[77] The uncanny represents a phenomenon with two sources, one in external reality, the other in the mind; one apparent, the other not.[78] In the uncanny, objects and events whose significance and identity one ordinarily takes for granted begin to behave as though motivated by and signifying something altogether different. They become symbols, but unreadable ones; looking at them, one registers the fact of representation but not its content.[79]

Wordsworth's matter-of-factness behaves just so. His poems, invested with the energies of an unconscious representation their matter-of-factness is constructed to deny, often seem haunted. Like ghosts, they mean everything and nothing. Once-familiar material returns in unfamiliar and sometimes threatening or uncontrollable form, conveying an emotional power that seems out of proportion to its unpromising appearance. Ordinary objects radiate an extraordinary significance.[80] The charge that would ordinarily attach to the plot, especially to the climax of the plot, returns attached to things one would not expect to be able to carry it. Nonevents, unnoticeable objects, and trite sayings—the text's "familiars"—carry an enormous freight. Wallace Jackson describes it in this way:

> The poet or his surrogate is subjected to unusually unsettling experiences arising from what may appear initially as a rather ordinary occasion. The formula is: nothing is below suspicion; everything is valuable, particularly the obvious. But if we accept the premise that Wordsworth was interested in creating new experience, then he had to begin with what is below ordinary experience, below in the sense of insufficient importance as well as in the psychological sense of that which lies beneath. Both meanings come together in the proposition that from the insignificant the significant arises.[81]

The energy that would ordinarily go into following a sequence of events focuses on a single unpromising event or object. Narrative, collapsed to a point from which it may or may not unfix itself, reveals its kinship with that most radical condensation of plot, the epitaph. The ultimate achievement of Wordsworthian matter-of-factness, Wordsworthian propriety, is the epitaphic coincidence of property and identity at the spot (*topos*) at which the earth is not only *where* but also *what* one is.

Wordsworth's renunciations and repudiations—of sensationalism, of specifically poetic language, of the uncanny, of Coleridge—are all parts of his plan to exorcise poetry of its impropriety by grounding it in matters of fact. They express his interest in demonstrating the natural foundations of poetry but also his desire to create an original literary property for himself, a poetry he could claim as his own. In turning the *Lyrical Ballads* into such a property, Wordsworth seems to achieve what every serious student of propriety dreams of: the creation of a self-realizing fiction, a rhetoric that proves its own truth. The poems about property written for the 1800 edition of the work, analogues of the property they imagine, suggest the power of imagination to create its own sources and its own home.

Wordsworth did not create himself, however, at least not singlehandedly: the origins of the poetic property to which he was so eager to affix his name were tainted, and the matter-of-factness he cultivated was still no more than a trope for the material language no poet can hope to attain. By treating the *Lyrical Ballads* as a piece of literary property, he pretended to have achieved a poetry in which words coincided with things, in which words *were* things, in which there was no disturbing gap between tropes and the proper names they covered—hence no room for haunting.

But this was itself a fiction. As the Coleridgean part of him knew, the property he celebrated was only a figure for the propriety whose internal contradictions he wished to heal and whose artificiality he wished to naturalize. The gesture of appropriation Wordsworth made in applying his name to the title page of the *Lyrical Ballads* would exercise no infallible authority over the contents of those pages or even over that other name written invisibly beneath it. The fact of Coleridge's anonymity renders Wordsworth's name itself subject to interpretation as a fiction, a catachresis, an impropriety, a haunted space.

In appropriating the work in his own name and suppressing both the name and the voice of his friend, Wordsworth intended to disown or expel the uncanny voice of the still-anonymous Coleridge. But the expulsion did not free the volume from the threat of the uncanny or the anonymous that Coleridge had come to stand for: they are only more severely repressed. The pressure of the anonymous, the arbitrary, the unowned, or the improper manifests itself most clearly at precisely those points where the poet is most determined to deny it. But before turning to Wordsworth's efforts to name the anonymous, let us take a look at what he had to contend with.

2

Voice and Ventriloquy in *The Rime of the Ancient Mariner*

The ordinary tale of the supernatural is like the magician's trick of pulling a rabbit out of a hat. It depends upon a false bottom, an illusion of sourcelessness. Bad metaphysics, it exploits our confusion about the relationship between cause and effect, appearance and reality, body and soul. The supernatural of *The Rime of the Ancient Mariner* pulls not rabbits out of hats but voices out of voices. It makes its home in the space between speaker and spoken, motivation and action, intention and meaning. Instead of pretending there is no source, it pretends there is one, that behind the Mariner-as-dummy there is a ventriloquist, a figure or language or system of meanings in the context of which the tale that comes out of the Mariner's mouth makes sense.

The *Rime* evades the question any reader asks upon opening to this first poem in the originally anonymous *Lyrical Ballads:* "Whose voice is this?" The *Rime,* one of the most deeply and elaborately anonymous poems ever written, comes to speech through the medium of an alien voice—archaic, inhuman, uncanny—in response to an impossible demand. "What manner man art thou?" the Hermit cries out in horror at the speaking corpse. It is a question derived anagrammatically from the answer the corpse is unable to give: man < manner < Mariner. The question contains the fragments of the word that, fleeing into anonymity, the Mariner leaves behind. "I am an Ancient Mariner" becomes "There was a ship." It is the first in a series of dislocations—translations, displacements, metonymies—that spring from the Mariner's refusal of his own name. It is a revelation of the anonymity whose power calls into being both the *Rime* and the collaborative project—the *Lyrical Ballads*—that the *Rime* inaugurates.

The impropriety of the *Rime*'s language, suited neither to the expression of anything we would regard as sound character nor to the evocation of any familiar system of reference, dares its audience to make sense of it.[1] We respond by talking about madness and the supernatural, notions that convert the failure of signification into evidence of significance and allow us to defer the unwelcome recognition of our interpretive helplessness. We sacrifice our belief in the Mariner's sanity on the altar of "character" or admit the possibility that spirits and demons cause the effects we cannot otherwise explain. Thus we attempt to rescue a purely ideal propriety.

Why can the Mariner not name himself? Perhaps because, as Wordsworth, obtusely accurate, seems to have been the first to notice, he is a man without "distinct character, either in his profession of Mariner, or as a human being."[2] He has no name because he has no identity. Ignorant of who he is, unable to recognize his fears and desires as his own or distinguish himself from his surroundings,[3] and practically devoid of conscious intention and affect, the Mariner apprehends the contents of his own psyche as alien and inexplicable, perceptible only in the forms of an unnatural nature, frightened and hostile men, and spirits. Everywhere he looks he sees with no recognition versions of himself, the human and natural worlds he moves in functioning as agents of his psyche,[4] their energies and actions displacements of his own.[5]

The Mariner's empty world is crowded with what he cannot own, cannot distinguish, and therefore cannot name; anonymity is the common linguistic condition of people and things in his tale. There are strangely few proper names here; the Mariner identifies almost no one, and names even of simple abstractions elude him. Despite the excesses of his later speech, his relation to language is, like that of so many of Wordsworth's early protagonists, that almost of an aphasic. With the single exception of his painful exclamation at the sight of the spectre ship, "A sail! a sail!", the Mariner seems to say nothing during the length of his voyage. When he does speak, he speaks like a man suffering from what Roman Jakobson describes as a similarity disorder.[6] How appropriate that the Mariner's cry should trope Coleridge's own standard example of synecdoche:[7] "A sail" for "a ship" whose sails have rotted away.[8]

The Mariner's difficulties with language and his reluctance to abstract judgments from the mass of discrete observations he presents may signal intellectual deficiency, but they could also indicate the impossibility of such identifications and judgments as we are accustomed to expect. We cannot discount the possibility that what look like distortions of language and logic in the Mariner's rendition reflect truly the incoherence of the world he has passed through.

> The Sun came up upon the left,
> Out of the Sea came he:
> And he shone bright, and on the right
> Went down into the Sea.
>
> Higher and higher every day,
> Till over the mast at noon—[9]

Unlike the Wedding Guest, who beats his breast in an agony of impatience, we may recognize in the Mariner's somewhat pedantic attention to days and directions an attempt to defend against cosmic derangement. But readerly dependence upon the Mariner—an obviously unreliable narrator—limits our ability to distinguish with any degree of certainty between psychological or linguistic and physical or metaphysical effects; we have a hard time deciding how much the tale's oddity has to do with the oddity of its teller and how much it has to do with the oddity of its material. Ultimately, however, the tale dissociates itself from both teller and theme and takes its place *en abyme,* generating its own linguistic origins and constituting itself as the object of its own signification.

As Arden Reed remarks, the Mariner is "more the effect of the 'Rime' than its cause," "the by-product of a text that wills its own repetition."[10] The Mariner's relation to his tale is tautological, at once totally arbitrary and totally determined. The Mariner tells his tale to explain that he is the man who tells the tale in order to explain what manner man he is. It is only after the end of his marine adventures, when the Hermit questions him, that the Mariner becomes aware of the unnaturalness of his relation to the story he tells:

> Forthwith this frame of mine was wrench'd
> With a woeful agony,
> Which forc'd me to begin my tale
> And then it left me free.
>
> Since then at an uncertain hour,
> Now ofttimes and now fewer,
> That anguish comes and makes me tell
> My ghastly aventure.
>
> [611–18]

A "strange power of speech" forces him out of silence. His aphasia violently reverses itself as language steps into the role of persecutor left vacant by the avenging *genii loci,* vestigial guardians of the proprieties the Mariner has violated.[11] An alien spirit thus comes to inhabit the body of the Mariner's speech, which, endlessly iterated and claiming no source in the Mariner's will, must be regarded as enclosed in invisible quotation marks. The tale that comes out of his mouth is not his. Prophet rather than source, the Mariner is only the perpetual, helplessly uncomprehending audience to the tale that speaks itself through him.[12]

Clearly, the Mariner's recital is no mere history. He does not choose his words; he suffers them, reliving what he tells. Who can tell whether he does not relive even his impulse to kill?

> "God save thee, ancyent Marinere!
> "From the fiends that plague thee thus—
> "Why look'st thou so?"—with my cross bow
> I shot the Albatross.
>
> [77–80]

The fiends that plague him may be simultaneously those of bitter remorse and those that tormented him at the time of his original violence: the penitential representation comes very close to repeating the crime the Mariner is trying to expiate. No wonder the penance must be repeated so often. As Homer Brown puts it, "The tale that repeats the crime 'repeats' it in a double sense: it tells the story which identifies the self-assertion of the crime with the self-assertion of the telling—the killing of the albatross with the usurpation of the Wedding Guest."[13] In the words of Jonathan Arac, "Repetition solicits repetition."[14] The effect is to implicate the ancient Mariner so deeply in the circumstances of his younger self as to discredit the authority of his final moral summing up: its lesson is either irrelevant or impermanent; it cannot save the Mariner from an endless repetition of his agony, from being possessed by the voice of the past.

But the Mariner is not the only victim of his voice. In this poem founded upon the power of quotation, quotation marks are strangely unreliable indices of the borders of speech. The Minstrel indicates when the Mariner is speaking with "quoth he" and "thus spake on that ancient man," and he consistently punctuates the openings of speeches by the Wedding Guest, the spirits, the Hermit, the Pilot, and the Boy. But he is not always careful to mark the end of a speech. To a reader careless of the convention—not observed in every poem in this volume[15]—that places a quotation mark in front of every line in a quoted speech and one last mark at the end of the final line, one voice may seem suddenly to become two.

> He holds him with his skinny hand,
> Quoth he, there was a Ship—
> "Now get thee hence, thou grey-beard Loon!
> "Or my Staff shall make thee skip.
>
> He holds him with his glittering eye—
> The wedding guest stood still
> And listens like a three year's child;
> The Marinere hath his will.
>
> [13–20]

A punctuational lapse, the absence of a closing quotation mark, allows the reader also to hear the two voices as one and so to perceive the dialogue as monologue.[16] The story dissolves the distinction between the roles of speaker and audience: both here are equally in thrall to the tale, the Wedding Guest no more capable of closing his ears against the tale than the Mariner is of closing his mouth against it.

It hardly seems to matter who speaks the words the tale requires;

for the purposes of vocalization, one character is as good as another. Characters confuse their own identities and voices with those of others, and so, in matters of revision, does Coleridge. In 1798, for example, the Mariner and the reanimated body of his nephew are pulling together at one rope when the Mariner's horror of zombies suddenly becomes a horror of himself:

> The body and I pull'd at one rope,
> But he said nought to me—
> And I quak'd to think of my own voice
> How frightful it would be!
>
> The day-light dawn'd—they dropp'd their arms,
> And cluster'd round the mast:
> Sweet sounds rose slowly thro' their mouths
> And from their bodies pass'd.
>
> [335–42]

In 1800 the nephew remains silent. But instead of the Mariner's fears, we get the Wedding Guest's:

> "I fear thee, ancient Mariner!"
> Be calm thou Wedding-Guest!
> 'Twas not those souls who fled in pain
> Which to their corses came again,
> But a troop of spirits blest:
>
> [345–49]

Fearing at that uncanny moment the sound of his own voice, lest it *not* be his, the Mariner hears instead the Wedding Guest's, whose ventriloquy gives voice and fulfillment to the Mariner's fears. Taken by itself, the 1800 text provides reassurance for the reader who, with the Wedding Guest, fears that the Mariner might be a ghoul; the Mariner's reply to the Wedding Guest[17] allays his suspicions. But the relationship between the revised and the original text lends support to the possibility that the words of 1800 deny. As the spirits bless'd work through the bodies of the crew, so the spirit of the Mariner speaks through the Wedding Guest. Both men become functions of the tale whose telling they must endure and to whose impersonal power they must bear witness.

Having begun by crossing the boundaries of speech and character ordinarily marked by punctuation, the anonymous voice of this self-propagating tale develops into full-scale ventriloquism. What we register as a linguistic problem, however, the tale's characters register as a demonological one; they see the Mariner himself, and not the tale that he tells and that they enter, as the problem. Instrument rather than author of the tale he tells, the Mariner appears to them a dead man possessed by a demon of loquacity.

To the Hermit, the Pilot, and the Pilot's boy, who assume that the body they draw from the sea at the sinking of the ship is that of a corpse, the sight—or sound—of the Mariner's attempt to speak is uncanny:

> Stunn'd by that loud and dreadful sound,
> Which sky and ocean smote:
> Like one that hath been seven days drown'd
> My body lay afloat:
> But, swift as dreams, myself I found
> Within the Pilot's boat.
> . . . .
> I mov'd my lips: the Pilot shriek'd
> And fell down in a fit.
> The holy Hermit rais'd his eyes
> And pray'd where he did sit.
>
> [583–88, 593–96]

They do not recover from their horror when he takes the oars. They do not react with relief that one they mistook for dead should prove still to be alive. Nothing the Mariner does convinces them that he is a living man. And although the Wedding Guest, not having seen him rise from the waters, is not as immediately or as forcibly affected as they are, he also soon becomes uneasy. Something, presumably, in the Mariner's manner—his mesmeric power, the unnatural concentration of vitality in his glittering eye and his unstoppable mouth, perhaps—causes the Wedding Guest to wonder what sort of creature he has before him. Nor can he believe that the tale the Mariner tells can be told by a living man. Hence his fear that he may be talking to a zombie.[18] Hence too the question that calls forth the tale.

By giving the Mariner the air of a zombie, the poem forces the reader to confront a radical split between speaker and speech, both of which seem haunted. The connection between possession and ventriloquy is made explicit late in the poem, when the spirits that have been inhabiting the dead bodies of the crew take the form of embodied imitative voice:

> The day-light dawn'd—they dropp'd their arms,
> And cluster'd round the mast:
> Sweet sounds rose slowly thro' their mouths
> And from their bodies pass'd.
>
> Around, around, flew each sweet sound,
> Then darted to the sun:
> Slowly the sounds came back again
> Now mix'd, now one by one.
>
> [339–46]

It would be a display of exquisitely acrobatic voice-throwing if the voices had an origin to be thrown from, but the circumstances forbid us to locate the source of voice in its apparent speakers; these voices no more belong to the crew out of whose mouths they pass than the tale belongs to the Mariner.

Were it not for the fact that the Mariner is but the first victim of the tale's compulsive repetitions, we might attribute his behavior to hysteria. But he is not the tale's only teller; his story is enclosed and repeated by others over whom the Mariner (as opposed to the tale) has no influence. That the later narrators are even more deeply anonymous than the Mariner himself (whose appearance, social demeanor, and history we know) is, of course, a problem; their retellings can neither authorize the truth of the original tale nor enable us to sort out its errors. But unless we decide that everyone who tells or retells the tale is mad in precisely the same way, we cannot read the tale's peculiarities as symptoms of pathology either psychological or ethical. Indeed, the framing of the tale calls into question the very notion of character upon which considerations of psychology and ethics—and hence, of course, propriety—depend.

The reduction of the poem's characters to reflections and echoes of the tale-ridden Mariner could, one imagines, be the work of the minstrel who narrates the tale that the antiquarian would gloss. But the tale's curse is not so easily explained; it exercises its power on figures whom one would like to assume stand beyond its reach, outside its fictional space—on those figures precisely who determine the boundaries of the tale. Both minstrel and antiquarian are absorbed into the mechanism of the tale's telling. With no punctuation distinguishing the minstrel's voice from the Mariner's, both voices seem to emanate from the same source, and the poor minstrel, his independence thus undermined, transmits to the antiquarian (not yet, in 1798, brought into being) the compulsion to repeat.

The poem's strange power to bring itself to voice against the knowledge or will of its sometimes arbitrary subjects is something other than a simple fiction: it affects Coleridge too.[19] As the Mariner is subject to a "strange power of speech" that forces him to repeat his tale endlessly, so the poet himself lay under a similar though more limited compulsion to repeat himself, revising the poem in 1800 and again in 1817, when he doubled it with a prose gloss in the style of a learned seventeenth-century antiquarian. "Each revision," writes Homer Brown, "is an apparent attempt to define and control the wandering meaning—in a sense the reading—of the poem. . . . And each version of this tale is allegorical in relationship to the one prior to it."[20] The gloss attempts to prop up the original narrative, making explicit what the Mariner either left implicit or, perhaps, missed. The brief "Argument," though tracing little more than the ship's movements and holding out the bare lure of "strange things that befell," does in little what the gloss does in full. Both repeat to rationalize or explain—to reclaim sense from apparent nonsense. But an uncanny motive behind the retellings gives itself away; rationalization reveals itself as an attempt to conceal the nature of the Mariner's story.

For the reader who accepts the authority of the gloss and the connections the gloss makes, the commentary is the completion of an otherwise incomplete structure. Walter Jackson Bate speaks for these readers when he asserts that Coleridge added "the beautiful gloss in order to flesh out the otherwise skeletal bones of the supernatural machinery and also to help smooth the flow of the narrative."[21] If we can take Bate's words more seriously than he meant them, the gloss humanizes the supernatural, animates the dead—worthy aims both, from the Wordsworthian perspective. But Bate's image suggests an unwitting interpretive necromancy, for the literary critical raising of bones merely repeats one of the *Ancient Mariner*'s objectionable wonders. The gloss does to the poem what the spirits do to the bodies of the crew, and what the spirits do to the crew the tale does to its explicators. A structure of nested quotations, the poem behaves in linguistic terms like its own ventriloquist, appropriated by and taking possession of one voice after another: the Mariner's, the minstrel's, the antiquarian's, the critic's. Acknowledging no author, the tale dominates its speakers. To encounter it is to be infected.

The *Rime*'s ventriloquisms are both fictions and realities. When the Wedding Guest, preternaturally sensitive to the presence of linguistic demons, realizes that the voice that has been telling him about the strange death of the crew could not belong to the terrifying body whose glittering eye and rigid hand have immobilized him, we should listen carefully:

"I fear thee, ancyent Marinere!
"I fear thy skinny hand;
"And thou art long and lank and brown
"As is the ribb'd Sea-sand.

"I fear thee and thy glittering eye
"And thy skinny hand, so brown—
Fear not, fear not, thou wedding guest!
This body dropt not down.

[216–23]

It is the body, and particularly the hand, that terrifies the Wedding Guest, and it is about the body, though not the hand, that the Mariner tries to reassure him. But he says nothing about the voice. In fact there is an alien voice, and even an alien hand, in the vicinity; it belongs, as Coleridge points out in a note appended in 1817, to Wordsworth, who contributed the lines about the Mariner's ghoulish appearance. Coleridge's uneasiness about the Wordsworthian lines he uses finds expression in the Wedding Guest's cry of apprehension; the Wedding Guest—or is it Wordsworth?—serves as ventriloquist to voice Coleridge's fears of ventriloquy. But if Wordsworth is the ventriloquist here, he is only the nearest to hand; there are others behind him.

The voice that repeats the *Rime* is strange not only because it is mysteriously motivated, and not only because it fails to explain anything more than its frame or the reason it is being told, but also because it is archaic, as indeed is the language of the entire poem. The style of the *Rime* seems strange because its familiarity goes too far back for us to recognize it. "A Dutch attempt at German sublimity," Southey called it,[22] his desire to poke fun accidentally leading him in the direction of a truth. An earlier English style[23] has returned sounding almost foreign.

So carefully did Coleridge set about archaizing the vocabularies of the poem and establishing plausibility of the historical details that scholars can guess with fair assurance when the voyage was supposed to have been undertaken,[24] when the minstrel was supposed to have made the Rime,[25] and when the commentator was supposed to have written the gloss.[26] But Coleridge's scholarly success worked against him. His contemporaries, responding not to the authenticity of the details but to the fact of their unfamiliarity and their suggestion of stylistic ventriloquism, reacted to the poet the way the Hermit reacted to the Mariner: with deep suspicion about the source of so obviously unnatural an utterance. Speaking anonymously for the *Critical Review,* Southey objected to what he regarded as the inauthenticity of the poem:

> We are tolerably conversant with the early English poets; and can discover no resemblance whatever, except in antiquated spelling and a few obsolete words. This piece appears to us perfectly original in style as well as in story.[27]

Others took exception to the diction while appreciating the overall style. An anonymous critic for *The British Critic* wrote,

> The author . . . is not correctly versed in the old language, which he undertakes to employ. "Noises of a *swound,*" . . . and "broad as a *weft,*" . . . are both nonsensical; but the ancient style is so well imitated, while the antiquated words are so very few, that the latter might with advantage be entirely removed without any detriment to the effect of the Poem.[28]

When he revised the poem in 1800, Coleridge did change the phrases to which critics had raised particular objections.[29]

Perhaps one reason for the critics' displeasure at the language of the *Ancient Mariner* as it appeared in 1798 is that others before Coleridge had drawn so heavily upon archaic and pseudo-archaic English as to have given the public a disgust for the style. During the 1780s and 1790s sophisticated writers of "ballads of simplicity" had their productions "encrusted with a patina spuriously induced by consonants doubled at random and superfluous *e*'s" in order to make them seem older than they really were.[30] The fraud was not always so transparent. Lowes remarks that

> nine out of ten of the archaisms which went into the earliest version of "The Ancient Mariner" had already imparted a would-be romantic flavour to the pages of Chatterton, and Shenstone, and Thomson, and of such smaller fry as Mickle, and Wilkie, and William Thompson, and Moses Mendez, and Gilbert West.[31]

Some readers were tired of antiquity. Others had never had a taste for it. Charles Burney, speaking for the eighteenth century generally,[32] expressed uneasiness about poetic regression:

> Would it not be degrading poetry, as well as the English language, to go back to the barbarous and uncouth numbers of Chaucer? Suppose, instead of modernizing the old bard, that the sweet and polished measures, on lofty subjects, of Dryden, Pope, and Gray, were to be transmuted into the dialect and versification of the XIVth century? Should we be gainers by the retrogradation? *Rust* is a necessary quality to a counterfeit old medal: but, to give artificial rust to modern poetry, in order to render it similar to that of three or four hundred years ago, can have no better title to merit and admiration than may be claimed by any ingenious forgery.[33]

Yet the style of the *Ancient Mariner* would fool no reader into thinking the poem ancient. Even the 1798 version, its archaic words and spellings not yet removed, would have looked odd to a sixteenth-century reader, for, despite its curiosities of diction, the basis of the poem is the English of 1798.[34] To use Coleridge's own distinction,[35] his poem was meant to imitate and not copy ancient poetic language. It seems to have been this mixture of the strange and the familiar, more than the strangeness itself, that disturbed contemporary readers.

Coleridge himself may have been uneasy about the unnaturalness of his imitation-antique language. He disparaged badly managed archaisms in others' poems, expressing particular dislike for "their inverted sentences, their quaint phrases, and incongruous mixture of obsolete and spenserian words."[36] Praising the ballad in Monk Lewis's *Castle Spectre,* a work he otherwise disparaged as "a mere patchwork of plagiarisms," he wrote,

> The simplicity & naturalness is his own, & not imitated; for it is made to subsist in contiguity with a language perfectly modern—the language of his own times, in the same way that the language of the writer of "Sir Cauline" was the language of *his* times. This, I think, a rare merit: at least, *I* cannot attain this innocent nakedness, except by *assumption*—I resemble the Dutchess [sic] of Kingston, who masqueraded in the character of "Eve before the Fall" in flesh-coloured Silk.[37]

If to copy "innocent nakedness" is lascivious, to copy primitive language is sophisticated. In both cases the imitation offends because it pretends to imitate what is valued precisely for its freedom—as object and as subject—from the taint of imitation. It offends because it acts out of awareness of that which must be unconscious.

But the objects of the *Rime*'s mimetic intentions are hardly innocent victims. Deeply and consciously involved in echoes and ventriloquies, the *Rime* derives from, or echoes, sources that are themselves perplexed. It is not simply the echoic structure that denaturalizes the language; the earlier voices are no more natural than those they haunt. There was never a first time the Mariner recited his *Rime.* From the outset the tale was a repetition—of the experience itself, which the Mariner relives as he retells it, of the words in which he retells it, and of other words, with which Coleridge and Wordsworth had been telling or trying to tell other tales during the last half-dozen years. The poem's obvious and exotic anachronisms cover more recent and more local influences, particularly "The Wanderings of Cain" and "Salisbury Plain."

The *Rime* was the result of two separate collaborative failures. It was meant to be a joint project, like the *Lyrical Ballads* to which it gave rise. As Wordsworth told Isabella Fenwick the story of the poem's inception and early development, he, Dorothy, and Coleridge were on a walk when they decided to write a poem in order to finance a tour. Parts of the idea for it came from the dream of a Mr. Cruikshank; other parts, such as the shooting of the albatross, the navigation of the ship by the dead men, and the spirits' revenge, were suggested by Wordsworth, who also contributed a few lines. But "as we endeavoured to proceed conjointly (I speak of the same evening) our respective manners proved so widely different that it would have been presumptuous in me to do anything but separate from an undertaking upon which I could only have been a clog."[38] Thus even before the poem took definite shape it was already a conversation turned monologue; years before the gloss was written there were voices other than the narrator's telling versions of parts of the same tale. The final form recapitulates what would otherwise seem to be irrelevant facts about its production.

The plan Wordsworth tells about was already a repetition of, or substitution for, an earlier plan. In his "Prefatory Note" to the fragmentary "Wanderings of Cain," Coleridge writes:

> The work was to have been written in concert with another [Wordsworth], whose name is too venerable within the precincts of genius to be unnecessarily brought into connection with such a trifle, and who was then residing at a small distance from Nether Stowey. The title and subject were suggested by myself, who likewise drew out the scheme and contents for each of the three books or cantos, of which the work was to consist, and which, the reader is to be informed, was to have been finished in one night! My partner undertook the first canto: I the second: and whichever had *done first,* was to set about the third. Almost thirty years have passed by; yet at this moment I cannot without something more than a smile moot the question which of the two things was the more impracticable, for a mind so eminently original to compose another man's thoughts and fancies, or for a taste so austerely pure and simple to imitate the Death of Abel? Methinks I see his grand and noble countenance as at the moment when having despatched my own portion of the task at full finger-speed, I hastened to him with my manuscript—that look of humourous despondency fixed on his almost blank sheet of paper, and then its silent mock piteous admission of failure struggling with the sense of the exceeding ridiculousness of the whole scheme—which broke up in a laugh: and the Ancient Mariner was written instead.[39]

Coleridge's account of the poem's "birth, parentage, and premature decease" (as he calls it) inadvertently suggests a parallel between the writing and the story being written. In stressing the absurdity of one man attempting to offer what is not his to offer, Coleridge's account cannot help but remind us that Abel the shepherd was killed because his offering of sheep was accepted while Cain the farmer's offering of grain—he had no sheep to sacrifice—was not. The brother poets proved unable to cooperate on a story centering around the fratricidal consequences of that unequally regarded sacrifice. It is no coincidence that so many of the poems on which Wordsworth and Coleridge tried to collaborate concern violence and envy.

As so often is the case, Coleridge's remarks on textual history provide a key to reading the text as an allegory of its own production. His remarks raise questions about the authenticity of expression that "The Wanderings of Cain" and its successor will dramatize. Though it may be ridiculous for one man "to compose another man's thoughts," Coleridge found the possibility of such an impersonation sufficiently intriguing to make it one of "Cain"'s major themes. Ventriloquism may be no proper source of poetry, but the *Rime,* "Cain"'s stepchild, depends on it, internalizing the relationship that Coleridge now writes off.

"The Wanderings of Cain" matters to a reading of the *Rime* because of the relationships among its history, its subject, and its formal structure—if one can call a text so confused, so nonsensical, either formal or structured. In "The Wanderings of Cain" as in the *Rime,* different voices and different versions of the same story compete with one another. The relationship among the introductory verse stanza Coleridge claimed to have reconstructed from memory ("Encinctured with a twine of leaves," etc.), the prose version of canto II, and the "rough draft of a continuation or alternative version . . . found among Coleridge's papers"[40] is not clear. It is hard to say whether we are dealing with different versions of the same events or with different, although perhaps similar, events—a problem the reader of the *Rime* and its gloss should recognize.

Though the plot of "The Wanderings of Cain" is too baffling to recount, it is—happily—not as a narrative but as a collection of themes, images, and questions about representation that "The Wanderings of Cain" finds its way into the *Rime.* "The Wanderings of Cain" contains the raw materials for the *Rime:* killing, punishment by solitude, spirits, trances, the sacrifice of blood from an arm, and wandering. It contains passages that translate almost immediately into the words of the later poem. One such passage follows:

> And Cain lifted up his voice and cried bitterly, and said, "The Mighty One that persecuteth me is on this side and on that; he pursueth my soul like the wind, like the sand-blast he passeth through me; he is around me even as the air! O that I might be utterly no more! I desire to die—yes, the things that never had life, neither move they upon the earth—behold! they seem precious to mine eyes. O that a man might live without the breath of his nostrils. So I might abide in darkness, and blackness, and an empty space! . . . For the torrent that roareth far off hath a voice: and the clouds in heaven look terribly on me; the Mighty One who is against me speaketh in the wind of the cedar grove; and in silence am I dried up."

Cain's complaints resemble the Mariner's: he is persecuted by storm and by freakish winds; he wishes he could die; he learns to love the slimy things that crawl with legs upon the slimy sea; the bodies of the dead crew move with no breath in their nostrils; he is alone, alone, on a wide, wide sea; he can hear the winds roaring far off; drought silences him. Both Cain and the shape of Abel resemble the Mariner: Cain whose eye "glared . . . fierce and sullen" and whose "countenance told in a strange and terrible language of agonies that had been, and were, and were still to continue to be"; and the shape of Abel, who cries, "Woe is me! woe is me! I must never die again, and yet I am perishing with thirst and hunger." The Mariner is in part a composite of Cain and the delusive representation of the brother he murdered, uncertain what god or what spirits may have dominion over him now.

In neither poem is it apparent whether the cosmos *is* a cosmos, united under a single, benevolent God, or a place of warring and delusive spirits. We see the spirits and hear their reports, but are they reliable? The Mariner asserts the unity of God and the universality of His laws of love, but the evidence suggests that the shape of Abel may have spoken the truth when he talked of another God ruling over the nightmare world of sin and death. "The Wanderings of Cain" articulates the heresy that the *Rime* rehearses to deny.

A work of Wordsworth's variously entitled "A Night on Salisbury Plain," "Adventures on Salisbury Plain," and "Guilt and Sorrow" looks like another possible source for the *Rime.* Coleridge saw a draft of this larger work, which was begun probably in 1793, about a year before he began the *Rime.*[41] Like "The Wanderings of Cain" and like *The Ancient Mariner,* "Adventures on Salisbury Plain" lacks a single authoritative narrator or narrative,[42] repeating the same story in different voices and with different sets of characters, trapped in representations of the past. Like the *Rime,* it is deeply concerned with traumatic repetition.

The protagonist, long the victim of official injustice, becomes an agent of private injustice himself, robbing and killing a man on his way home after years away at sea. This crime, which he commits near his own doorstep, drives him back into exile, now self-imposed: dreading to show himself to his family as a murderer, he wanders anxiously, wearily, over Salisbury Plain as over a stage on which his past is being continually reenacted and his future—or lack of it—continually foreshadowed. Making his way through a storm to "the dead house of the Plain," he encounters a Female Vagrant, who, after briefly mistaking the guilty sailor for an unburied corpse, tells him the story of her own wanderings. Her life, which Wordsworth excerpted to print as "The Female Vagrant" in the 1798 *Lyrical Ballads,* only a few pages further on from the *Rime,* is guiltless but apparently cursed in much the same way as the Mariner's; she remembers her anguish and her calm at sea in words almost identical to those in which the Ancient Mariner remembers his. At dawn the two leave the dead house and come upon a beaten child lying as if dead on the ground. For an instant the sailor sees in the child a reflection of the man he himself has killed: the murder seems to have repeated itself before his eyes and accused him of his crime. The child's father frightens them off. Walking on, they meet an ailing woman who proves to be the sailor's wife, driven from her home by her neighbors' suspicions of her husband's involvement in the murder. Recognizing her long-lost husband, she is overcome with emotion and dies of joy. A couple of innkeepers realize at that instant who the sailor must be and urge him to surrender to the law. He does so and is hanged.

The killing of the traveler, like the killing of the albatross, is a form of what the gloss to the *Rime* calls inhospitality. Both murderers are hosts,[43] and both are punished with homelessness for their offenses against hospitality. Yet neither crime is a narrative turning point. Although their punishment is wandering, both are already wanderers. Their crimes change things less than one might expect; indeed, it is that changelessness of things that is their true punishment. Both men are doomed to inhabit a time that cannot progress normally and a space that turns in every direction to the scene of the crime. Instead of returning to his family, the sailor enters a world in which everyone and everything is related to him; he becomes the traveler he kills and the hanged man he sees; he looks at his victim bleeding again in the guise of a child and hears himself as a brutal father threaten himself with the gallows. The vagrant's story of a family lost through war is a counterpart to his own.[44] His reunion with his wife kills her, and the hospitality of the innkeepers kills him. Although the sailor himself never tells his tale except (out of our hearing) to the judges, the stories everyone else tells echo the story he could have told.

Despite its contemporary social relevance, "The Female Vagrant" was almost as much an anachronism in that volume as the *Rime.* Wordsworth's poem participates in Spenserian patterns of behavior, confronting men with aspects of their own motives and destinies. Its stanzas, aspects of its style,[45] and its symbolic space[46] are Spenserian, too. But, unlike *The Ancient Mariner* and unlike *The Faerie Queene* or *The Shepheardes Calendar,* "Salisbury Plain" does not flaunt its archaism. Samuel Schulman observes that "Wordsworth's use of the Spenserian mode in a poem like this—contemporary, socially advanced, anti-war—is a repudiation of the antiquarian sensibility that had, up to now, cherished and promoted the appreciation of Spenser."[47] By the time Wordsworth came to write "Salisbury Plain" its Spenserian stanzas no longer brought Spenser to the mind of the average reader, who was more familiar with the neoclassical derivative than with the bewildering original.[48] No anonymous seventeenth scholar glosses its antique meaning; no E. K. remarks upon its "straungenesse." "Salisbury Plain" establishes no distance between barbarous past and barbarous present.[49] It reminds us how history uncannily persists, bringing itself to voice through the voices of strangers, reenacting itself in fragments, defying the silence of its protagonist.[50]

"The Wanderings of Cain" and "Salisbury Plain" provided Coleridge with a store of material to use in the *Rime.* Some of this material was available elsewhere (in *The Borderers,* in "The Destiny of Nations"); much of it was simply in the air between the two poets. The poems also provided examples of a puzzling aspect of the relationship between representation and repetition: the multiplication of signs and the splitting of their referents. But perhaps the particular content or the particular source matters less than what it all represented for Coleridge: material that arrived between quotation marks, fuel for a literary machine that could transform problems of intertextuality into problems of intratextuality.

The Ancient Mariner's uneasiness at the sound of his voice expresses Coleridge's own uneasiness. Both know the tale they tell is of alien origin, and for both of them, though for different reasons, this fact comes laden with anxiety. The *Rime*'s archaism, like its thematic ventriloquism, expresses the poet's consciousness of what he owes to his sources—one of whom was himself. But the anxiety he feels is not the kind that can be soothed by acknowledgment; his sources suffer from the same embarrassments he does. If the contest of voices within the *Rime* acts out that poem's relation to its sources, what is one to say about similar contests in the sources themselves? It is not the borrowing of material that generates the *Rime*'s anxiety, for the anxiety was there in the original; it is part of what Coleridge borrows. So is the penitential repetition. Cain and the sailor both sinned before Coleridge sat down to his *Rime.* No matter how much he tries, the Mariner cannot expiate a sin committed before he was created.

A summary of the *Rime,* a transcription of a recital of a repeatedly ventriloquized tale, might go, "“"'I' can't stop talking."”" The Mariner's compulsive self-quotation, which calls into question the self he quotes, expresses on the level of individual character a compulsion to repeat that constitutes not just the poem's psychology and genealogy but also its morphology. Stanzas, lines, phrases, and even individual words reveal the same penchant for repetition and self-quotation as do the poem's ancestors, inhabitants, and redactors.

Echoes and patterns of imagistic repetition ordinarily invite comparisons: we take them as indices—straight or ironic—of continuity, coherence, or analogy. Some of the *Rime*'s echoes—verbal, imagistic, and structural—behave as we expect them to; others do not. As Arden Reed points out,

> The process of doubling in the "Ancient Mariner" operates in two directions. One is the creation of resemblance or identity out of difference, when the poem demonstrates how two things that seem unrelated or even opposite can come to mirror each other. . . . But . . . the poem is also engaged in splitting identity (the presence of the word to itself, for instance) into differences, in turning the singular "rime" into two meanings that are not necessarily commensurate. This second process may be related to a more general fragmentation that marks the entire poem. Both of these operations, the making and unmaking of congruence, take place throughout the text and are woven together; but they do not form any regular, much less any dialectical pattern.[51]

Through much of the poem, the tendency to repeat disguises itself as balladic repetition:

Water, water, every where,
And all the boards did shrink;
Water, water, every where,
Nor any drop to drink.

[115–18]

Traditional balladic repetitions depend for their effect either upon their rhythmic value alone or upon their ability to unfold an irony or a revelation. *The Rime*'s repetitions sometimes seem to function the same way, as forms of punctuation laden at once with musical and with thematic value. One of the more accessible of such clusters involves interruption. The "loud bassoon" that announces the entrance of the bride into the hall interrupts the Mariner's tale just when the ship has reached the equator, where twice later its voyage will be interrupted. The voyage is interrupted first by a deadly calm that brings the specter ship bearing Life-in-Death, whose appearance parodies the bride's. It is interrupted again by the changing of the spirit-guard that makes the ship pause and rock and lunge. The "roaring wind" that approaches the becalmed ship makes "the upper air burst into life" and sets "fire-flags sheen" and stars dancing in a fashion that anticipates the conclusion of the wedding, when "what loud uproar bursts from that door!" at the singing of the bride and her maids. These echoes hint at a relationship of inverse analogy between the Mariner's journey and the wedding that his tale prevents the Wedding Guest from celebrating.

Clusters such as this one, much favored by those who insist upon the organic unity and Christian implications of the poem, lend themselves to analysis into categories of life and death, vitality and stasis, love and hate, good and evil. Taken by themselves, these patternings seem to set human life and love into the context of universal life and love, giving cosmic overtones to the wedding and affirming the universality of the human moral and epistemological codes. They suggest that what happens in the middle of the ocean remains comparable to what happens in ordinary English villages and remains interpretable by terrestrial rules. But of course the analogy can work the other way around as well, suggesting that what happens in the villages is properly interpretable only in terms of what happens to unlucky mariners at sea. It is a disturbing thought, but when—as here—the alternative is total unreadability, even a sinister interpretation may be better than none at all.

Most of the *Rime*'s repetitions are neither unmeaning "hey nonny noes" nor clues whose meaning will have become clear by the end of the poem but passages in which the mere mechanism or materiality of language seems almost—but not quite—to deny the possibility of sense. "Alone, alone, all all alone, / Alone on a wide wide Sea," laments the Mariner. The cry approaches the condition of a wordless moan. At the same time, it dramatizes a solitude that seems to imply its absoluteness by verbal necessity. The line resembles both a stutter, mere sound haunted by its own terrifyingly arbitrary and disparate possibilities, and an oxymoron, "all" being an unfinished "alone," "alone" being a portmanteau of "all" and "lone" or "one." The barely articulate wail contains its own comfort and the germ of one of Coleridge's favorite intellectual convictions, that the "all" and the "one" could be reconciled. But little other than wistful thinking holds the line's paradoxical echoes together; and even so it is unclear whether the wistful thinking is the critic's or the Mariner's.

Many of the *Rime*'s apparent echoes and symmetries resemble accidents rather than analogies. These repetitions, instances of what one might call the *instance de la lettre,* suggest primarily the power of images to recur and the powerlessness of the Mariner or the narrator to dispose of them. They seem not merely the objects of obsession but agents of contagion, infecting those who behold them. Their metonymy exercises a metaphoric, even metamorphic, effect. For this reason both looking and speaking can be dangerous activities.

In the *Rime* you become what you meet. This principle dictates the poem's structure and plot. The hypnotic power the Mariner exercises over the Wedding Guest he has absorbed, painfully, from the dead crew, who, having met Death and Life-in-Death, experience the meaning of the first and enact the meaning of the second:

All stood together on the deck,
For a charnel-dungeon fitter:
All fix'd on me their stony eyes
That in the moon did glitter.

The pang, the curse, with which they died,
Had never pass'd away:
I could not draw my een from theirs
Ne turn them up to pray.

[439–46]

The Mariner's ship displays a similar vulnerability during its transformation into an image of the two things it encounters at sea, the albatross and the specter ship. By the time it returns to port, the Mariner's ship is inhabited by Death in the several persons of the crew and Life-in-Death in the person of the Ancient Mariner, an apparent corpse still capable of both speech and movement. The ship itself, says the Hermit, "hath a fiendish look": "The planks looked warped! and see those sails, / How thin they are and sere!" It has become a skeleton ship. Though it does not plunge and tack and veer, it does, like the specter ship, move "without a breeze, without a tide," powered by supernatural forces.[52] The wind that blows as it comes to land has no navigational use:

But soon there breath'd a wind on me,
Ne sound ne motion made:
Its path was not upon the sea
In ripple or in shade.
....

Swiftly, swiftly flew the ship,
Yet she sail'd softly too:
Sweetly, sweetly blew the breeze—
On me alone it blew.

[457–60, 465–68]

The ship shares too the fate of the albatross, whose behavior foreshadows elements of the coming catastrophe. "It ate the food it ne'er had eat," as the Mariner will shortly after, although perhaps a diet of blood is not strictly comparable to one of biscuit worms. The ship, doomed to go "down like lead" when the Hermit approaches it in his boat singing "godly hymns," suffers a fate not unlike that of the albatross, which falls into the sea at an "unaware" blessing from the Mariner. The ship sinks to the sound of underwater thunder that "split the bay." Its sinking creates a whirlpool in which the Hermit's boat "spun round and round." Both ships together thus reenact in a sinister fashion the scenes in which the playful albatross first comes to the frozen ship: "round and round it flew: / The Ice did split with a Thunder fit; / The Helmsman steer'd us thro'" (66–68).[53]

It is not necessary, however, actually to encounter a physical object in order to feel its metamorphosing influence. Sometimes a merely verbal encounter is enough. Passing through the neighborhood of a simile or even a submerged metaphor puts you (even, perhaps, you the reader) at risk; the words are capable of realizing themselves at your expense. So the ship's very setting off is a sinking, as it "drop[s] / Below the Kirk, below the Hill, / Below the Light-house top"; its final moments realize in literal terms the implications of its first ones. The cracking and growling and roaring and howling of the ice at the south pole, "like noises of a swound," anticipate the trance in which the Mariner later hears two spirits discussing his past and his future. And the first hint that the Mariner is in trouble comes before the commission of the crime, when the Mariner compares the force of the storm that drives the ship south to the violence of persecution. In 1798 a fairly impersonal tempest "play'd us freaks." In 1817 the tempest became a hostile spirit:

And now the STORM-BLAST came, and he
Was tyrannous and strong;

He struck us with o'ertaking wings,
And chased us south along.

With sloping masts and dipping prow,
As who pursued with yell and blow
Still treads the shadow of his foe
And forwards bends his head,
The ship drove fast, loud roared the blast,
And southward aye we fled.[54]

When the albatross appears, as Paul Magnuson points out, "the mariner unconsciously associates the albatross with the storm while he and the crew outwardly receive the bird as a member of their Christian community.[55] The shooting of the Albatross, which most readers regard as the single event that produces the more dramatic misfortune that follows,[56] may have been a consequence of that unconscious association; alternatively, it may have been an attempt to produce belatedly a reason for what would otherwise lack explanation. A figure of the effect produces the reality of its own cause.

But to speak of before and after, anticipation and fulfillment, may be inappropriate here, where chronology is a blur, events are metalepses, and what drives the plot is the conversion of figures into literal realities and sometimes back into figures again. Chronology does not really apply to the events of this poem: its temporality is rhetorical. The same scenes—or at least the same figures—are always before our eyes, even if we cannot see them or understand what they represent. Things we never saw before are greeted like sudden recognitions, as if successful interpretation had called them into being. Thus the odd sense of familiarity at the appearance of the specter ship:

Alas! (thought I, and my heart beat loud)
How fast she neres and neres!
Are those *her* Sails that glance in the Sun
Like restless gossameres?

[173–76]

This itself echoes the gesture of recognition that opens the poem. "It is an ancient Mariner," says the narrator, as if we had already seen "it" and wanted to know what it was.[57] The lack of antecedent is no obstacle to recurrence in a poem like this, in which a figure may generate its own *etymon* and interpretation precedes its own object.

While the *Rime* deprives its declared and undeclared origins of originality, it also produces the image of a linguistic genesis of sorts. At the heart of the poem (if it can be said to have such a thing) one finds a passage in which the poem's principal obsessions and paradoxes converge. The appearance of the specter ship, an emblem of what he is about to become, inspires the Mariner to invent a rash method of what the gloss calls "free[ing] his speech from the bonds of thirst":

I bit my arm and suck'd the blood
And cry'd, A sail! a sail!

[152–53][58]

The lines intimate a close relation among naming, violence, and death. Bloodshed, after all, is bloodshed: with the killing of the albatross so recently past, the Mariner's desperate attempt to quench his thirst cannot help but suggest murder.[59] Even worse, the bloodsucking conjures up superstitions about how the dead prey upon the living. But although the poem elsewhere provides what may be evidence for such a reading, one need not think solely in terms of vampires and ghouls. Odysseus offered bloody oblations to the most respectable shades in Hades in order to release them from speechlessness.[60] When he drinks his own blood, the Mariner puts himself in the position of one already dead, and this despite the fact that Death and Life-in-Death are only at that moment coming over the horizon. Whereas in Homer the dead drink blood so that they can address the living, the Mariner drinks blood in order to hail the dead.

The act is a parody of the archaic rite, itself a Hadean inversion of divine inspiration: drinking blood in the underworld is a necessary prelude to true speech, just as inhaling divine breath is—or was—the necessary prelude to true song. In either rite, one takes into oneself the essence of another's life or spirit.[61] If the drinking of his own blood can be considered the Mariner's version of inspiration and not merely a novel way to clear his throat, then the source of his inspiration is not a higher being but himself.

Paradoxically, the traditional gesture of poetic dependence has become an assertion of vocal and imaginative autonomy. It is the physiological equivalent of self-quotation and the literary equivalent of suicide.[62]

This is not the first time the Mariner has been inspired by the blood he sheds. It was the killing of the albatross that first enabled him to identify himself, at least retrospectively, as an "I"; it may have been what provided him with a self to refer to.[63] This second shedding of blood functions like the first, enabling the Mariner to identify an inchoate "something" as a ship. It provides him too with the words that will prove to be the germ of his tale, the vocabulary (a literalization of an earlier vehicle) with which he will later try to answer the Hermit's question about his own identity. "A sail! a sail!" becomes the first line of the Mariner's autobiography: "There was a Ship."

The moment that brings into view that incarnation of the principle of uncanniness, Life-in-Death, brings also the mind's recognition of its own originary power. What answers to the Mariner's cry is an engine of autonomy and the first violation of the laws of nature. The specter ship moves without wind, without indeed any apparent motive power at all—as fits the instrument of retribution for a motiveless crime. When the Mariner's ship becomes spectral itself, it moves the same way, powered by the absence of wind, which in this case is something other than mere stillness.

> And soon I heard a roaring wind:
> It did not come anear;
> But with its sound it shook the sails,
> That were so thin and sere.
> ....
> The loud wind never reached the ship,
> Yet now the ship moved on!
> Beneath the lightning and the Moon
> The dead men gave a groan.
>
> They groaned, they stirred, they all uprose,
> Nor spake, nor moved their eyes:
> It had been strange, even in a dream,
> To have seen those dead men rise.

The helmsman steered, the ship moved on;
Yet never a breeze up-blew. . . .

[309–12, 327–36, 1817 ed.][64]

Natural wind exists as a constant moving away from itself; its condition, like that of language, is differential. This wind, curiously independent of the movement of air, affects things not by presence, not by absence, but—so to speak—by the absence of that natural absence in which normal wind consists: only the sound or voice of its roaring ever reaches the ship. It behaves like a metonymy of its own metonymic potential, a deconstructive metalepsis that leaves nature, causality, and identity behind. Its appearance amounts to a confession of allegory, voice that lives in despair of its object.

The association between wind and language is, of course, ancient and universal.[65] Traditionally, poetic wind, bearing the voice and breath of the muse into the very body of the human singer, guaranteed the truth of song: it testified to a metaphysics of presence. And so Coleridge was content to regard it until as late at least as 1795, when he imagined it sweeping, "Plastic and vast, one intellectual breeze, / At once the Soul of each, and God of all," over a world of Eolian harps.[66] A similar ideal, albeit expressed in the mode of despair, would lie behind the "Dejection" ode, whose wind the poet imagines no longer as an ecstatic, impersonal power but now as the magical counterpart to his own blocked voice, capable not only of expressing all he cannot but also of reviving that lost state in which nature and consciousness were one. He wants, in Frost's words, not "copy speech" but "original response," neither inspiration nor an interpreter but an echo that reestablishes his dialogue with what now he only gazes at "—and with how blank an eye!" Though he argues that "from the soul itself must there be sent / A sweet and potent voice, of its own birth," the priority of the internally generated voice is uncertain; the poet still yearns for the "wonted impulse" of a storm that "Might startle this dull pain, and make it move and live!" By the time the storm has risen and Coleridge has realized that he has recovered his voice, the wind has become his double, and it is impossible to locate the origin of the voice it represents.

The *Rime*'s uncanny wind, like those of the "Eolian Harp" and the "Dejection" ode, is allied with language and with spirit, but in uncomfortable ways. It is not life-giving, truthful, or cathartic, and the way it raises spirits is not cheering. Though it takes the form of spirits, it is not spiritual: insisting upon its independence, it usurps upon the souls and bodies of those it occupies, substituting voice for intentionality and turning those it inspires into zombies. It is a demonic version of the force the two conversation poems invoke, an allegory of influence, enacting the horrors against which those more traditional representations are meant to defend.[67]

The *Rime,* like the Mariner, is obsessed with its need to talk about itself and its relation to speech but never quite manages to name its subject. The poem is filled with emblems and allegories of its history and constitution: the Mariner possessed by his "strange power of speech" and the dead crew whose bodies house the spirits that sometimes sing and sometimes sail are working through aspects of inspiration, influence, and intertextuality. Just how terrifying these issues could seem to Coleridge we may see in a passage that appeared in the 1798 edition before being suppressed. The Mariner has just encountered the specter ship. Life-in-Death whistles, and a wind responds by whistling back at her through Death:

A gust of wind sterte up behind
And whistled thro' his bones;
Thro' the holes of his eyes and the hole of his mouth
Half-whistles and half-groans.

[195–98]

It plays upon him as upon some ghastly Aeolian harp—a strange power of speech indeed. These lines, along with some other details of grossly Gothic character, were purged from the poem by 1800 in an attempt to placate the critics,[68] whose voices, like so many others, found lodging in Coleridge's text. But the mysterious behavior of the wind, something hostile critics pounced upon as "absurd or unintelligible"[69] and even friendly readers found disturbing,[70] remained in place.

Like the wind, the *Rime* denies its origins: no original language, no language of spirits, no motivation, no proper causes. It gives us imitations, repetitions, representations—but no originals. It constitutes its own motivation; its telling demands the explanation its retelling, like the reenactment of Freudian transference, fails to provide. Yet the surprising thing is not, finally, that the *Rime* feels and fears the influence of outer or earlier voices, that its originality is open to question, but that the poem works so hard to put itself in second place, to confess and exhibit its secondariness. It shudders at alien voices, but it shudders at its own voice—thoroughly haunted, possessed, dispossessed, and characterless, and thereby most deeply and characteristically Coleridgean—most of all.

Divided from himself as from other men, inhabiting a world of baffling disjunction, and speaking a language neither whose motive force nor whose meaning is apparent, the Mariner is in no position to tell who he is. In a world where identity fails to coincide with character, where motivations are external and apparently autonomous, the difficulty of naming himself would be enormous. Perhaps the *Rime* really is the shortest answer to the Hermit's question, demonstrating the difficulty of saying "I am" in one's own voice.

3

The Poetry of Property

Despite his part in its composition, Wordsworth regarded the *Rime* as an embarrassment and held it to blame for the cool reception accorded to the *Lyrical Ballads*. When he reissued the volume in 1800, he removed the *Rime* from its position of prominence at the head of the volume to the deep obscurity of the penultimate spot, just ahead of "Tintern Abbey." A note provided his readers with an exposition of the ambivalence the poem aroused in him:

> I cannot refuse myself the gratification of informing such Readers as may have been pleased with this Poem, or with any part of it, that they owe their pleasure in some sort to me; as the Author was himself very desirous that it should be suppressed. This wish had arisen from a consciousness of the defects of the Poem, and from a knowledge that many persons had been much displeased with it. The Poem of my Friend has indeed great defects; first, that the principal person has no distinct character, either in his profession of Mariner, or as a human being who having been long under the controul of supernatural impressions might be supposed himself to partake of something supernatural: secondly, that he does not act, but is continually acted upon: thirdly, that the events having no necessary connection do not produce each other; and lastly, that the imagery is somewhat too laboriously accumulated. Yet the Poem contains many delicate touches of passion, and indeed the passion is every where true to nature; a great number of the stanzas present beautiful images, and are expressed with unusual felicity of language; and the versification, though the metre is itself unfit for long poems, is harmoniously and artfully varied, exhibiting the utmost powers of that metre, and every variety of which it is capable. It therefore appeared to me that these several merits (the first of which, namely that of the passion, is of the highest kind,) gave to the Poem a value which is not often possessed by better Poems. On this account I requested of my Friend to permit me to republish it.[1]

Wordsworth can hardly have believed that such remarks would serve to recommend the *Rime* to its readers, nor can he have intended that they should do so. The poem's defects, like its merits, are beside the point: the note is an exercise not so much in critical judgment as in proprietary power, directing attention away from the *Rime*'s still curiously unnamed author and toward its self-proclaimed patron. In disclaiming authorial responsibility for the poem, Wordsworth makes a proprietary gesture: it is to him and not to Coleridge, he tells us, that we owe whatever gratitude we may feel for the poem. He takes possession of a literary property whose proper owner would not own it and whose anonymity had become a source of increasing uneasiness.

The note is the natural consequence of Wordsworth's decision to place his name on the title page of what had two years before been an anonymous and therefore unowned work. It bespeaks a new interest in literary appropriation,[2] an interest that would shape and dominate this second volume of the *Lyrical Ballads,* belying the poet's contention that he had abjured his private poetic inheritance in favor of a share in communal linguistic property. The volume as a whole enacts a retraction of the anonymity implied by the preface but practiced only—and ambivalently—in the earlier volume. Its acts of nomination, which begin on the title page and end on the last page of the volume, are acts of self-authorization.

Like the volume of 1798, that of 1800 contains a number of poems about economics. The issues of property that occupy "Hart-Leap Well," "The Brothers," "Andrew Jones," "The Two Thieves," the "Poems on the Naming of Places," "Michael," and a number of lesser poems of the same kind allow the poet to show his characters in that state of excitement which, as he tells us in the preface, generates truly poetic language. Other issues might have served such a purpose equally well. But between 1798 and 1800 the significance of the economic theme had subtly changed; property had revealed itself as a potential figure for poetry itself. In this volume, particularly in the "Poems on the Naming of Places" and "Michael," property functions not just to elicit poetic utterance but to represent the value of that utterance.[3] By the end of the volume, to write about property is tantamount to writing about writing.

Although Wordsworth was concerned with the distress of the poor, the reality of economic hardship goes only so far in explaining the poet's interest in the theme. Proceeding through the second volume of the *Lyrical Ballads,* the reader will find matters of property and its loss invested with a significance that would have puzzled Wordsworth's rural neighbors. The tendency in the volume is toward an allegorization of economics rather than a socially responsible analysis of it.

The poems in this volume were not the first in which Wordsworth spoke of imagination in economic terms. "Tintern Abbey," occupying in the 1798 volume the same position that "Michael" would occupy in the second volume of 1800, presents itself in part as a meditation on the economics of sensation. The landscape of his youth

> had no need of a remoter charm,
> By thought supplied, or any interest
> Unborrowed from the eye.—That time is past,
> And all its aching joys are now no more,
> And all its dizzy raptures. Not for this
> Faint I, nor mourn nor murmur: other
> Gifts have followed, for such loss, I would believe,
> Abundant recompense.

Though the poet makes no explicit claim to the landscape he so carefully locates,[4] his absorption of that landscape into himself—his conversion of a cataract into a passion, a mountain into an appetite—suggests that he regards it as an annex to his identity, a form of psychological property. And so he treats it, offering it to his sister that she may build upon it "a mansion for all lovely forms," "a dwelling-place / For all sweet sounds and harmonies," a resting-place for his memory, a tomb for his spirit.

The landscape "Tintern Abbey" surveys is partly external, partly internal, and partly textual. Looking down over the scene and into the past, it also looks back over the volume it concludes. Here Wordsworth steps out from behind his anonymity and reveals himself as author and proprietor—in the absence of anything similar from Coleridge, *sole* author and proprietor. Without actually naming himself, Wordsworth manages to lay implicit claim to the entire

1798 volume, taking calm possession of even its uncanniest contents.[5]

As the theme of property becomes explicit in the second 1800 volume, however, it becomes disconcerting. The poetry represents property as a morally ambiguous thing, founded upon guilt or fear. "Hart-Leap Well," for example, the poem that opens volume II of the 1800 *Lyrical Ballads,* picking up where "Tintern Abbey" left off, returns to the terms of the earlier poem in such a way as to stress their darker implications. The "heart" that Nature never did betray in "Tintern Abbey" is echoed here by the hunted "hart"; the "mansion" that the poet in "Tintern Abbey" hoped his sister would build in her mind becomes here the mansion Sir Walter erects on the spot where the hart dies. Like "Tintern Abbey," "Hart-Leap Well" concerns a return to origins that is simultaneously an imaginative appropriation, but that appropriation becomes the source of uneasiness.

"Hart-Leap Well" returns not only to Wordsworthian but also to Coleridgean sources. It looks back not only to "Tintern Abbey" but also to the *Rime,* which occupied in the first volume (1798) the same spot "Hart-Leap Well" does in Volume II of the work in 1800. Here we are again in the midst of supernatural vengeance exacted for an offense against supernatural order. Pursuing the hart, Sir Walter fails to notice the "doleful silence in the air," an ominous sign of the unhappiness among the spirits of the place observing "This race . . . [that] looks not like an earthly race":

> This beast not unobserv'd by Nature fell,
> His death was mourn'd by sympathy divine.
>
> The Being, that is in the clouds and air,
> That is in the green leaves among the groves,
> Maintains a deep and reverential care
> For them the quiet creatures whom he loves.

Tutelary spirits, akin to the albatross's avengers, quietly destroy Sir Walter's Pleasure-house. Though the killing of the beast cannot be undone, the architecture that commemorates it can be: the revenge is not as dramatic as that which turned the Mariner's vessel into a specter ship, but it is equally thorough.

As in the *Rime,* the fascination of the story is contagious and morally contaminating. Sir Walter's memorial effort erased what it pretended to preserve; his architecture paid tribute not to the hart he has destroyed but to his own prowess in destroying it. As his efforts at interpretation buried their object, so, perhaps, do the poet's.[6] To look for the ruined mansion is to "Hunt . . . for a forgotten dream"; to interpret the pillars Sir Walter has set atop the hart's hoof marks is to repeat his own remarks and reenact his crime. Interpretation is identified with what it would interpret and implicated in the original crime. It is impossible to distinguish the commemorative motive from the appropriative or to free either from the taint of the other. And as we shall see, the difference between staking a claim and digging a grave is slight.

Wordsworth's interest in poetic appropriation becomes explicit only in the "Poems on the Naming of Places." Naming the hills and valleys around him, he exercises Adam's prerogative, taking dominion over the earth by means of nomination.[7] The poet's claims in these poems are bold and unembarrassed, though circumscribed; he speaks here in his own name, taking evident pleasure in the power of his own voice to create real, albeit modest, social facts—for the poems make it clear that the names have a social power. The poet hopes that all who dwell near him will know the places he has written about by the names he has given them and use the names as he and his circle use them, as practical labels for places in the neighborhood.[8] He would seem, at first glance, to have resolved the ambivalence toward property evident in "Hart-Leap Well" and the poems that followed it, an ambivalence reflecting, perhaps, an awareness that any act of appropriation, even one directed toward what one believed to be one's own rightful property, is liable to involve a trespass. But his boldness is involved in a paradox: there can be no question of trespass where there is no property, and, as far as the reader can tell, these places belong to no one either before or after the poet names them.[9] Although the act of naming implies appropriation, writing a poem giving a glade to one friend or a mountain peak to another does nothing to change the legal status of the place and gives the recipient of the poet's generosity no recognized rights over it. It is hard, then, despite the transparency of their intentions, to know how to take these poems. Are they serious or are they not? What kind of authority does this exercise of verbal appropriation signify? What kind of claim is Wordsworth really making?

About *Home at Grasmere,* Wordsworth's long celebration of domestic appropriation and poetic settlement, a poem begun about the same time as the "Poems on the Naming of Places," Lore Metzger has remarked a "fairytale romance" quality, a fantastic disregard for the real hardships suffered by the people whose families had always lived on the land and who were now being forcibly deprived of their economic independence by (among other things) acts of enclosure. *Home at Grasmere,* she says, "reveal[s] nothing about the process by which an individual living in an age of dislocating political, social, and economic changes could gain such undefiled wholeness, such undiminished self-realization" as Wordsworth describes himself as enjoying at Grasmere.[10] One might convict the place-naming poems of the same culpable oblivion.[11] But what shocks us is not so much the fact of the poems' self-absorption as the audacity of their self-enclosure. Simultaneously demanding and refusing contextualization, the poems defy us to make sense of their self-conscious nonrelations with the social world. They seem to be engaged in an attempt to transcend their own material pretexts.

Wordsworth might have justified his poems by appeal to local practice. "In the North," writes Coleridge, "every Brook, every Crag, almost every Field has a name,"[12] and among Wordsworth's community the crags and fields tended to bear the names of friends. But in the "Advertisement" to the "Poems on the Naming of Places," Wordsworth chooses to follow a slightly different line of argument, one that disregards the fact of tradition:

> By Persons resident in the country and attached to rural objects, many places will be found unnamed or of unknown names, where little Incidents will have occured, or feelings been experienced, which will have given to such places a private and peculiar interest. From a wish to give some sort of record to such Incidents or renew the gratification of such Feelings, Names have been given to Places by the Author and some of his Friends, and the following Poems written in consequence.[13]

Insisting he gives names where no one had bothered to give names before or bothered to remember the names if given, Wordsworth effectively erases all rival local names from the official record. In so doing he arrogates to himself and his close friends the credit for what we know was a more widespread practice.[14] But in representing the verses as essentially private, Wordsworth seems to minimize his claims. The poems are "records" of things of no particular intrinsic importance, humble mementos that would have little value for anyone outside the poet's immediate circle. They are not impressive pieces of verse; probably the friends to whom they were dedicated were their most gratified readers. The "Advertisement" apologizes for something that seems hardly to be regarded as poetry at all.

Despite the apparent modesty of the "Advertisement" to the place-naming poems, however, the program it suggests is not dissimilar to the program of Wordsworth's greatest poetry,[15] in which he invests an unpromising object or form with as much significance as it can bear while providing as little story or explanation as is possible. The suppression of story in Wordsworth's other poetry may be compared with the suppression of the logic of naming in these poems. As James Averill describes it, "The inevitable event toward which the poem has been moving and from which it radiates is left blank."[16] It is this that makes it hard to gauge the magnitude of the poetic endeavor here, to determine whether these are merely fanciful verses or poems of seriousness amounting to arrogance. Although the poet presents his namings as if they were the consequences of logic, he denies the reader an explication of what that logic is: he gives us nothing to judge. Common sense alone cannot authorize or account for the namings. "What a pleasant spot," he says; "how delightful it is to sit under this fine tree and look at the hills; *therefore* I shall name this place after so-and-so." But why after so-and-so and not what's-her-name? Despite his "therefore" and his "because," the reason for his namings frequently remains obscure.

If there is no connection between the place and the person other than what the poet creates by his naming, the poem may be regarded as a gracious but gratuitous offering of something the poet does not possess and cannot give: "This is a beautiful place, and so I name it for you"—"and so" representing the wishful reasoning of generous affection. "Our thoughts at least are ours," the poet says to himself in "It was an April Morning," as if within the confines of the imagination one were free to name anything as one pleased, or as if the circumstance of naming were so private that no one need concern himself with another man's preference in the matter.

If names matter, if names are indeed the whole point, it is hard to know what to make of the manifest aversion to real names in these poems. Refusing to tell the very thing that the poet pretends he wrote the poems to tell, they give partial or false versions of the names. "It was an April Morning" names a valley "Emma's Dell" after the poet's sister Dorothy; though in his poetry she does occasionally appear under this pseudonym, it seems odd somehow to find her still bearing a false name here. "To Joanna" gives the real first name of the woman for whom Joanna's Rock is named, but no one outside the group of friends would know that Joanna was Joanna Hutchinson. "To M. H." must have posed a similar problem to contemporary readers, who would gather that the "M" must stand for "Mary" but who would not know what the "H" stood for. "There is an Eminence" gives the reader enough information for him to come up with either "Wordsworth's Peak" or "William's Peak," but the poem does not itself pronounce either name. "A narrow girdle of rough stones" names its place "Point Rash-Judgment"—but then, that is nobody's name. Withholding names, the place-naming poems become paradoxes. What remains when the names are gone is voice dissociated from reference. One must ask, then, why names at all? What name matters here?

For those readers who knew little about Wordsworth and less about his friends, his decision to disguise names would have meant nothing. Had they known about it, they might have considered the substitution a means of protecting privacy. Those who knew the people and their names, however, must have felt a slight shock: what ought to have been familiar was not. If the point of the place-naming poems was to enable friends and neighbors to recognize people and places, the decision to disguise the names thwarts that purpose; the referentiality upon which much of the charm of these pieces depended was undermined. But perhaps it was the idea of referentiality rather than its practical realization that interested Wordsworth: the idea of a name rather than the recognition it usually makes possible. The place-naming poems name a landscape that exists partly in England but more in the realm of language. Attempting to establish not only a human home but also a ground for the imagination,[17] the poems inhabit that region in which the human is not always distinguishable from the inhuman, the fancied from the real, the meaningful from the meaningless. The ground the poet names is the territory around his house, but it is also the territory of the poetic imagination. For this reason, and despite their evident homeliness, the poems create an uncanny effect. This uncanniness was not Wordsworth's own invention. It had its origins in the history of property itself.

From ancient times, appropriating land meant more than simply putting a fence around it. It involved ritual consultations with the gods and precautions against transgressing the will of the gods or the dead, who were regarded as the original—and potentially jealous—custodians.[18] Possession was a reciprocal relation; its symbolism reminded the new owner that in staking a claim to nature he was submitting to the claim that nature staked in him.

The rituals that grew up around the acquisition of property were acknowledgments of one's creaturely origins, obligations, and ends. They were simultaneously attempts to impute one's own needs and desires to nature, which thereby acquired a mouth, an appetite, a voice, and a body. In classical times, for example, one of the first steps involved in founding a city was the building of a *mundus*. This meant digging a hole and casting into it the first fruits and some earth from the settlers' home cities. The *mundus* seems to have been consecrated to the infernal deities and to have been "a shrine of the *manes,* the propitiated souls of the dead." It may also have been regarded as the mouth of the underworld.[19] The Greeks and Romans invested with divinity the very stones that marked the boundaries of their public and private properties—the archaeologically authenticated counterparts to Puttenham's rhetorical rock heaps and Amphion's inanimate audiences. Unlike those fabulous stones, however, these *horoi* or *herms* displayed a "hierophantic character" and were endowed with voice, at least with ventriloquisms, housing gods who sometimes spoke through first-person inscriptions. The *herm* was "a square stone, sometimes garnished with a head or male pudenda, or both." It could take the form of a *hermax,* which was "a heap of stones, with one stone erect in the middle or on top. Such heaps could be landmarks, boundary stones or tombs, and herms remained a familiar form of tombstone."[20] These stones, suggesting both tombstones and huge fertility symbols, represented a "divinely ordered compact between sky, earth and man,"[21] and provided a passageway between the underworld and the heavens.[22] Thus the boundary marker provided continuity between human and divine, between past and present. For the ancients, the ground was haunted and property was sacred.

Wordsworth's place-naming poems and "Michael" focus on the modern equivalents of these classical constructions, sites at which property becomes prosopopoeia and the ground seems to speak. Exercises in the creation of property, the place-naming poems and "Michael" covertly acknowledge the fact of prior ownership: the ground they inscribe seems already to be inhabited—or haunted.[23] It would have to be, if the poet's demands are to be answered, if the landscape is to submit to his naming and authorize his claims with claims of its own.

Seen from one perspective, the poems seem to be gestures of affection and compliment, pointing to the continuity of generations and the endurance of communal memory; seen from another, they are reminders of the inevitability of oblivion and death.[24] The funerary aspect is most pronounced in two place-naming poems not to be found in the *Lyrical Ballads:* "When to the attractions of the busy world" and "Inscription for a Seat by the Road Side Half-Way up a Steep Hill Facing South." "When to the attractions of the busy world"[25] became a real elegy when Wordsworth's brother John, for whom he had written the poem, died at sea. Circumstances, not form, distinguish it from the other "Poems on the Naming of Places." The exaggerated morbidity of "Inscription for a Seat by the Road Side,"[26] however, arises from its explicit function as a *memento mori.* Despite the particularity of the title, the place seems unimportant except as a moral emblem, a place of meditation along the road of life. The poem's "rather obvious piety"[27] overwhelms the literal reality of its subject. The inscription calls upon an imaginary young passerby to think of the aged, the weak, and the ill who stop at "this sod, and this rude tablet" to rest and, "well-admonished, ponder here / On final rest." For them the place is both a refuge and a *memento mori*—perhaps the former because the latter, providing refuge because imaging a final rest. The inscription exhorts this young man to consider their ends and his own. As the place should remind him of their mortality, so they should remind him of his own:

> And if a serious thought
> Should come uncalled—how soon *thy* motions high,
> Thy balmy spirits and thy fervid blood
> Must change to feeble, withered, cold and dry,
> Cherish the wholesome sadness!

Keeping in mind that he will one day be in the same condition as the others who stop here, the young traveler should try to internalize not just the lesson but also the place and become a living version of this "seat of sods" for others:

> And where'er
> The tide of Life impel thee, O be prompt
> To make thy present strength a staff of all,
> Their staff and resting-place—so shalt thou give
> To Youth the sweetest joy that Youth can know;
> And for thy future self thou shalt provide
> Through every change of various life, a seat,
> Not built by hands, on which thy inner part,
> Imperishable, many a grievous hour,
> Or bleak or sultry may repose—yea, sleep
> The sleep of Death, and dream of blissful worlds,
> Then wake in Heaven, and find the dream all true.

"Bethou me," the inscription seems to say, and even its author finds the invitation compelling. When Coleridge published the piece in the *Morning Post* he signed it "Ventifrons," which is dog-Latin for "Windy Brow," the place where he, Wordsworth, and Dorothy made the seat of sods. In this early version of the place-naming poem, the place names the man (but which man? perhaps it does not matter) rather than the other way around.[28] The signature itself implies that the author speaks from out of the ground.[29]

Whereas several of the other poems in the *Lyrical Ballads* focus on attempts to read signs already present in the landscape,[30] the "Poems on the Naming of Places" attempt to put signs there for others to read. The poet seems ambivalent, however, about being caught in the act of inscription, which is also in this case an act of forgery, for he tries to represent his poems as issuing out of a natural rather than human authority. He wants nature to endorse his words. If he can interpret a mountain's natural signs as the meaning of his words, he can present himself as nature's prophet, not so much creating meaning as articulating a meaning already present in the landscape. Because the meaning he wants ratified is that of his own authority, however, his maneuvers involve him in a paradox: nature must confer on him a title that, to be legitimate, he must create himself.

If the places named in the "Poems on the Naming of Places" are meant to reflect anyone, that anyone is more often the poet than the friend for whom he names the place. Standing at the head of the "Poems on the Naming of Places," "It was an April Morning" self-consciously tests the power of the poet's voice, presenting the valley it names as an image of voice—as an image of the young man who writes about it.[31]

It was an April Morning: fresh and clear
The Rivulet, delighting in its strength,
Ran with a young man's speed, and yet the voice
Of waters which the winter had supplied
Was soften'd down into a vernal tone.
The spirit of enjoyment and desire,
And hopes and wishes, from all living things
Went circling, like a multitude of sounds.

The poet is more prominent here than his subject. His celebration of the brook sounds like a thinly disguised celebration of himself, poetic voice, and the power of desire. The brook is like a young man and a poet, softening or making subtle the old voice of winter while keeping its mature strength. And as if to confirm the association, the poet describes not "a multitude of sounds" but "hopes and wishes . . . like a multitude of sounds." The simile we might have expected has been turned inside out. The inversion serves notice that the reality of the landscape now depends upon the imagination of the poet. The imagination has become the ground of the ground.

As one might expect where the poet's mind has established its priority over the place, the scene begins to reflect not what is but what is yet to be. The landscape expresses the youthful impatience of one eager to take possession of some promised gift. The dell becomes a visible prolepsis:[32]

> The budding groves appear'd as if in haste
> To spur the steps of June; as if their shades
> Of *various* green were hindrances that stood
> Between them and their object . . .

Although the poet returns from his imaginings to nature, restoring tenor and vehicle to their conventional relationship, he fills nature with a desire to overleap itself. Yet

> meanwhile,
> There was such deep contentment in the air
> That every naked ash, and tardy tree
> Yet leafless, seem'd as though the countenance
> With which it look'd on this delightful day
> Were native to the summer.—

The winter trees are so content in their leaflessness they look like summer trees. The contentment is oxymoronic, a contentment with what is not yet, a contentment that functions like effective denial. Like any hungry infant hallucinating milk, impatient nature dreams its own fulfillment. Transcending the need that brought it into being, imagination satisfies its own desires.

Into this fane of an untrodden region of the mind, following the vocal brook back towards its source, walks the poet. He comes

> to a sudden turning . . .
> In this continuous glen, where down a rock
> The stream, so ardent in its course before,
> Sent forth such sallies of glad sound, that all
> Which I till then had heard, appear'd the voice
> Of common pleasure: beast and bird, and lamb,
> The Shepherd's dog, the linnet and the thrush
> Vied with this waterfall, and made a song
> Which, while I listen'd, seem'd like the wild growth
> Or some natural produce of the air
> That could not cease to be.

Again the source of the voice is hard to pin down, becoming the voice of the whole landscape and by contrast or contagion making the earlier voices "common" too, diffused into all of nature. The poet imagines this voice of the air, this "wild growth / Or . . . natural produce of the air," to be immortal or timeless, not this time overleaping the present but now extending it indefinitely.

But the poem turns away from its own implications, allowing reality to reassert itself.

> Green leaves were here,
> But 'twas the foliage of the rocks, the birch,
> The yew, the holly, and the bright green thorn,
> With handling islands of resplendent furze:
> And on a summit, distant a short space,
> By any who should look beyond the dell,
> A simple mountain Cottage might be seen.

Nature, or perhaps the poet, defers fulfillment and settles for less later for someone else rather than more now for me. This is still a wintry landscape; its green is the permanent green of the hardiest plants. The solitary cottage, too, almost lost in the catalogue of wintry green things, is minimal, and it lays a minimal claim on the landscape. It is there more to be seen than itself to see; it does not possess the landscape but suggests the notion of possession that the poet takes up only to relinquish, as he determines with a gesture of perverse largesse to dedicate the place to his sister:

> I gaz'd and gaz'd, and to myself I said,
> "Our thoughts at least are ours; and this wild nook,
> My EMMA, I will dedicate to thee."

At the moment he puts himself in a position to seize and bestow this landscape, he does two things: he distinguishes his voice from nature's, and he insists upon the property he has in his own mind, if nowhere else. He quietly concedes the limitations of his power; his is not the voice of nature, nor is nature his to dispose of as he pleases. But his concession is also an assertion of the imagination's independence from nature. Having declared his independence, the poet is prepared to take possession:

> Soon did the spot become my other home,
> My dwelling, and my out-of-doors abode.

And, of the Shepherds who have seen me there,
To whom I sometimes in our idle talk
Have told this fancy, two or three, perhaps,
Years after we are gone and in our graves,
When they have cause to speak of this wild place,
May call it by the name of EMMA'S DELL.

Although his audience is small and undistinguished, consisting of a few shepherds, he looks forward to the time when their voices will continue his vocal effort, lending his voice a retrospective authority and his claim a retrospective antiquity. The poem reaches out to influence those who will live after the poet and who can make his naming, if not his name, immortal.

At stake in the survival of Emma's name is the survival of the poet's voice. Despite his dedication of the spot to his sister, the place is more his than hers—he does not say it became Emma's second home, nor is Emma's name (or pseudonym) really important. The point of this exercise in naming seems to be the assertion rather of his voice than Emma's name, rather the fact of his speaking and analogizing than the content of his speech and analogy. The name must stick in spite of the contrary analogy between the place and the poet and in spite of the falsity of the name he gives; the poem tests not poetic logic or coherence but pure voice. The act of naming takes precedence over the particular name it uses; in effect what the poem tries to make the landscape remember is not Emma but the source of voice, the poet himself. If the name "takes"—if the shepherds use it—the land itself will seem to own or speak the name it has been given, a prevenient epitaph for the poet and his sister. The name must survive not in spite of death but almost because of it.

The slightly morbid tones of the conclusion to "It was an April Morning" become unmistakably eerie in "To Joanna." This, the second of the "Poems on the Naming of Places," may be the only one in the group that does not lend itself to being read as a poem of light compliment. Behind the "therefore we have named this place for you" with which most of the poems in this group end is the affectionate desire to remember a friend in some beautiful spot. Behind the logic of the naming of Joanna's Rock is the recognition of natural necessity; the mountains have recognized

Joanna's voice and taken it into theirs. It is something of a shock, then, to discover that the logic of this naming is based on fiction; this is the only one of the "Poems on the Naming of Places" that has no basis in reality—that has, so to speak, no ground.[33] Here the literal, matter-of-fact source seems unimportant. Even if we accept the poem's account, Joanna's laughter seems in retrospect too trivial to count as a source; its echoings and reechoings confuse the matter, and by the time the mountain uproar has died down it is no longer clear where the voice came from. The actual source seems to matter less than what becomes of it, the way it is echoed, quoted, and revised. To name the place "Joanna's Rock," after all this, seems ironic; this is the place where Joanna momentarily lost her voice to nature and heard it come back to her no longer her own and meaning something more than she had meant. She may own a rock in the landscape, but her ownership of her own voice is open to question.

As the opening lines make clear, Joanna is no worshipper of nature and has little patience for people "Who look upon the hills with tenderness, / And make dear friendships with the streams and groves." Yet those who love nature love her too, and in the two years she has been gone, the opening verse paragraph goes on to say, they have missed her and talked about her. This provides the pretext for introducing the story. The Vicar recently stepped out of his house to ask the poet how Joanna was and to demand why the poet,

> like a Runic Priest, in characters
> Of formidable size had chiselled out
> Some uncouth name [as the Vicar sees it] upon the native rock,
> Above the Rotha, by the forest-side.

The story he tells the Vicar is about Joanna's amazement at the spectacle not of the natural beauty of a spring morning but of his own apparent stupefied response to it. Finding the man more interesting than the landscape, she laughs; and nature, proving itself stranger than she suspected, echoes her laughter. The sound terrifies her. Returning to the place a year and a half later and remembering "affections old and true," the poet carves his friend's name into the "living stone," which now he and his friends call "Joanna's Rock."

As the poet has it in his conversation with the Vicar, Joanna's laughter seems to wake nature from sleep and to humanize the mountains, which not only reflect the voice but seem to respond to it, augmenting it with their own voices, so that while sometimes it sounds like the same sound Joanna uttered, sometimes it sounds completely different, "a mountain tone" or the noise of a speaking-trumpet:

> The rock, like something starting from a sleep,
> Took up the Lady's voice, and laugh'd again:
> That ancient Woman seated on Helm-crag
> Was ready with her cavern; Hammar-Scar,
> And the tall Steep of Silver-How sent forth
> A noise of laughter; southern Loughrigg heard,
> And Fairfield answer'd with a mountain tone:
> Helvellyn far into the clear blue sky
> Carried the Lady's voice,—old Skiddaw blew
> His speaking trumpet;—back out of the clouds
> Of Glaramara southward came the voice;
> And Kirkstone toss'd it from his misty head.

John Wordsworth told Mary Hutchinson that his brother the poet believed that "To Joanna" and "Nutting" "show the greatest genius of any poems in the second volume" of the *Lyrical Ballads,*"[34] and certainly haunting genii abound in this poem.[35] But whether the genii belong to nature or to the poet is not clear. The poet doubts whether

> this were in simple truth
> A work accomplish'd by the brotherhood
> Of ancient mountains, or my ear was touch'd
> With dreams and visionary impulses
> Is not for me to tell. . . .

He is unsure of what has happened. Both he and the mountains have been dreaming. He half suspects that the voices were directed not randomly or at Joanna but at him and that their sound emanates from his own consciousness. If the sound comes back as almost uncannily familiar to the poet, it comes back as uncannily strange to Joanna. At the sound Joanna drew by his side "as if she wished to shelter from some object of her fear." It sounds as if the poet did not know what frightened her, as if he did not associate the "loud uproar in the hills" with her at all at that moment. The echoes made both of them feel isolated and a little anxious, each suspicious that the noise had to do with him or with her alone.

Not only the sound but the entire experience is uncanny. The voice leaves its source behind, and the experience repeats itself, in a milder way, as the poet tells the story to the Vicar. Joanna laughed out of innocent incredulity at the poet's reaction to the colors of the stones and the flowers arrayed

> Along so vast a surface, all at once,
> In one impression, by connecting force
> Of their own beauty, imaged in the heart.
> —When I had gazed perhaps two minutes' space,
> Joanna, looking in my eyes, beheld
> That ravishment of mine, and laughed aloud.

She was amused by something she did not understand. Listening to the story and hearing about how the mountains echoed that laugh, the Vicar "in the hey-day of astonishment / Smiled in my face"—reacting to the surprising behavior of nature as Joanna had reacted to the surprising behavior of her friend. He has caught something of the mood of the storyteller himself, who has begun his tale feeling "those dear immunities of heart / Engendered between malice and true love." The framing of the story not only contains but also extends the echoes of Joanna's laughter. Perhaps it is as an assertion of authority over his own voice that Wordsworth constructs his poem around an extended self-quotation, itself full of the mountains' quotations of Joanna's laughter. Unlike Joanna, whose voice gets away from her, the poet has control over the way his words are repeated, because he repeats them himself. Yet the poet's voice does threaten to take on a life of its own, as Wordsworth suggests in a notebook entry:

> . . . I begin to relate the story, meaning in a certain degree to divert or partly play upon the Vicar. I begin—my mind partly forgets its purpose, softened by the images of beauty in the description of the rock, and the delicious morning, and when I come to the 2 lines "The Rock like something" *etc.,* I am caught in the trap of my own imagination. I entirely lose sight of my first purpose. I take fire in the lines

> "that ancient woman". I go on in that strain of fancy "Old Skiddaw" and terminate the description in tumult "And Kirkstone" *etc.*, describing what for a moment I believed either actually took place at the time, or when I have been reflecting on what did take place I have had a temporary belief, in some fit of imagination, did really or might have taken place. When the description is closed, or perhaps partly before I waken from the dream and see that the Vicar thinks I have been extravagating, as I intended he should, I then tell the story as it happened really; and as the recollection of it exists permanently and regularly in my mind, mingling allusions suffused with humour, partly to the trance in which I have been, and partly to the trick I have been playing on the Vicar.[36]

In carving Joanna's name into the "living" rock, the poet seems to wish to domesticate or humanize the scene, but, as in others of the "Poems on the Naming of Places," the naming or inscription either emerges from or suggests a sense of mortality: by inscribing "Joanna" on a rock the poet has made his friend an epitaph. The carving marks the place where Joanna's voice has been absorbed into the larger voices of nature and ceased to be hers. Nor is the survival of the poet's own nominative powers guaranteed by the sacrifice of Joanna's name: the poet's inscription falls instantly into the decay of illegibility. The fact of inscription remains evident and so, oddly, does its meaning, but the letters themselves are lost. To the eyes of the Vicar, who understands the inscription without understanding that he does so, the uninterpretable markings suggest "some uncouth name" of archaic aspect. One might judge from his unconscious connection of the rock with the idea of Joanna that the engraving is more legible than it appears or that, alternatively, its power to put the Vicar in mind of Joanna proves how naturally appropriate the place-naming was. One might with equal plausibility, however, conclude that here language has fallen utterly out of any preestablished scheme of propriety and shown its power—that of an unbound and unappropriable imagination—to mimic the possessive intentionality of the poet it dispossesses.

In its suggestion that the poet may fall victim to nature—or to language—"To Joanna" counters the tendency of most of the other place-naming poems, which is to emphasize the power and propriety of the poet's voice. With the third of the "Poems on the Naming of Places" Wordsworth returns to this simpler and more gratifying theme. Here the poet is no longer in competition with the object of his gallantry. The opening words of "There is an Eminence" suggest with embarrassing immediacy the rationale for the naming it treats: "There is an Eminence,—of these our hills / The last that parleys with the setting sun." Of course the "Eminence" is named for the poet, and of course the poet does his best in the lines that follow to disown the analogy implicit in those words. Instead of considering the possible likeness between a mountain and a sublime poet, Wordsworth shifts the poem's attention away from the hill's eminence and toward its relationship with things around it.

> We can behold it from our Orchard-seat,
> And, when at evening we pursue our walk
> Along the public way, this Cliff, so high
> Above us, and so distant in its height,
> Is visible, and often seems to send
> Its own deep quiet to restore our hearts.
> The meteors make of it a favorite haunt:
> The star of Jove, so beautiful and large
> In the mid heav'ns, is never half so fair
> As when he shines above it.

Despite its great distance and great height, it stands in a special relation to the poet and his friends—a relation purely visual, but not inconvenient and not unsatisfying. Despite its impersonality, the mountain provides comfort: it is visible from everywhere. In its relation to the heavens too it is amiable, the object of meteor-love and planet-love, and it seems to bless Jupiter with beauty. For all its eminence and separateness, it seems a sociable mountaintop. But the poet is still intent upon distinguishing himself from it; its solitude, however agreeably figured, is still threatening to the poet.

> 'Tis in truth
> The loneliest place we have among the clouds.
> And She who dwells with me, that no place on earth
> Can ever be a solitude to me,
> Hath said, this lonesome Peak shall bear my Name.

Perhaps the "And" that links the description of the mountain's loneliness to the decision to name it implies no connection; perhaps it pretends to no necessary logical force but is simply, casually, conversational: "This is what the place is like, and now it is mine." Perhaps the place does not much matter because it is chosen not as an emblem of the poet but as a blank space convenient to write a name upon. But the intensity with which the poet appreciates the difference between the mountain's situation and his own suggests he feels too the threat of their resemblance. The connection between them is paradoxical, simultaneously implying and denying their kinship in solitude. The passion in these lines reflects the magnitude of what is at stake in the poet's choice between community with the mountain and human community: it is the force of the poet's analogizing voice that overcomes the loneliness of the mountain, putting into the relation of likeness what was without analogy before. But the poet finally chooses to emphasize the difference between the "lonesome Peak" and himself. Binding himself to his sister rather than to the rock, he averts the threat of his own somewhat sinister analogy and refuses—only here, in this one place-naming poem—to acknowledge death.

The next poem, however, more than compensates for this lack. In its explicitly allegorical intentions, "A narrow girdle of rough stones" resembles the "Inscription for a Seat by the Road Side" more closely than any other of the place-naming poems. The poem tells of a mistake the poet and two friends make one misty September morning. Idling along the side of a lake, they hear the sounds of a harvest in progress, and, as the mist suddenly clears, they see ahead of them the outline of a peasant fishing. They blame him for being so "'Improvident and reckless'" as to

> lose a day
> Of the mid harvest, when the labourer's hire
> Is ample, and some little might be stored
> Wherewith to cheer him in the winter time.

Then, as they come closer, still complaining, he looks at them and they see that he is ill and thin, barely able to stand and hold his fishing pole, never mind take part in the harvest. They regret their thoughtlessness, reproach themselves for their lack of tact and charity, and name the place "Point Rash-Judgment" in memory of their mistake.

David Simpson points out that the naming "simply repeats in a finer tone the prior nomination of the old man as an emblem of idleness. The gesture of self-correction is thus implicated in the same problems as determined the initial crime."[37] The three friends have not learned to refrain from the temptation of turning things and people into symbols but have indulged again in "an act of selfish appropriation and wilful intentionalizing." For Simpson, the poem becomes an implicit criticism of its own act of naming and offers an undercutting of its own interpretation.[38]

But it is also possible to see the naming as a refusal to acknowledge the landscape's potential meaning. The poet reads the scene in terms of human error so as not to read it in terms of death. When the poem opens, the poet and his friends (Coleridge and Dorothy) are strolling by the lakeside and looking at the "dry wreck" of leaves and twigs the lake has washed up. What they see is real enough, but it has a dreamlike quality:

> in our vacant mood,
> Not seldom did we stop to watch some tuft
> Of dandelion seed or thistle's beard,
> That skimmed the surface of the dead calm lake,
> Suddenly halting now—a lifeless stand!
> And starting off again with freak as sudden;
> In all its sportive wanderings, all the while,
> Making report of an invisible breeze
> That was its wings, its chariot, and its horse,
> Its playmate, rather say, its moving soul.

The three friends seem to find the antics of the seed amusing, but the image is uncanny: the floating seed seems now "lifeless" and now "sportive," the source of its life (if life it can be called) invisible and mysterious. The sight seems at the same time to be an introspective vision, a glimpse of the mental landscape in which the friends' vacancy and aimlessness is figured in the wandering fluff. Indeed, the structure of the sentence allows the reader some moments of doubt about whether it is the seed or the walkers who suddenly halt or start off again with a sudden freak.

By the time the poet has glimpsed the fisherman through the

mist, he has shown himself at his least admirable, a sentimental tourist who is liable to glorify water weeds by thoughtless comparisons to the "queen Osmunda" or to a "Naid by the side / of Grecian brook, or Lady of the Mere, / Sole-sitting by the shores of old Romance," and who is apt to blame an old man for the appearance of idling.

Seeing in the man a reflection of their own idleness exaggerated to blameworthy proportions, the company treats him as something which they are at liberty to condemn. They err in regarding him so familiarly. The turning of his head brings a sudden revelation of his condition and exempts him from their criticism. It also makes it impossible for the poem to continue as a tour description. What looked like an ordinary peasant escaped from the labor of the harvest turns out to be a figure like the leech-gatherer in "Resolution and Independence" or the Cumberland beggar, a figure hardly human any more:

> we saw a man worn down
> By sickness, gaunt and lean, with sunken cheeks
> And wasted limbs, his legs so long and lean
> That for my single self I look'd at them,
> Forgetful of the body they sustain'd.—
> Too weak to labour in the harvest field,
> The man was using his best skill to gain
> A pittance from the dead unfeeling lake
> That knew not of his wants.

Had they seen this figure in the harvest field, they would have had no difficulty recognizing his kinship with Death the Reaper. Looking into a landscape they have appropriated in idle fancy and onto which they have projected their own characteristics, the walkers face a reminder of mortality. The man's presence comes as a revelation of the meaning of the landscape: in him the suggestion of the "wreck" of withered weeds on the shore, the "lifeless[ness]" of the "sportive" seed, the "dead calm" of the lake, and the reaping of the harvest come together.

The *memento mori* is a mirror for those who look into it. Its power is the power of self-knowledge. But the poet backs off from the image and refuses to own the interpretation his own imagination has suggested, returning instead to the ordinary and the manageable:

> The happy idleness of that sweet morn,
> With all its lovely images, was changed
> To serious musing and to self-reproach,
> Nor did we fail to see within ourselves
> What need there is to be reserved in speech,
> And temper all our thoughts with charity.

By interpreting what has happened in this way, they avoid the need to worry either about the plight of the man or about the threat of the uncanny. They have now identified the meaning of the landscape with a Christian moral, making the man into something that has been placed there to admonish them and safely absorbing what had the potential to disrupt their self-absorption. The naming enforces this interpretation, limiting the implications of the disturbing vision:

> Therefore, unwilling to forget that day,
> My Friend, Myself, and She who then receiv'd
> The same admonishment, have call'd the place
> By a memorial name, uncouth indeed
> As e'er by Mariner was given to Bay
> Or Foreland, on a new-discover'd coast;
> And POINT RASH-JUDGMENT is the Name it bears.

"A narrow girdle of rough stones" is the only one of the "Poems on the Naming of Places" that names a place after something other than a human being. Precedents for naming places after moral qualities are not hard to find. The geographies of allegory are filled with such places as the Castle of Perseveraunce, the Slough of Despond, and the Wood of Error. The poet thus has support from the poetic tradition and religious tradition when he names a Point Rash-Judgment; the very figure of the fisherman, less realistic than fantastical, seems to authorize a name of that kind, if not that name in particular. But the presence of the fisherman in the poem, and of the poem in the sequence, emphasize the anachronism of Wordsworth's enterprise. The poet is a latecomer here, and the landscape itself rises up to rebuke him. The taking of such property demands human investment, human sacrifice, and perhaps the ground is already too crowded with spirits to admit any more.

The final poem in the series moves away from the growing egotism of the earlier poems and toward a recognition of the claims that others may make. Here at last the poet releases the landscape from the obligation of mirroring him and allows it to reflect someone else. "To M. H." begins with a description of a walk "far among the ancient trees," following a natural path made by the shade of the trees "checking the wild growth / Of weed and sapling" below. This path of natural control leads to "a slip of lawn / And a small bed of water" where, the poet thinks, flocks and herds must come to drink. Here nature is generous to nature:

> nor did sun
> Or wind from any quarter ever come
> But as a blessing to this calm recess,
> This glade of water and this one green field.
> The spot was made by Nature for herself:
> The travellers know it not, and 'twill remain
> Unknown to them . . .

The place seems almost magically protected from evils, an unexotic paradise that suffers not even from the internal threat of unbridled fertility. It is secret but not inaccessible:

> it is beautiful,
> And if a man should plant his cottage near,
> Should sleep beneath the shelter of its trees,
> And blend its waters with his daily meal,
> He would so love it that in his death-hour
> Its image would survive among his thoughts . . .

That the glade should remind the poet of death does not come as a shock to the reader; this *memento mori* is oddly comforting or reassuring, making death seem rather an occasion for pleasant remembering of love than a loss of being. Although secluded and apparently protected from the harshness of weather, the glade's blessing is based not on an exclusion of darkness and death but on a domestication of their terror.

Though when he wrote this Wordsworth was not yet a declared

suitor, and though he does not speak in his own name ("this still nook . . . *we* have named for you"), it is hard to forget that within a few years M. H. would be the poet's wife and hard not to see the poem as a larger and more solemn version of "Roses are red, violets are blue." In retrospect the poem's final lines appear to complete an amorous simile: "And, therefore, my sweet MARY, this still nook / With all its beeches we have named for you." Feminine in every aspect and associated with privacy, love, and calm, the place is an image of Mary Hutchinson; the naming seems appropriate.[39]

This is the only place-naming poem that accomplishes its naming without violence or strain. The poet seems rather to be accepting a fact of nature than imposing his will; yielding to the name, he seems to bow to something as reasonable and as inevitable as death. "That which in the earlier poems was disturbingly other is here reassuringly so," remarks Heather Glen.[40] The logic of this poem is tolerant rather than inexorable. Perhaps because by this time the poet has succeeded in proving his voice and need no longer struggle to assert it, perhaps because now he is motivated by the thought of a dear friend rather than by anxieties about himself, perhaps because he has come to value the beauties of the landscape for their own sake, this poem shows a new generosity of spirit. The poet no longer tries to make the landscape remember him; now he imagines remembering it on his deathbed, his memory affording it survival. But to put it like that overstresses the personal. Wordsworth abstains here from naming himself even as an "I"; in this most touching and most persuasive of the "Poems on the Naming of Places," he relinquishes the desire for appropriation, expressing instead only a desire to give.

I have been arguing that the naming of the "Poems on the Naming of Places" reflects the naming that occurs on the title page and that the appropriation of these pieces of ground stands for the appropriation of a literary territory. That most public of namings at the front of the volume was also a confirmation of another man's anonymity; and the exclusion Wordsworth effected there has an analogue here as well. The "Poems on the Naming of Places" include no place-naming poem for Coleridge. If Wordsworth expected Coleridge to make a poem himself for inclusion in this section,[41] he misjudged his collaborator: Coleridge could not have made such a gesture in his own behalf. His relationship to property was always marginal or parasitic; he always preferred to occupy someone else's house and sit at someone else's table. Fittingly, then, his name was carved, along with Sara Hutchinson's, Dorothy's, and perhaps Joanna's and Wordsworth's, into Sara's Rock, not into one of his own. Fittingly, too, what stands in place of his place-naming poem comes after the conclusion of the "Poems on the Naming of Places" and commemorates not the success but the failure of an imaginative appropriation. Like the others, the last of the "Poems on the Naming of Places" goes by a pseudonym. It is called "Michael."

4

"Michael," "Christabel," and the Poetry of Possession

Literary history suggests a significant intertextual relation between Wordsworth's "Michael" and Coleridge's "Christabel," two poems not ordinarily read together. "Michael" was written during the autumn of 1800 in order to provide a conclusion to the second volume of the 1800 *Lyrical Ballads* after Coleridge's "Christabel," earlier intended for that position of honor, was expelled from the volume. "If Coleridge had been able to finish 'Christabel' Wordsworth would never have written 'Michael,'" Stephen Parrish remarks,[1] and indeed there would have been no reason for "Michael"'s hasty composition had not the removal of the perhaps unfinishable "Christabel" left such a hole in the volume. "Michael" is a poetic stopgap, a literary placeholder. It acts simultaneously to suppress and to supplant, to revise and to memorialize Coleridge's poem, thematizing the displacement in which it participates and reflecting upon its relationship to the text it replaces. Coleridge's poem about demonic possession gave way to Wordsworth's poem about financial and familial dispossession; a poem whose loss of place may have prevented its author from completing it gave way to a poem about unfinished work. "Michael" acts, then, as a commentary upon "Christabel" But "Michael"'s authority, like its pastoral serenity, is precarious, as if it were haunted by what it displaced, for "Christabel" is more than "Michael"'s unsuccessful predecessor; it is also its prophet. "Christabel" seems to predict its own fate, in which "Michael" plays such an important part.

Intending to suppress a tale of the preternatural, Wordsworth made it come true. But whose doing is this? The substitution of Wordsworth's poem for Coleridge's, Wordsworth's appropriation of Coleridge's literary place, can be interpreted as one of "Michael"'s meanings—and also one of "Christabel"'s. "Michael" and "Christabel" connive at the realization of the same fantasy. The relations between the rival poems form part of the text of the greater collaborative work that the two individual poems frame.

The circumstances surrounding "Christabel"'s lapse from acceptability are mysterious. Although critics tend to assume it was withheld from publication because it was not ready, its completion was not yet, during the autumn of 1800, despaired of. And according to Dorothy Wordsworth's laconic journal entries, the only record of its reception in the Wordsworth household, Wordsworth does not seem to have disliked the poem. From late August to early October of 1800 she notes the poem's progress and the pleasure it gave her and her brother to hear Coleridge read it. But suddenly on October 6 she writes, "Determined not to print *Christabel* with the L. B."[2] Who determined this and why, she does not say. A few days later Wordsworth began work on "Michael," which was finished in December of that year and printed as the last poem in the second volume of the *Lyrical Ballads*.

Wordsworth's explanatory letter to his publisher throws a little light on the decision to remove Coleridge's as yet unfinished poem from the *Lyrical Ballads:*

> A Poem of Mr Coleridge's was to have concluded the Volumes; but upon mature deliberation, I found that the Style of this Poem was so discordant from my own that it could not be printed along with my poems with any propriety.[3]

We saw in Chapter 1 that, in appealing to the concept of "propriety," Wordsworth may well have had in mind not so much what belongs to the context as what belongs to the proprietor—"propriety" in the sense of "property." The ambiguity of the concept served Wordsworth's ambivalence; the polite sense could mask a selfish one. Wordsworth seems to have felt uneasy about the presence of another man's poems, in another man's style, within a collection that, in spite of its original anonymity, was increasingly being recognized as his. Coleridge deemed his own an alien voice in this work, on whose title page, it had recently been decided, Wordsworth's name alone would appear. He habitually spoke of the volumes as Wordsworth's,[4] and, years later, after he had finally published "Christabel," he judged that among the mass of Wordsworth's contributions to the *Lyrical Ballads,* "my compositions, instead of forming a balance, appeared rather an interpolation of heterogeneous matter."[5]

Coleridge's poems simply did not belong there. Had he chosen to write about sheep or distressed villagers, his contributions might have fared better. But his subjects—demonic possession, ventriloquism, and loss of identity—drew attention to the difficulties that his poems' inclusion in a volume of Wordsworth's would have produced. His poems made intolerable explicit the threat they posed. If readers expected Wordsworth's poetic voice, then the voice of "Christabel," eerily incantatory in a way no poem of Wordsworth's in the volume is, would have shocked them much as Geraldine's hisses, coming out of Christabel's mouth, shocked the Baron.

As it was, "Christabel"'s eventual publication in a volume exclusively Coleridge's disturbed readers. Contemporary reaction (the squeamish flinched at the poem's "mastiff bitch"; the cynical spread rumors that Geraldine was a transvestite) suggested that the poem's perceived impropriety was rather a matter of content than of context. But that the problem was simple vulgarity or obscenity is doubtful.[6] The difficulty of speaking properly in or about "Christabel" seems essential rather than accidental. Literary propriety, conformity with the rules governing what is fit for a particular speaker to say about a particular subject, depends upon the security of the speaker's identity and the stability of the subject's meaning. Neither this security nor this stability is available in "Christabel," where mimicry undermines identity and nothing is quite what it seems. There can be no coincidence of things and their meanings when the things hardly coincide even with themselves; there can be no language proper to an undefinable subject.

Unlike "Christabel," "Michael" seems the very model of poetic propriety, a poem almost ostentatiously well grounded in the real world and the forms of expression it seems naturally to generate. An almost organic relationship between objects and their meanings characterizes even the difficult composition of the poem. Thus Dorothy Wordsworth remarks in her journal on "Michael"'s progress in terms that suggest the equivalence of words and things. October 11: "After dinner we walked up Greenhead Gill in search of a sheepfold. . . . The Sheepfold is falling away. It is built nearly in the form of a heart unequally divided." October 21: "Wm. had been unsuccessful in the morning at the sheepfold." November 9: "W. [?] burnt the sheepfold." And November 11: "William had been working at the sheepfold. They were salving sheep."[7] Her entries make no distinction between the structure of stone and the structure of words, composition and hard physical labor. It sounds as if the poem were made out of the same stuff as the landscape.

Within the poem the relationship between words and things is the same. The beginning of "Michael," at least, allows both poet and reader the comfortable belief that natural objects speak their own changeless significance. Meanings inhere in material things whose durability is legendary. Tradition and frugality alike ensure that the lamp by which Michael and Isabel work in the evenings will not be replaced by a newer one; sheep may die but will never cease being sheep; and although the land suffers slight changes over time, the landscape endures. The stability of this physical world supports a semiotic economy so rich, so generous, that, at least at the beginning, at least apparently, its symbols seem as solid and as proper as its matters of natural fact.

The poem opens upon a scene that practically allegorizes itself.[8]

If from the public way you turn your steps
Up the tumultuous brook of Green-head Gill,
You will suppose that with an upright path
Your feet must struggle; in such bold ascent
The pastoral Mountains front you, face to face.
But, courage! for beside that boisterous Brook
The mountains have all open'd out themselves,
And made a hidden valley of their own.
No habitation there is seen; but such
As journey thither find themselves alone
With a few sheep, with rocks and stones, and kites
That overhead are sailing in the sky.

[1–12][9]

With its pastoral mountains, brooks, and stones, the valley is real enough, but here and there an odd phrase suggests that the place is made as much out of moral meaning as out of rock. For a moment an "upright path" (l. 3) through this area of utter solitude looks like the kind of path an upright man must tread, one that needs courage and self-reliance to follow; it suggests a spiritual rather than a merely geographical ascent. Urging the reader to follow this path to "one object which you might pass by, / Might see and notice not" (ll. 15–16),[10] the poet seems to promise two things at once, both a realistic history, "ungarnish'd with events" (l. 19), of how a heap of stones came to be sitting in the middle of such an isolated place, and a moral fable about uprightness. There is no tension in the double promise. Just as the "upright path" can be steep both literally and figuratively, and just as the man whose feet struggle with it can be both physically and morally sturdy, so the unfinished sheepfold to which this upright path leads can be at once a real heap of stones and a symbol of something: its matter-of-factness does not preclude spiritual significance. Such a world Wordsworth had in mind when he wrote, in the Preface to the *Lyrical Ballads,* about the origins of true poetic language in the contemplation of the permanent forms of nature.

The link between the two, poem and landscape, is property. Natural in substance, human in significance, property is what Wordsworth wishes his poetry to resemble, as he makes clear at the beginning of the poem. The economic model works to ground the incredible in the indubitable, but it also undermines the perfect propriety of which property appeared at first to be the natural expression. What seemed timeless and inevitable is revealed to be artificial, contingent, and of recent date. Revealing the price of what seemed given, the poem neutralizes its own naturalness.[11]

More than any other poem in the *Lyrical Ballads,* a work dominated by the theme of property, "Michael" epitomizes Wordsworth's attitudes toward the relationship between property and passion.[12] He describes the poem as

> a picture of a man, of strong mind and lively sensibility, agitated by two of the most powerful affections of the human heart; the parental affection, and the love of property, *landed* property, including the feelings of inheritance, home, and personal and family independence.[13]

In addition to having social and moral value, property is associated in Wordsworth's eyes with writing; it figures a kind of textuality. Describing the "small independent *proprietors* of land here called *statesmen,*" Wordsworth writes,

> Their little tract of land serves as a kind of permanent rallying point for their domestic feelings, as a tablet upon which they are written which makes them objects of memory in a thousand instances when they would otherwise be forgotten.[14]

Marked with the graves of ancestors and perhaps of children as well, land serves as history, reminding its inhabitants of those from whom they inherited it, those whom their labor upon it supported, and those who will in their turn inherit it. Property is mnemonic. In Wordsworth's words, it is a "tract," a "tablet" upon which family history and social feelings are written—though by whom they are thus written is not clear. If Wordsworth's maneuvers to gain control over and credit for his published poems suggest that texts are a form of property, his remarks on statesmen suggest that, conversely, property is a form of textuality.

The two concepts, property and textuality, share a dependence upon the idea of handing down or tradition. Michael values his land not for its price in the marketplace and not for the minimal wealth it enables him to accumulate but for its power to symbolize and strengthen family bonds. This land, where Michael's family is buried and where he expects to be buried too, is literally the dust of his ancestors, the embodiment of patriarchal authority, received from one's ancestors and to be passed on to one's sons. It sustains the continuity of a way of life, binding generation to generation, an index not of its owner's autonomy so much as of his connection with other people. In this it resembles a story, which is valued not as it is hoarded but as it is shared. In order to mean anything, to be worth anything, a story must be told, listened to, and—the teller hopes—told again. Its value, created in the handing down, lies in its ability to become significant to others. "For Wordsworth," writes Kurt Heinzelman, "the basis of poetic value is also a contract which burdens the reader with the need to labor in order to sustain that (poetic) inheritance which is a necessary part of existence."[15]

In talking about the landscape, a lost property that was for

Michael "like a book" (l. 70), Wordsworth is led almost immediately to talk of his own place in the poetic economy. The story, he says, was the first to teach him to appropriate "passions that were not my own" (l. 31),[16] to feel the human sympathy one needs in order to understand "the heart of man and human life" (l. 33). It taught him, in other words, about emotional property. Thus the poet presents himself as Michael's emotional or literary heir.[17] A substitute for the son who failed his father, Wordsworth receives Michael's story as a literary property that he intends to hand on in his turn to "youthful Poets, who among these Hills / Will be my second self when I am gone" (ll. 38–39). The landscape with which the poem opens is apparently empty of any rival claimant: "No habitation there is seen" (l. 9). Wordsworth takes for his own a poetic territory that would otherwise, he suggests, go uncultivated. But would it? Has Luke, the natural heir, really forfeited his claim to the poet who displaces him?

Wordsworth's poem exhibits a guilty anxiety on the subject of the heir. The object of his father's deepest love and the instrument of family disaster, Luke is nevertheless oddly obscured as a human subject. In the nearly five hundred lines of the poem, Luke speaks not a single intelligible word. We are told that as a baby he utters "without words a natural tune" and that as a youth he shouts at the sheep, but when the crisis comes and his father says goodbye to him, he can only sob aloud. Inarticulate to the last, he is sent away from home for reasons that, despite their urgency, remain vague and unpersuasive. Once he is out of sight, his reality fades, and with it fades the reality of his story. If Luke's temporary success is hard to imagine, his failure, in the context of the rest of the poem, seems a naive fantasy, lurid because so nearly empty of content, so abbreviated. His catastrophe occurs in the space of six lines that are as solemn as they are uninformative. The poet disposes of him summarily:[18]

> Meantime Luke began
> To slacken in his duty, and at length
> He in the dissolute city gave himself
> To evil courses: ignominy and shame

Fell upon him, so that he was driven at last
To seek a hiding-place beyond the seas.

[451–56]

Luke's end represents precisely the kind of narrative Wordsworth rejects in the "Preface" to the *Lyrical Ballads:* sensational, unsubtle, and characterless. Never entirely present to the reader's imagination, Luke here becomes utterly unreal, a bad son out of melodrama. His evil has no content, no definite form, other than that final flight from England and from the possibility of returning to the sheepfold; his sin seems to lie not so much in his London excesses as in his failure to come home, or even perhaps in his simply being away from home in "the dissolute city."[19] But the particulars of Luke's behavior[20] seem to matter less than the opportunity they give the narrator to have done with him. The important thing is that the heir is now gone—out of England, out of our moral class, out of the poem. His place is now vacant.

The abrupt treatment of Luke is typical of the poem's narrative style, which seems frequently uneasy about the events it has to relate and determined to get away with telling as little and as late as possible. It was part of Wordsworth's program in the *Lyrical Ballads* to avoid sensational narrative. But where "Michael" differs from the other poems in the volume is in the embarrassment with which it tries, unsuccessfully, to dodge its narrative obligation. The poet stalls repeatedly before revealing the news that causes Michael to decide to send his son away, and when he does finally tell us what the matter is, we may be nearly as incredulous as Michael himself.

Long before the time
Of which I speak, the Shepherd had been bound
In surety for his Brother's Son, a man
Of an industrious life, and ample means,
But unforeseen misfortunes suddenly
Had press'd upon him, and old Michael now
Was summon'd to discharge the forfeiture,
A grievous penalty, but little less
Than half his substance. This un-look'd for claim
At the first hearing, for a moment took
More hope out of his life than he supposed
That any old man ever could have lost.

[219–30]

To the reader no less than to Michael, the crisis, this news of distant financial failure portending Michael's ruin, is incredible,[21] it is not made real the way the mountains, the work, and Michael's feelings for his son have been made real. Into a poem controlled by dignified realism there enters an air of the fantastic. The narrative, like the bad news it brings, seems to come from elsewhere, challenging not only Michael's control over his life but the poet's control over the propriety of his poem.

The disaster is distinctly un-Wordsworthian: not a case of simple financial reverse, the result of a war-damaged economy or the enclosure of a commons, this has to do, apparently, with credit, a concept one would have thought alien to Wordsworth's poetic economy. It drops us out of pastoral and into melodrama, becoming real only as it imposes on our belief in Michael's natural propriety as a landowner. Too late we learn that Michael has not always owned his land:

> These fields were burthen'd when they came to me;
> 'Till I was forty years of age, not more
> Than half of my inheritance was mine.
> I toil'd and toil'd; God bless'd me in my work,
> And 'till these three weeks past the land was free.
>
> [384–88]

A couple of hundred lines have gone to assuring the reader of the strength of the ties that bind Michael to his land. This work is undone in an instant. Michael's familiar property and home is revealed to have a not altogether familiar or homely past: as even etymology suggests, the problems of *economy*, the *law of the house,* were there from the beginning. The effect is like that of palimpsest: a suppressed writing begins to disturb what is written over it.[22] A repressed past begins to shape the present in its own image. The most homely and domestic of Wordsworth's poems becomes, at this instant, uncanny.

The hero, like the poet, tries hard to resist the newly apparent threat to his authority, and, like the poet, he fails. In an attempt to keep his property, Michael decides to send his son to London. Although it is not entirely clear why he does not consider keeping Luke with him to work off the debt,[23] Michael assumes that the crisis is temporary; working with a kinsman, Luke is to earn money and then return to a home that will be the more securely his own. It is in every way a bad decision. For Michael and for the poet, the land is bound up with memories of ancestors and hopes for descendants; it signifies and embodies the continuity of generations. The decision to send away the heir so that the inheritance may remain clear privileges the symbol of the filial relation over the actual son. The exchange of Luke for the land, the division of the symbol from what it symbolizes, deprives both of their meaning and their value. It destroys the basis of that remarkable propriety of language in which the poem began.

Before Luke goes, Michael takes him out to the spot near the brook where he has piled together stones for the building of a sheepfold. Michael asks his son to lay the first stone and to remember what it stands for:

> "When thou art gone away, should evil men
> Be thy companions, let this Sheep-fold be
> Thy anchor and thy shield; amid all fear
> And all temptation, let it be to thee
> An emblem of the life thy Fathers liv'd,
> Who, being innocent, did for that cause
> Bestir them in good deeds. Now, fare thee well—
> When thou return'st, thou in this place wilt see
> A work which is not here, a covenant
> 'Twill be between us—but whatever fate
> Befall thee, I shall love thee to the last,
> And bear thy memory with me to the grave."
>
> [416–27]

The sheepfold Michael proposes to build as the sign of his covenant with Luke—the pile of stones rather, since it never succeeds in becoming a sheepfold—represents, despite Michael's intentions, confusion. Michael wants the stones to signify the continuity of generations. He wants it to serve the function of a *herm,* the stone or pile upon which one founds a great property. But a *herm,* as we saw in the previous chapter, could be a morally and socially ambiguous construction, at once a symbol of fertility and a place of sacrifice. In the western tradition, moreover, any heap of stones associated with a covenant inevitably refers also to the altar on which Abraham would have sacrificed the son of his old age, Isaac, had not God allowed a ram to be substituted at the last minute.[24] Stones set up to commemorate the absence of a beloved relative and affirm belief in an eventual reunion will naturally put one in mind of tombstones as well as altars. Michael intends to inscribe the spot with one set of meanings, but it is already inscribed with a contrary set: the stones signify interruption, substitution, and death before they signify continuity, fidelity, or reunion. So Michael's inscription of the landscape, like the poet's tale, attempts an erasure of an older text that neither poet nor hero wants to acknowledge. Both poem and sheepfold are attempted displacements of original meanings. By this point, symbols no longer seem natural; meaning is no longer self-evident. Something has come between the natural world and its human significance. The poem's original poetic propriety has broken down.

The poem's narrative evasions and redoublings, like Michael's attempt to evade the meaning of the stones he gathers and impose on them a new significance, suggest a struggle with material alien to the poet's design, sensational story that, both tempting and threatening, resists expulsion and domestication alike. At the heart of this pastoral lies a melodrama, a form for the city, not for the fields. According to the poem itself, its sensational story comes from afar, where the unreliable nephew lives, and it moves rapidly away again, first to London and then overseas, where the poet cannot follow. Geographical foreignness tropes literary foreignness; the story of the danger posed by the foreign has itself a foreign origin—an origin in an imagination other than Wordsworth's. The way "Michael" handles the Luke episode—the unassimilable center of the poem—reflects Wordsworth's handling of another story about the threat of the foreign, the poem whose alien presence in the *Lyrical Ballads* Wordsworth found intolerable.

Reading the self-thwarting narrative structure as evidence of Wordsworth's real uneasiness with what he has done, I have tried to portray "Michael" as a work of usurpation. Whether that usurpation was conscious or not remains uncertain. There is no direct evidence that Wordsworth intended his poem as a reworking of his friend's. No letters or notebook entries provide any hint that there is more to the relationship between the poems than the accident that both were written for the closing pages of the *Lyrical*

Ballads. Five humorous ballad stanzas discovered some years ago in the notebook containing the earliest version of "Christabel" suggest the possibility, however, of a verifiable link between Coleridge and the figure of Michael. There has been some controversy over whether these stanzas represent an early draft of "Michael," a humorous frame for "Michael," or perhaps simply a parody both of a poem that was proving itself troublesome and of Wordsworth and Coleridge as poets:[25]

Two shepeherds we have the two wits of the dale
Renown'd for song satire epistle & tale
Rhymes pleasant to sing or to say
To this sheepfold they went & a doggrel strain
They carved on a stone in the wall to explain
The cause of old Michaels decay.[26]

The "doggrel" they write tells of a man critics have associated with the subject of Wordsworth's "A Character in the antithetical Manner,"[27] who may be Coleridge, a man named Robert Jones, or perhaps a figure compounded of them both.[28] That "A Character" may be a sketch of Coleridge does not mean that Michael must be Coleridge. Indeed, that the vulnerable, talkative, neurotically dependent poet should be portrayed as a rugged, taciturn, self-reliant shepherd seems improbable. But the circumstances suggest a connection in Wordsworth's mind between Coleridge and the half-absurd, half-pathetic subject of this one version of the "Michael" story who "thinks and does nothing at all."[29]

"Michael" is about Coleridge, but it is also about "Christabel" and about Wordsworth's relationship to them both.[30] In the story of Michael and Luke, Wordsworth represents the obscure offense against property that the defense of "propriety" mentioned in the letter to Longman has led him to commit. "Michael" dispossesses "Christabel" in part by imitating that poem; it not only takes "Christabel" 's place but also assumes some of its moral, thematic, and structural features. "Michael" incorporates such details of Coleridge's work as "Christabel" 's oak tree, faithful dog, troubling dream, and morally emblematic lamp. It also contends with the thematic implications of the earlier poem's failure of voice. "Christabel" 's fragmentary state, its mistrust of representation, and its fear of the foreign become problems for Wordsworth's poem, which must struggle with itself in order to speak.

First the more obvious parallels. The families in both poems are destroyed by pleas for help from the children of brothers.[31] Sir Leoline is snared through his regret for having quarreled with an old friend whose daughter Geraldine says she is; Michael is drawn into catastrophe through a bond of surety to his brother's son. Both poems end with the natural children alienated from the parents whose pity or, in Michael's case, irritable sense of duty toward other men's children led them to hurt their own.

In both poems, the evil associated with the old friend's or kinsman's child corrupts the son or daughter whose immediate welfare is sacrificed to the old tie. The rival child displaces the true child from his secure place in the family, and the true child, abandoned, takes on the characteristics of the rival. Luke ends up no better than the nephew whom Michael suspects has been "false to us;" Christabel assumes through "forced unconscious sympathy" the viperish "look of dull and treacherous hate" she sees in Geraldine's eyes, and she begins to hiss, expressing the evil that is—we assume—properly Geraldine's. Christabel's passive imitation of her guest is the most dramatic instance of the confusion of the two characters, who have switched and shared roles from the beginning.[32] Inviting Geraldine to spend the night with her, Christabel speaks as if she were the suppliant guest asking her hostess for a place to sleep: "'I beseech your courtesy, / This night, to share your couch with me'" (ll. 121–22). It is Geraldine who seems horror-stricken by her own deformity, shuddering as she bares her withered bosom and dreading to enter Christabel's bed; Christabel herself says nothing and, as far as the reader knows, feels nothing either. But in the morning the technically innocent girl, whose blackest sin seems to have been her readiness to be duped, murmurs, "Sure I have sinn'd!" (l. 381).

Both poems struggle against their own narrative. In "Michael" what barely resists suppression is the story of Luke and his fall; in "Christabel" it is the story of what happens to Christabel after Geraldine comes to bed.[33] Geraldine herself, the subject of the story that cannot be told, is the apparent threat to speech in Coleridge's poem. Her enchantment seems to hold not only Christabel but Coleridge too in thrall. Incapable of analyzing the force of censorship, he falls victim to it as hopelessly as his heroine.

Yet despite the foregoing list of parallels, the poems do not seem much alike. It is unlikely that even the most strenuous efforts to keep in mind the points of similarity will enable a reader to feel that "Michael" is derivative of "Christabel." To the contrary: If either poem looks derivative, it is "Christabel." That this should be so suggests perhaps the thoroughness and power of Wordsworth's revision of Coleridge's materials and structure. So successfully has Wordsworth's poem renaturalized the other's supernaturalism and reappropriated its concerns that "Michael" seems more original—closer to nature, less aesthetically sophisticated—than "Christabel."[34]

It will not do to turn "Christabel" into "Michael"'s victim. "Christabel" did not merely suffer exploitation; it is not in any simple sense a source of Wordsworth's poem. "Christabel," like its heroine, is too good a victim to be quite innocent. The poem, like the girl, seems to court destruction. Critics frequently observe that Geraldine is on some level a creature of Christabel's unconscious, a figure empowered to enact the fantasies of a girl intent upon preserving her purity. "Christabel" allegorizes the failure of an independent voice in the presence of a greater power and dramatizes its own dispossession. In taking possession of Coleridge's materials, "Michael" does no more than enact the story "Christabel" tells, revealing Coleridge's poem to have been an accurate prediction of its own fate.

The prose apology that accompanied "Christabel"'s publication sixteen years after "Michael"'s appearance is the clearest possible evidence of Coleridge's uneasy awareness that something about the poem made it vulnerable, liable to be mistaken for an imitation. Although written ostensibly for the purpose of convincing skeptical readers of the poem's originality, the preface's assertions of chronological priority are strangely self-thwarting, raising more doubts about the poem's relationship to originality and imitation than they allay. In fact, the preface introduces a consideration of the perverse imitation that constitutes the subject of the poem itself.

But the problem of the poem's chronology is a genuine concern. Before Coleridge published his poem, he allowed it to circulate in manuscript among his friends, many of whom admired it, some of whom tried to reproduce its effects. Sir Walter Scott incorporated elements of "Christabel" into his "Lay of the Last Minstrel," and an anonymous poet published a "Gothic Tale" entitled "Christobell" that offered a completed version of the Christabel story. By the time "Christabel" itself finally appeared, aspects of the story were already familiar to the public, and there was some danger that the poem would appear to be one of its own imitations. Scott would cheerfully acknowledge Coleridge's originality and his indebtedness. Nevertheless, it was a worried Coleridge who informed his readers that he had begun the poem in 1797 and added to it in 1800.

> It is probable that if the poem had been finished at either of the former periods, or even if the first and second part had been published in the year 1800, the impression of its originality would have been much greater than I dare at present expect. But for this I have only my own indolence to blame. The dates are mentioned for the exclusive purpose of excluding charges of plagiarism or servile imitation from myself.[35]

The words are those of a guilty man whom we know to be innocent. As is so often the case with Coleridge, anxiety exceeds its occasion. Perhaps by the time he finally published "Christabel" pangs of conscience had become habitual and the disclaimer of literary wrongdoing a tic. Whatever the reason, Coleridge behaves as if he expects the judgment to go against him. He protects himself by so phrasing the imagined charge that, if he is convicted, he will be found guilty of victimizing only himself. His image of self-robbery implies an identification or confusion of derivative and source. Thus in the process of defending his originality Coleridge undermines it.[36] And, indeed, as the preface continues, this implication becomes overt, as though he could articulate it only in the denial. Not just the originality of this one poem is in question but the possibility of originality in any poem:

> For there is amongst us a set of critics, who seem to hold, that every possible thought and image is traditional; who have no notion that there are such things as fountains in the world, small as well as great; and who would therefore charitably derive every rill they behold flowing, from a perforation made in some other man's tank. [*CPW*, pp. 214–15]

His gestures of appeasement look like further evidence of a bad conscience:

> 'Tis mine and it is likewise yours;
> But an if this will not do;
> Let it be mine, good friend! for I
> Am the poorer of the two.
>
> [*CPW,* p. 215]

He concedes the weakness of a strong case, begging equal credit as a charity rather than as a right. His citation of dates seems to have been inadequate even for the purpose of self-reassurance.

Why this uneasiness? Coleridge could not clear up the problem of "Christabel"'s origins because the confusion of the poem's chronology was no accident. Dates prove nothing; the poem's lateness, its publication after long silence, is part of its meaning as a performance.

The opening lines, written two decades earlier, gloss the poet's anxiety about indeterminate beginnings. The poem opens upon a scene of anachronism. As the castle clock strikes midnight a rooster, awakened by owls, begins to crow as if it were dawn:

> 'Tis the middle of night by the castle clock,
> And the owls have awakened the crowing cock;
> Tu—whit!—Tu—whoo!
> And hark, again! the crowing cock,
> How drowsily it crew.
>
> [1–5]

And although it is April by the calendar, "Spring comes [so] slowly up this way" (l. 22) that "naught was green upon the oak / But moss and rarest mistletoe" (ll. 33–34); indeed, "one red leaf, the last of its clan" (l. 49), still remains on the tree from the previous fall. What we see and hear is at odds with what we know. The natural calendar does not correspond to the human one. When the poem begins, it is earlier, but also later, than it seems, an effect reinforced by the wobbling of the verb tenses throughout the poem. Shifting without apparent reason between present and past tenses, the poem renders uninterpretable the relationship between them and makes it impossible to distinguish between story time and reading time. We cannot always separate *then* from *now*.

The poem's tenuous hold on narrative temporality is severely strained by the coming of Geraldine, whose presence is signaled, appropriately enough, by an "it" without an antecedent:

The lady sprang up, suddenly,
The lovely lady, Christabel!
It moaned as near, as near can be,
But what it is she cannot tell.—
On the other side it seems to be,
Of the huge, broad-breasted, old oak tree.

[37–42]

The syntactical disturbance heralds a narrative disturbance. What should be first arrives second; subsequence must supply the lack of antecedent. The story Geraldine tells of the events preceding her appearance behind the oak anticipates the events about to befall the woman who saves her. Geraldine's past is Christabel's future.[37] Christabel, like Geraldine's storied self, will be rapt from her familiar world, will be forced to cross "the shade of night," will lie "entranced," and will have her cries "choked . . . with force and fright." The possibility that the story Geraldine tells may be a fraud makes the foreshadowing all the more sinister: a fiction involving one character overtakes the audience innocent enough to believe its truth. Geraldine's story, like the antecedentless "it," is merely a placeholder for something that has not yet come into existence. Like a Greek oracle, it refers to its own fulfillment through the efforts of its interpreters: Christabel, Sir Leoline, Coleridge, Wordsworth, and finally us.[38]

Geraldine is a vampire of the semiotic variety. She steals not blood but likeness, for she has none of her own. She poses the dread threat of false representation, destroying by mimicry. In Bard Bracy's dream, a dove named Christabel lies fluttering on the ground. Stooping to see what the matter is, the Bard

saw a bright green snake
Coiled around its wings and neck.
Green as the herbs on which it couched,
Close by the dove's its head it crouched;
And with the dove it heaves and stirs,
Swelling its neck as she swelled hers!

[549–54]

Like the snake, Geraldine is a thief of identity and voice. She injures Christabel by imitating her so neatly as to make the girl herself seem inauthentic. The original, unable to compete with so wonderful an imitation, becomes derivative herself, suffering the apparent "plagiarism or servile imitation from [her]self" that Coleridge mentioned in connection with himself. But even more terrifying than Geraldine's imitation of Christabel is her subordination of the girl to the expression of her own evil.

Coleridge made the evidence against Geraldine impossible to read, going so far as to suppress the only direct evidence of what is the matter with her.[39] In the manuscript version of the poem, when Geraldine "unbound / The cincture from beneath her breast" and her silken robe fell to the floor, "Behold! her bosom and half her side / Are lean and old and foul of hue." But it was "A sight to dream of, not to tell!"[40] For when the poem was printed the clue given by the manuscript was deleted. Geraldine's evil is thus literally unspeakable; Coleridge can no more tell us about it than Christabel can after Geraldine enchants her. All we are left with is Geraldine's prohibition:

"In the touch of this bosom there worketh a spell,
Which is lord of thy utterance, Christabel!
Thou knowest to-night, and wilt know to-morrow,
This mark of my shame, this seal of my sorrow;
  But vainly thou warrest,
    For this is alone in
  Thy power to declare,
    That in the dim forest
  Thou heard'st a low moaning,
And found'st a bright lady, surpassingly fair;
And didst bring her home with thee in love and charity,
To shield her and shelter her from the damp air."

[267–78]

What her version of the story omits is what Coleridge's version omits, but Geraldine deletes the evidence of the deletion, too. She functions as a figure of censorship who cannot be described and who prohibits her story from being fully told.[41] She censors both her deformity and the fact that she censors it.[42] Like "Michael"—

and like "Christabel"—she seems too innocent to be true. Her evil manifests itself through its own invisibility. We find we suspect her because we have no reason to do so. We know she is bad because she does not look it, because the evidence against her is obviously missing, and because Christabel begins to misbehave. We hold her responsible for Christabel's derangement; we begin to read Christabel's apparent hypocrisy as if it were Geraldine's.

Although presumably Christabel is simply being framed, appearances are so very much against her that we must wonder whether we really can blame her bad behavior on her guest. But if Christabel's hissing and herpetoid faces refer to Geraldine's nature rather than a new corruption in her own, what do they signify? What is Geraldine's evil? Her evil seems to reside in her phenomenological duplicity, her failure to appear as she is. She is not merely hypocritical, however. She does not exactly misrepresent herself. She has, in fact, no independent identity to represent. Her constitution involves an infinite regress of meanings: she is not what she seems, and what she is is what she does not seem to be. She differs from herself perpetually.

Geraldine's evil lies, then, partly in her deformity, partly in her concealment of it, but mostly in her powers of displacement, which reveal her to be essentially linguistic in nature. A bit of language given a woman's name and dress, she behaves not according to any moral code but according to the rules that govern systems of signs. No more than a single phoneme can she be interpreted out of context. It would be a mistake to examine her in isolation from Christabel; neither can be represented, apparently, except in relation to the other. Once they are separated, the poem breaks off, as if it could represent them only through one another, as if language were rendered impossible by their parting. Geraldine is evil because she enforces the condition of allegory, turning those around her into signifiers of the identity she depends upon them to supply and depriving them of the power to make known the truth about themselves. She makes intolerably clear what representation implies: not self-evidence, as Wordsworth wanted to believe, the natural expression of one's own being, but the subversion of identity. This is what happens when Geraldine makes snakes' eyes at her victim:

The maid, alas! her thoughts are gone,
She nothing sees—no sight but one!
The maid, devoid of guile and sin,
I know not how, in fearful wise,
So deeply had she drunken in
That look, those shrunken serpent eyes,
That all her features were resigned
To this sole image in her mind:
And passively did imitate
That look of dull and treacherous hate!
And thus she stood, in dizzy trance,
Still picturing that look askance
With forced unconscious sympathy
Full before her father's view—
As far as such a look could be
In eyes so innocent and blue!

[597–612]

Experiencing a bizarre form of sympathy, Christabel becomes, at least for a moment, what she sees. She images what threatens her. For her, representation is equivalent to demonic possession.

Certainly demons are not the same as fields, but possession is a common ground for both. If, as I have shown, property is analogous to textuality for Wordsworth and if, as "Christabel" makes evident, demonic possession is primarily figured by the disturbance of voice and referentiality, then "Michael"'s "property" can be said to be a conceptual pun on "Christabel"'s "possession." What "Michael" holds to be the necessary condition for composition is "to feel / For passions that were not my own . . . for the sake / Of youthful Poets, who among these Hills / Will be my second self when I am gone" (ll. 30–31, 37–39). The basis of his narrative is sympathy, the ability to represent within himself the passions of others and to find or create images or representations of himself in those who will listen to his tale—only a less terrifying, less humiliating form of the possession that afflicts Coleridge's characters. This capacity for sympathy, for creating a "second self," enables Wordsworth to inherit and to pass on his literary property. It is the basis of his power as a literary agent. It is also what enables him to take the ruin of Coleridge's poem and complete it with his own, domesticating its uncanniness, transforming a potential threat to identity into a force of social connection. But Wordsworth's poem can save the proprieties that "Christabel" menaces only through an act of literary violence that, paradoxically, mimics the objectionable impropriety of its victim.

Who, then, is finally responsible—the imitator or the imitated? Whose story is it, anyway? Casting "Christabel" out of the *Lyrical Ballads,* substituting his poetic voice for another's, Wordsworth simultaneously silences and imitates the censorious, ventriloquistic Geraldine. "Michael" acts as both usurper and usurped, taking on—like Christabel—the features of what it undertakes to exorcise, its poetic purity corrupted by the object of its cathartic intentions. Who is to say whether Coleridge fell victim to Wordsworth's story or Wordsworth to Coleridge's? Who even will insist it is necessary to apportion blame? The two poems, each one a Geraldine to the other's Christabel, take mutual possession of one another, undermining the very notion of exclusive poetic property.

5

The Haunted Language of the Lucy Poems

The economy of the Lucy poems involves neither property nor, in any obvious sense, possession. It figures no struggle for ground, no exorcism of previous inhabitants. For such loss as these poems record—emotional rather than financial or literary—there can be, it would seem, no recompense. The poems confound both poet's and critics' accounting.

But although issues of property never become explicit here, the economically-worded Lucy poems exhibit the same kinds of behavior and raise the same sorts of issues we have seen in the poems more openly concerned with possession and dispossession. Concerned with the uniqueness of his loss, the poet finds his own words turned against him, his voice usurped upon by its own simulacrum or by silence. Self-reduplicating, autoventriloquistic, and plagued by rivals who are also doubles, the poems generate an uncanniness that looks more Coleridgean than Wordsworthian. They rehearse the formal problems of *The Ancient Mariner;* they anticipate the difficult dynamics of "Michael" and "Christabel." But now there seems to be no one within their range to blame or credit for the disturbance of propriety and univocality. This group of poems was not one of the poets' joint projects. Bookless[1] in Goslar, freezing with his sister among a people whose language he had decided he could not learn,[2] and separated from Coleridge in Ratzeburg by over one hundred miles of frozen German roads and a resolution to save money, Wordsworth must have felt almost as isolated as Lucy herself. The only plausible source of literary disturbance was Wordsworth's own *Prelude,* then in genesis.

Despite the poems' agonistic behavior, then, the problem seems to be wholly internal, generated by Wordsworth's relation to his own language. It is the power of the Lucy poems to subject the poet to the conditions of his own texts that links them with the uncanniest of Coleridge's poems. The language of the Lucy poems, like that of "Christabel" and *The Ancient Mariner,* takes possession of its speaker, revealing him to be bound by his own dicta, his poetic freedom straitened by the letter of a text he never meant so literally. Incorporating, like Coleridge's uncanny poems, their own interpretive and literary historical contexts, these poems exhibit a textuality indistinguishable from intertextuality. With his own words suddenly resistant to his attempts at interpretive domestication, behaving as though they came from elsewhere, the poet becomes one of his own characters, overtaken at his desk by his own plot.[3]

It is these most un-Wordsworthian of poems that carry to its logical conclusion the program Wordsworth avowed in the Preface to the *Lyrical Ballads,* employing the smallest possible stimulus to move his readers' imaginations and sympathies. Here as in the other *Lyrical Ballads,* Wordsworth works to produce that "certain coloring of imagination, whereby ordinary things [are] presented to the mind in an unusual aspect," taking care to keep within the bounds of his newly defined poetic propriety, in which "the feeling . . . developed gives importance to the action and situation, and not the action and situation to the feeling":[4]

She *liv'd* unknown, and few could know
  When Lucy ceas'd to be;
But she is in her Grave, and Oh!
  The difference to me.

Seeking to thwart the "craving for extraordinary incident," the "degrading thirst after outrageous stimulation" that readers accustomed to "sickly and stupid German Tragedies, and deluges of idle and extravagant stories in verse" might bring to his work, the poet goes far toward purging incident altogether from these poems, turning what might have been a story about the death of a beloved woman into a story about his own awakening from careless contentment into grief.

In his insistence that the real story is internal and perhaps not even really a story at all, the poet of the Lucy poems goes further than the poet of, say, "Simon Lee"; for where in "Simon Lee" there is nothing to tell, in the Lucy poems there is: the poet simply does not tell it. Grief—one presumes[5]—cripples the poet's syntax ("O mercy!" to myself I cried, / "If Lucy should be dead!") and leaves him effectively speechless. A tombstone would be more informative. Radical understatement, the pathos of the words' helplessness to convey fully the poet's feelings, substitutes for the pathos of Lucy's death and the poet's inability to do anything about it. When the poet does speak at length, the force of vocal inhibition keeps his voice low: "I will dare to tell, / But in the lover's ear alone, / What once to me befel." Instead of Lucy's struggle to live, the poems offer us scenes of the poet's struggle to speak. But when the force of vocal inhibition manifests itself in the cancellation of whole stanzas, as it does in "Strange fits of passion" (whose final stanza was abandoned) and "She dwelt among th'untrodden ways" (which lost its first and third stanzas), it exceeds its dramatic justification. Wordsworth does not merely impersonate a taciturn lover; he suffers the censorship he wields.

Like the rest of the *Lyrical Ballads,* the Lucy poems leave conspicuous room for voices other than that of the poet. They leave room particularly for the reader, who is invited to supply his interpretation in place of the story the poet refuses to tell. Narrative and syntactic fragments, the Lucy poems depend upon their readers' interpretive efforts to fill them out. What we are asked to interpret in these texts is itself an act of interpretation in which the poet reads his own words as if they had been spoken by another. The poet makes himself out to be only the belated interpreter of what are, after all, his own poems. He calls upon the reader to aid him against, or perhaps merely to witness, the stranger he discovers in himself, his own internal poetic rival, who speaks a language the poet recognizes as foreign—as indeed, in Goslar, it was.

The Lucy poems demonstrate almost programmatically the axioms of the Preface to the *Lyrical Ballads;* they also epitomize its problems. What Wordsworth describes in the Preface is an experimental redefinition of the borders of poetry in such a way as to include everything vital and exclude the artificially sensational. He seeks to marry the language of art to the language of life. But the Lucy poems discover in that theoretically purifying and hypothetically revivifying connection only confusion and death. The meeting of the two languages, that of the unselfconscious man and that of the self-conscious poet, is catastrophic. Describing in the "language really used by men" a dead woman "Roll'd round in earth's diurnal course / With rocks and stones and trees," the Lucy poems show with terrifying literalness how "the passions of men are incorporated with the beautiful and permanent forms of nature." Following to the letter the prescriptions of the Preface intended to ground poetry in the common and the familiar, the Lucy poems fall, ironically enough, into a gothicism even ghostlier than the one Wordsworth meant to avoid.

Each Lucy poem is only a synecdoche of the same occluded narrative of loss, repeating what we already know from hearing it not quite told by the others. They inhabit what Geoffrey Hartman calls "the ghostly interstices of narrative,"[6] haunted not only by Lucy but also by the ghost of her story. Read collectively, they suggest a narrative whose outlines, like those of any respectable ghost, are hazy: we cannot tell exactly where it begins, what it includes, or where it ends. We know there are a number of Lucy poems, but we do not know exactly how many because we cannot tell what counts as a Lucy poem and what does not.[7] Although critics are fond of arranging the poems in sequences,[8] it is no use deciding that "Strange fits of passion" must go first when one can't figure out whether "I travelled among unknown men" belongs to the sequence or whether "Louisa" could be a member of the group traveling under an alias. Part of the difficulty arises from Wordsworth's failure to treat the poems as members of the same family or to distinguish them in any formal way from their neighbors. Four of what we now think of as the Lucy poems were printed in the second volume of the 1800 *Lyrical Ballads:* "Strange fits of Passion," "She dwelt among th'untrodden ways," and "A slumber did my spirit seal" were sandwiched between "Ellen Irwin, or the Braes of Kirtle" and "The Waterfall and the Eglantine." Readers of the time may have imagined "Ellen Irwin," a slight ballad-like poem about a girl who dies for her lover, to be the first and most intelligible of a short sequence of poems on the tendency of amiable young women to die. They may not have connected these poems with "Three years she grew in sun and shower," which appeared further on in the volume. When Wordsworth collected and classified his poems in 1815, the Lucy poems suffered a fresh dispersal. "Strange fits" and "She dwelt" were printed side by side in "Poems Founded on the Affections," between "Louisa" and "I travelled among unknown men," both of which have been linked to the Lucy group. "A slumber" and "Three years she grew" went together into "Poems of the Imagination," flanked by "O Nightingale!" and "I wandered lonely as a cloud," neither of which has ever been considered a candidate for inclusion among the Lucy poems.

Like most readers, I take "Strange fits of Passion," "She dwelt among th'untrodden ways," "A slumber did my spirit seal," and "Three years she grew" to be the central Lucy poems; I omit "I travelled among unknown men" partly because it does not appear with the others in the *Lyrical Ballads.* Deciding to accept the conventional grouping is a matter of convenience, not conviction; although it is impossible to draw precisely the borders of the group, it is equally impossible to talk about them without making some gesture in the direction of any such demarcation. Nevertheless, it is important to recognize that the blurring of the poems' identity is one of their chief characteristics and an effect Wordsworth worked to create, not only by scattering them, not only by leaving Lucy sometimes anonymous, but also by providing the poems with delusive doubles.

Of these doubles "Lucy Gray" is perhaps the most notorious. Both "Lucy Gray" and Lucy Gray function as literary ghost effects, afterimages of the proper Lucy poems. Surely undergraduates are not the only ones beguiled by the similarities between this Lucy and the other. "Lucy Gray" seems at first glance to offer an explanation of what the other Lucy poems leave so mysterious: So this is what happened! So this is what she was like! But it is finally as difficult to grasp the meaning of this girl as of the other. Lucy Gray the ghost, like "Lucy Gray" the poem, comes into being as the residue of desperate interpretation, what is left after her parents have traced the "print" of her feet to the middle of a bridge:

> downward from the steep hill's edge
> They track'd the footprints small;

And through the broken hawthorn-hedge,
And by the long stone-wall;

And then an open field they cross'd,
The marks were still the same;
They track'd them on, nor ever lost,
And to the Bridge they came.

They follow'd from the snowy bank
The footmarks, one by one,
Into the middle of the plank,
And further there were none.

By continuing beyond the print, "Lucy Gray" provides its heroine with an afterlife, which is, perhaps, the only life ever available to her. For in some sense Lucy Gray was already, even before her loss, a ghost; her inability to cross the bridge, to cross water, should have told us as much. Her body is never found because there is no body to be found; the only thing anyone can recover is that textual "print," which leads her parents and us to that blank space in which the other Lucy, too, died.

"Lucy Gray" supplies an aetiology for the ghostly melancholy of the central Lucy poems; it tells a story about what it is like to look for a girl who has fallen out of the text and thereby eluded interpretation. If she could be found, she could be mourned; but what blocks mourning blocks understanding as well. Not her death but rather her elusiveness binds this poem to the other, less overtly baffling, Lucy poems, whose interpretive frustrations the curiously extratextual ghost of Lucy Gray epitomizes.

The literal corpselessness of "Lucy Gray" corresponds to a figurative corpselessness in the proper Lucy poems, whose blank, practically nameless heroine hardly seems real enough to die. We tend to think of life as capable of representation and death as beyond language, but Lucy's life was the impossible figure for her death. As Frances Ferguson points out, Lucy exists largely as a cypher and an occasion for metaphor-making:

> The similes and metaphors are figural substitutions for Lucy which stand in for Lucy completely enough to suggest that there may be a fundamental category mistake in seeing her as a human being—she is, perhaps, a flower (or a simile, or a metaphor).[9]

It is not altogether clear that a girl who is a flower (or a simile, or a metaphor) can die at all, except figuratively. The poet takes care to erase from her representation any traces of genuine humanity she may have begun with,[10] and the facts of her death are studiously evaded. Although no body is ever explicitly missed, none is ever pronounced dead, either. It is always in the interim that Lucy dies: between one poem and another, between one stanza and the next, even (as in "A slumber did my spirit seal" or "Three years she grew") between an innocent image and its horrified deciphering.

Although we know she must be mortal, Lucy hardly seems susceptible to anything so punctual as death. While she lived, "She seem'd a thing that could not feel / The touch of earthly years," and while he is with her the poet seems to share a like immunity from anxious time. "A slumber did my spirit seal," he tells us, and he does seem to have enjoyed, while she lived, an extraordinary kind of temporal exemption, inhabiting, grammatically speaking, the subtle gap between the temporally imprecise imperfect, the tense of habitual and familiar truths, and the preterite, the tense of discontinuities, discrete events, and narrative. When in "Strange fits of passion" an abrupt awareness of the progress of the moon leads him to imagine Lucy's death, he is unable face the possibility that her death could occur as a dying:

> What fond and wayward thoughts will slide
> Into a Lover's head—
> "O mercy!" to myself I cried,
> "If Lucy should be dead!"

His subjunctive transforms what might have been an event into a condition, a capacity for death, something he must already have known about her. "If Lucy should be dead!" he cries, as if perhaps she had already died without his having realized it, or as if her death occurred somehow outside of time. But she isn't dead, at least not yet. A false alarm, a premature apprehension, distracts us from the imminence of the real thing.

This is the closest the poet comes to showing us the death itself, and he can do it only by presenting it as imaginary. Although by the time the reader moves on from this poem to any of the others the fiction will have been revealed to be true, an atmosphere of unreality clings to Lucy's nonstory. As Geoffrey Hartman has pointed out, it is as if her death were something that existed only within the poet's mind, an invention of his consciousness.[11] The poet has a curious emotional investment in the esoteric knowledge of her death:

> She *liv'd* unknown, and few could know
> When Lucy ceas'd to be;
> But she is in her Grave, and Oh!
> The difference to me.

The "difference" is so fine as to be nearly impossible for anyone else to register, and that, from the poet's point of view, is as it should be. His attitude seems a compound of doubt and jealousy: doubt that she really is dead, and jealousy lest others declare themselves his rivals in mourning her.

Such feelings would not be as inappropriate as they may sound. Freud describes the "work of mourning" as a slow accession to the reality of a loss that the mourner would gladly deny. In his reluctance to give up the beloved dead he may

> [cling] to the object through the medium of a hallucinatory wishful psychosis. Normally, respect for reality gains the day. Nevertheless its orders cannot be obeyed at once. They are carried out bit by bit, at great expense of time and cathectic energy, and in the meantime the existence of the lost object is psychically prolonged.[12]

Before the mourner manages to free his ego from its attachment to the dead, then, he is liable to see ghosts, whose appearance express his doubts about the reality of his loss and who seem to want to draw him into the grave with them. If he is to return to living in the living world, however, he must detach himself from the dead. Peter Sacks observes,

> Few elegies or acts of mourning succeed without seeming to place the dead, and death itself, at some cleared distance from the living. Hence, in part, the sense of distance marked by the processions in elegies or by such related items as the catalogued offering of flowers. These offerings, apart from their figurative meanings and their function of obeisance, also add to the temporal or spatial respite within the rites,

or within the poem itself; and the flowers, like the poetic language to which they are so often compared, serve not only as offerings or as gestures for respite but also as demarcations separating the living from the dead.[13]

In Sacks's words again, "The work of mourning . . . is largely designed to defend the individual against death."[14] The mourner mourns to save his own life; he must distinguish himself from the object of his grief and affirm his kinship with his fellow mourners, the living. But neither may he altogether renounce his ties with the dead, lest he be forced to renounce their legacy to him.[15] At the same time as he breaks either identification—with the other mourners or with the object of their mourning—he must reassert it, proving in the face of rival claimants his right to inherit, proving against the claims of the dead his right to live.

As an expression of the work of mourning, then, elegy is fundamentally a contest or struggle simultaneously against the dead and against the mourner's living rivals. The mourner finds himself involved in an emotional triangle whose dynamics recall those of the Oedipal triangle whose resolution first permitted him access to language. Thus Sacks:

> Each procedure or resolution is essentially defensive, requiring a detachment of affection from a prior object followed by a reattachment of the affection elsewhere. At the core of each procedure is the renunciatory experience of loss and the experience, not just of a substitute, but of the very means and practice of substitution. . . . In the elegy, the poet's preceding relationship with the deceased (often associated with the mother, or Nature, or a naively regarded Muse) is conventionally disrupted and forced into a triadic structure including the third term, death (frequently associated with the father, or Time, or the more harshly perceived necessity of linguistic mediation itself). The dead, like the forbidden object of a primary desire, must be separated from the poet, partly by a veil of words.[16]

If successful, mourning makes it possible for the mourner to name and figure the dead. Elegy brings poetic voice to birth at the side of the grave and at the expense of deathly silence.

Although the Lucy poems have sometimes been called elegies, they are not good—or at least not successful—examples of the genre. As bad elegies, the Lucy poems worry the work of mourning rather than accomplishing it. They refuse to confront the moment of death or the fact of the body; they fail to distinguish between what is inside the grave and what is outside it. Unable to forget Lucy, sometimes unable to name her, and incapable of providing credible witnesses to her death, the poet convinces us chiefly of his bitterness at having lost the girl to what sounds suspiciously like another suitor. With such a chief mourner, no wonder Lucy remains a ghost.

The difficulty of mourning was much on Wordsworth's mind during the winter of 1799–1800. He made it the subject not just of the Lucy poems but also of the so-called Matthew poems, two of which appeared in the 1800 *Lyrical Ballads* along with the four principal Lucy poems. Both the Lucy poems and the Matthew poems are abortive elegies, poems in which a man fails to detach himself from those he has lost and turn again to the living.[17] In both groups poetic voice—making analogies, creating figures—generates fears of treacherous substitution or rivalry. The poet must bite his tongue or whisper as he goes; it is dangerous to speak in the vicinity of the dead.

The most obvious similarity between the two groups[18] has to do with the nature of the sorrow that is their subject. In none of these poems is grief open to comfort; in all of them the sense of loss remains fresh and repels all efforts at consolation. The passage of time has no healing emotional significance in these poems. In "The Two April Mornings," Matthew remembers the pain he felt grieving for his daughter thirty years earlier:

Six feet in earth my Emma lay,
And yet I lov'd her more,
For so it seem'd, than till that day
I e'er had loved before.

And, turning from her grave, I met
Beside the church-yard Yew
A blooming Girl, whose hair was wet
With points of morning dew.

A basket on her head she bare,
Her brow was smooth and white,
To see a Child so very fair,
It was a pure delight!

No fountain from its rocky cave
E'er tripp'd with foot so free,
She seem'd as happy as a wave
That dances on the sea.

There came from me a sigh of pain
Which I could ill confine;
I look'd at her and look'd again;
—And did not wish her mine.

Though momentarily tempted by the resemblance between the passing girl and his lost Emma, Matthew refuses to succumb to the consolations of confusion; he will not allow anyone but Emma to be his daughter. The shape of his grief retains a strict integrity.

No substitutions, no consoling figurations, are possible for Matthew, not even for children who never existed. In "The Fountain" he laments not for his lost daughter, nor indeed for anyone in particular except, perhaps, himself; his grief has become anonymous but not therefore any easier to remedy. He complains of a grief so general it has become mere melancholy:

"My days, my Friend, are almost gone,
My life has been approv'd,
And many love me, but by none
Am I enough beloved."

"Now both himself and me he wrongs,
The man who thus complains!
I live and sing my idle songs
Upon these happy plains,

And, Matthew, for thy Children dead
I'll be a son to thee!"
At this he grasp'd his hands, and said,
"Alas! that cannot be."

The old man's dead will suffer no rivals. The sense of absorption we find here we find also in the Lucy poems, but the literalness of his grief is Matthew's own. Not for him is the poet's carelessness about the identity of his beloved; this man knows whom he has lost. The dead are not allowed to return in any shape. No "Emma Gray" lurks in the margins of these texts. But if the Matthew poems seem written in repudiation of rivals, revenants, and fictional doubles, they nevertheless stand in relation to the Lucy poems, like "Lucy Gray," in precisely the position of rivals, revanants, and doubles.

The Matthew poems and "Lucy Gray" form a ghostly poetic corona around the central Lucy poems, blurring the hardness of their edges and suggesting that Lucy may not be as distinct a figure nor her death as distinct an event as the speaker assumes. Against these unspoken insinuations the poet offers passionate but confused defense. Choking on his own voice, he insists upon the uniqueness of his loss, his frequently demonstrated taciturnity becoming, over the course of what for lack of a better word one might call the cycle, an irrepressible loquacity. But the more he insists, the more troublesome grow our doubts.

The poems' very multiplicity creates problems. Long and repetitious elegies we are used to—elegiac repetition is conventional, Sacks notes, and frequently "elegies are presented as being repetitions in themselves." The very length of an elegy says something about the difficulty of coming to terms with the death of someone beloved: the repetitions tend to create a sense of ceremonial continuity in the face of mortal discontinuity, and the iterations help persuade the mourner that his loss is real.[19] If the Lucy poems were the stanzas of a single larger elegy, we might understand their function in this light; for the terrible amplitude even of "In Memoriam" one can imagine excuses. But the Lucy poems, though not so wearyingly numerous as Tennyson's laments, are perhaps harder to justify because harder to integrate. The poems do not admit of addition, indeed of accumulation of any kind. There is no sense that they represent distinct moments in a process of mourning; between one poem and another there is no sense that the past has receded or the poet moved forward. On the contrary, the poet is unable to progress; he is forced, like the Ancient Mariner, to relive his loss and repeat his dismay. Things have changed and can never again be the same, he cries; but the iteration belies the cry. The time is always only an undifferentiated and static *afterwards.* Each poem, refusing to acknowledge the others, presents itself as the first, the only lament.[20]

As a result, the poems form a rivalry rather than a sequence or even a group. The structure of rivalry not only determines their relations to one another and to other poems standing proximate to them ("Lucy Gray," the Matthew poems) but also informs their emotional content. The poet sees rivals in death, in Lucy, and in himself. His grief is superimposed upon jealousy and self-doubt; he cannot always be sure who it is that he mourns or even who he is that finds himself mourning.

The rival the poet fears does not generally take the form one might expect.[21] He is rarely visible and not indubitably human. We surmise his existence because the poet does: he acts as if he has a rival and is willing to sacrifice a great deal in order to be able to repel the threat the rival poses; he is willing to sacrifice even Lucy herself.

Compared with the extravagance of the conventional elegy's praises, invocations, and offerings to the dead, this poet's gestures in Lucy's direction appear strangely grudging. Unlike the ordinary elegist, who calls upon nature to mourn and the dead to return to life, this poet seems to want to disperse the mourners and remind Lucy that there is nothing worth coming back for. Her life itself was nothing much—as the poet describes it, something between a quibble and a paradox. In "She dwelt among th'untrodden ways" Lucy was

> A Violet by a mossy stone
> Half-hidden from the Eye!
> —Fair, as a star when only one
> Is shining in the sky!

It is oddly half-hearted praise. The poet seems to suggest that Lucy was most beautiful when she was a little hard to see or at least when there was no one else around—that she did not stand up to comparisons well, or even direct inspection.

All this redounds, of course, to the credit of her modesty. But the lover's enthusiasm for his beloved's tendency to shrink from view suggests a desire to shield not only her but also himself from competition. Twice in the course of this brief poem he falls into awkwardness as he tries to deny the possibility that other men might notice her.

She dwelt among th'untrodden ways
Beside the springs of Dove,
A Maid whom there were none to praise
And very few to love.

It is possible to make sense of this, but only at the price of acknowledging that those few who love Lucy do not admire her. It is possible, too, by means of logical acrobatics, to make sense of the final quatrain:

She *liv'd* unknown, and few could know
When Lucy ceas'd to be;
But she is in her Grave, and Oh!
The difference to me.

When the poet says she "*liv'd* unknown," he does not mean it literally; it is the proximity of the second iteration of the word "know," used literally, that creates the initial confusion. But why so awkward? The thought that others may admire her drives him to overstatements that he is forced to retract. Judging by the logical and linguistic strain, one would be tempted to say that what threatens him is not so much her loss as the competition it seems to demand of him.

The poet catches his first glimpse of the competition in "Strange fits of passion," during a hypnotically slow ride toward Lucy's cottage one moonlit night.

When she I lov'd, was strong and gay
And like a rose in June,
I to her cottage bent my way,
Beneath the evening moon.

Upon the moon I fix'd my eye,
All over the wide lea;
My horse trudg'd on, and we drew nigh
Those paths so dear to me.

And now we reach'd the orchard plot,
And, as we climb'd the hill,
Towards the roof of Lucy's cot
The moon descended still.

In one of those sweet dreams I slept,
Kind Nature's gentlest boon!
And, all the while, my eyes I kept
On the descending moon.

My horse mov'd on; hoof after hoof
He rais'd and never stopp'd:
When down behind the cottage roof
At once the planet dropp'd.

It is like a problem in geometry. If we forget the horse for a moment, we find a triangle, with the poet on the ground, Lucy's cottage some distance away, and the moon up above. The triangle changes its shape as the poet rides on and the moon progresses across the sky, and finally, as the moon sets behind the cottage, it collapses. How we read the poet's bizarre response to this collapse ("O mercy!" to myself I cried, / "If Lucy should be dead!") will depend upon what we make of the triangle—and what we make of the moon. The most immediately obvious thing about the moon is its longstanding association with lunatics, of whom the poet may be one. The second most obvious thing about it is that the poet begins to confuse it with the human object of his quest.[22] Riding towards Lucy's cottage, he rides also toward the moon, his horse seeming to leave the earth behind as "hoof after hoof / He rais'd and never stopp'd." We cannot know whether the poet has begun to identify the moon with Lucy or whether he has allowed it to distract him from his thoughts of her, whether his moonstruck journey means fidelity or betrayal or (*Endymion*-style) both at once. But when the moon converges on Lucy's cottage and disappears, suddenly he imagines the girl has died.

If the moon is somehow Lucy's counterpart or rival, it is the poet's as well. It keeps pace with him, as the moon always does with a traveler, accompanying him as he heads toward Lucy's cottage, only descending as he ascends. Its movement reflects his movement; it *is* he; only, in beating him to his goal, this double becomes a rival, as doubles are wont to do.[23] The object of his desire and his narcissistic identification, his ideal self and the idealization of Lucy, turns out to be also the object of his envy. Its eclipse suggests simultaneously the success of a rival, the death of that rival, the death of his beloved, and the extinction of his double. The poet's instant and instinctive fears for Lucy's life must express even more terrifying fears for his own life, but only the threat to Lucy can be articulated. The complex nature of the doublings within the triangle allows the poet to survive the lunar menace: he can offer up Lucy as a sacrifice in his own place. One double seems to destroy the other. All that is clear is that in this poem both love and identity are inextricably involved with erotic triangularity—something we already knew from Freud.

The symbolic threat of the moon in "Strange fits" is the threat precisely of the symbol, of language even, with its tendency to set itself up in rivalry not only against its representations, the objects of its desires or significations, but also against its speaker, its desiring and intending subject. To speak is to betray oneself; the rival most to be feared shows himself as soon as one opens one's mouth in protest against him. Perhaps this is why the poet whispers; perhaps he really is afraid of the sound of his own (or is it his own?) voice. Each Lucy poem, like either Matthew poem, encounters death as a revelation of the rift between representation and desire. In the Lucy poems this disjunction is the source, apparently, of a consciousness the poet will not acknowledge as his own but that speaks through his words. In these poems the loss of individuality that death threatens comes in the form of vocal substitution. The poet experiences Lucy's death as a difficulty in saying what he means to say about her. His own voice shocks him.

In "A slumber did my spirit seal" we encounter a configuration similar to that we found in "Strange fits." The geometry of this shortest and most shocking of the Lucy poems involves a triangle involving the poet and two doubles: Lucy and an invisible but audible figure that turns out to inhabit the poet's own words.

A slumber did my spirit seal,
I had no human fears:
She seem'd a thing that could not feel
The touch of earthly years.

No motion has she now, no force
She neither hears nor sees
Roll'd round in earth's diurnal course
With rocks and stones and trees!

While Lucy was alive he had no need to think precisely about what she was. She was at once too ambiguous and too unambiguous: too changelessly herself to need a name, which implies the possibility of alteration or absence, and too much a part of the poet's own "I," which is also a "she," to warrant a separate term of identification.

On the other side of the white space the poet's unconsciousness has become Lucy's. As if his self-consciousness, his awareness of himself as distinct from Lucy, has required the most absolute of distinctions between them, his waking up means her death. Or, since Lucy never is treated as a character independent of the poet's consciousness, his awakening into self-consciousness is the equivalent of feeling as if someone had disappeared whose separateness he had never before noticed.[24] His "I" will no longer shade off into "she." Lucy, meanwhile, has been diffused into all external nature, no longer distinguishable from "rocks and stones and trees," as she takes on herself the burden both of the poet's earlier unconsciousness and his implicit belief in her—which means also his—immortality. The question whether the "she" of the third line refers to "my spirit" as its antecedent thus becomes irrelevant: either she carries off the threat of death by suffering it herself or else her continued existence in nature confirms how right the poet was to suspect that "she" was immune to change.

The poet's thoughtless innocence has become guilt, for his dream provided the literal terms of Lucy's death. Midway through the poem, between the first stanza and its uncanny mirror-image in the second stanza, the imagination is brought face to face with its imaginings. The horror of the second stanza depends upon a combination of the ironic and the uncanny. It is ironic that the poet's calm confidence in Lucy's immortality should have been betrayed so subtly, that death should turn out to have entered through a legalistic quibble or loophole. It is uncanny that his earlier thoughts and innocent words should return to him with a meaning he never meant. From the perspective of the second stanza, the first is haunted; when the poet speaks them it is something else that means them. What haunts the first stanza is literalness of a peculiarly reductive kind. The images of the first stanza seem, upon first reading, to stand on their own, plain enough, in no pressing need of interpretation. The second stanza arrives as the literal meaning that shifts the first stanza, as the poet and we are now uncomfortably aware, into the realm of the figurative, which we had not taken seriously enough. Lucy's death, which occurs as the metamorphosis of one kind of language into another, coincides with the self-interruption of the poem as it stops to interpret itself, to quote its own words in a new context that reveals the split between conscious intention and meaning. Here language itself is Lucy's ghost and the poet's deadly rival.

In "A slumber," as in "Strange fits" and "She dwelt," the poet is a latecomer in his own poem, arriving at the truth too late to rescue Lucy from his own Doppelgänger, which is also hers. The companionable moon or his own dreamy words betray him, leaving him not only bereaved but also obscurely guilty. He spoke the words that prophesied Lucy's death, and he followed the moon that killed her. His desire to keep her invisible to the world meant the end of her. In the last-written of the Lucy poems, however, the poet is blameless, a passive witness to the crime his rival commits. He does not speak, or ride, or wish; he merely quotes. For the first time, the rival shows himself for what he is: not a verbal parasite, not an ambivalence, not an optical illusion, but a powerful figure with a history and a voice of his own, before which the poet can only give way.

In "Three years she grew" the voice of Nature usurps the poet's control over his poem, interrupting him after only a line and a half and not letting him speak again until it has destroyed his subject.[25]

Nature is not what people who think of Wordsworth as a "nature poet" might expect. It is not just that this Nature speaks; nature frequently speaks in Wordsworth, but not usually in discrete or iterable words, and not usually as through a *prosopon.*[26] This Nature, an oddly articulate and thus oddly unWordsworthian character, presents himself as the linguistic creature of an earlier literary tradition—the same branch of tradition inhabited by Chaucer's Nature, regulator of avian matings in *The Parlement of Foules;* Spenser's Nature, epicene judge of Mutabilitie in *The Faerie Queene;* and Proteus, worker of metamorphoses, embodiment of allegory, greatest of ventriloquists.[27] He is also King of the Underworld, his opening words—

A lovelier flower
On earth was never sown;
This Child I to myself will take,
She shall be mine, and I will make
A Lady of my own

—suggesting echoes of the Persephone myth, filtered perhaps through *Paradise Lost:*

Not that fair field
Of Enna, where Proserpine gathering flowers
Her self a fairer flower by gloomy Dis
Was gathered, which cost Ceres all that pain
To seek her through the world.[28]

Daughter of Eve and Persephone,[29] the product, like Nature, of origins more literary than natural, Lucy listens—or fails to listen—while Nature sings an erotic invitation in the tradition of the Passionate Shepherd.[30] Wordsworth's Nature offers Lucy a more radical version of the innocent Marlovian pleasures "That valleys, groves, hills, and fields, / Woods, or steepy mountain yields." But unlike Marlowe's Shepherd, Wordsworth's swain does not admit the lady's right to refuse; there is no possible Wordsworthian "Nymph's Reply to the Shepherd."[31]

Nature never deviates very far from what an earthly lover might say to his mistress. Much of his language can be understood in terms of reverence and a desire for union; in his fond imagination, Lucy becomes a mythic creature, and he sees her against backdrops both picturesque and beautiful. But his courtly and amorous fancies tend toward an ambiguity of expression in which it is possible to imagine, at least momentarily, sinister possibilities. Take, for instance, the second stanza:

Myself will to my darling be
Both law and impulse, and with me
The girl in rock and plain,
In earth and heaven, in glade and bower,
Shall feel an overseeing power
To kindle or restrain.

What is Lucy doing "in rock and plain"? Has she been buried? Is she now a spirit? However disturbing the image that the phrase conjures, and whatever its meaning, the next few words buffer its power to shock, reinterpreting the rocks and earth of the "rock and plain" as an image of terrestrial life under the auspices of the divine. And having thus casually dispersed the odor of the chthonic and displayed Lucy at liberty in the upper world, Nature at last locates her in the places one would expect to find wooable maidens: glades and bowers. The darker implications now seem figments of a morbid imagination; except perhaps to the reader of Ovid or Spenser, glades and bowers hold no terrors.

Such is the pattern of much of what Nature says. His words slide between the covertly threatening and the courtly, but the shifts are subtle enough to make it hard for the reader to pin down anything in particular as sinister; Nature takes his own shady images and reinterprets them in terms either more conventional or less disconcertingly intelligible. When Nature tells us

> The floating clouds their state shall lend
> To her, for her the willow bend,

we cannot know whether he means a compliment (she is like the wind, and the very trees bow in worship of her), whether he is elaborately saying that even the "mute insensate things" of nature feel her glory, or whether he has in mind something less courtly than bizarre, Lucy's evaporation and the weeping of the willow, that funereal tree ("Sing willow, willow, willow"). Oddly enough, the literal sense—what the individual words taken seriously seem to suggest—comes across as more fantastic, more highly figurative, than the familiar or conventional figurative sense. The poem forces us to confront a human-sacrificial aspect of the apparently harmless language of courtship, making us think about the uncanny underpinnings of thoughtlessly conventional language.

While there is something threatening in the language Nature uses or parodies, the threat is veiled. The force of Nature's invitation is not immediately evident. His lines, composing a mere catalogue of delights, bespeak the happy contemplation of his desires: if he can win Lucy's love, they will be one in spirit, joyful and serene. His intentions, moreover, are honorable; he has in mind not so much a seduction ("This Child I to myself will take") as a marriage ("While she and I together live / Here in this happy dell"). And the future he describes—a future that instantaneously achieves perfected bliss without the bother of working toward it—seems to involve no pressure, not even that of sequentiality. The lack of temporal indicators ("first," "next," "then," "finally") and the fact that, within Nature's speech, stanzas 2, 3, 4, and 5 could be read in any order suggest that Lucy's choice will entail no binding consequences:

Myself will to my darling be
Both law and impulse, and with me
The Girl in rock and plain,
In earth and heaven, in glade and bower,
Shall feel an overseeing power
To kindle or restrain.

She shall be sportive as the fawn
That wild with glee across the lawn
Or up the mountain springs,
And hers shall be the breathing balm,
And hers the silence and the calm
Of mute insensate things.

The floating clouds their state shall lend
To her, for her the willow bend,
Nor shall she fail to see
Even in the motions of the storm
Grace that shall mould the Maiden's form
By silent sympathy.

The stars of midnight shall be dear
To her, and she shall lean her ear
In many a secret place
Where rivulets dance their wayward round,
And beauty born of murmuring sound
Shall pass into her face.

Lucy may choose from his prospectus, and after choosing she may choose again. Or so it seems.

But the delights Nature lists are not options, and it is not for Lucy either to choose them or to refuse. The sense of his proposals is that Lucy yield up her will and her identity. "My self will to my darling be / Both law and impulse," he declares, the lover's conventional desire to become one in spirit with his beloved revealing itself, in Nature's formulation, to be an ambition rather more radical and less gentle than mere erotic identification. The natural and the human will converge. Lucy takes on attributes of fawns, clouds, weather, the stars, and streams; and Nature (or, perhaps, merely lowercase nature) takes on attributes of human consciousness: law, impulse, restraint, grace, sympathy. According to Nature's scheme, the beloved internalizes her lover, who has come to reflect her inner being, taking his will—if it is his will—for her own. Perhaps for this reason there is no need for her to reply to Nature; it is impossible that she should have an autonomous voice.

In the process Nature describes, Lucy is not merely the object of Nature's will because she is also its manifestation and its source; she absorbs the will that works upon her and that makes the plans that Nature reveals. She shares Nature's power even as she is subjected to it. Dwelling "in rock and plain, / In earth and heaven, in glade and bower," she haunts the ground, moves the clouds, causes the trees to bow. She might be a *genius loci,* if only one could locate her precisely enough. But one cannot. She diffuses into the abstract landscape:

> she shall lean her ear
> In many a secret place
> Where rivulets dance their wayward round,
> And beauty born of murmuring sound
> Shall pass into her face.

Though the secret places and the rivulets may be particular and literal enough, the place shows itself to be subtly allegorized in these last two lines. In allegory it would not be impossible, as it is in the kind of reality Wordsworth is accustomed to depicting, for an abstract quality like "beauty" to detach itself from its context (here the sound of the murmuring rivulets) and take up residence in some new context, here Lucy's face. Lucy's situation is Spenserean (or even Coleridgean); what we take to be her spiritual condition is manifested in the landscape and figures around her. As Nature says, she cannot

> fail to see
> Even in the motions of the storm

Grace that shall mould the Maiden's form
By silent sympathy.

Lucy sees into the life of things, but in an oddly reflexive way. Looking out into the storm (like the Ancient Mariner catching sight of the specter ship), she beholds the contagious image of herself and her future.

But if this is allegory, it is an improper or at least an uninterpretable one. Wordsworth's landscape is not to be read in quite the same way as is one of Spenser's or Coleridge's; there is no one to tell us what the woods are named or what happened once by the rivulets. The history of this landscape is suppressed or nonexistent. These scenes, which have not yet received their names, are as yet pre-allegorical, merely Ovidian. There must be a metamorphosis before there is a myth. But is there a metamorphosis, or only a misapprehension?

Lucy starts out human, and it is not at all clear when she ceases to be so. At our last glimpse of her, which comes in Nature's deceptively urbane closing prophecy, she seems indubitably girlish:

And vital feelings of delight
Shall rear her form to stately height,
Her virgin bosom swell,
Such thoughts to Lucy I will give
While she and I together live
Here in this happy dell.

We find ourselves returned, if only momentarily, to the familiar world in which little girls do get bigger and can be said, in terms that everyone recognizes and understands to be dictated by convention, to be reared by delight. It seems clear that Nature is just being poetical, as he was when he told us that Lucy "shall be sportive as the fawn," as he was even when he told us that "A lovelier flower / On earth was never sown." Though we may not have an altogether precise understanding of what he means, we feel fairly certain that we know the basis of his comparisons, or at least that these *are* comparisons. There really do exist girls who remind their friends of fawns or flowers.

But the analogues that would make such understanding possible are not always available. The finite distance from literal sense that marks properly figurative language widens to infinity; metaphor shades off into catachresis. What can be the literal sense of Lucy's feeling "an overseeing power / To kindle or restrain"? How can one feel a power of sight? Is Lucy the wielder of this power or its object? What does the power kindle or restrain—or is the overseeing power itself to be kindled or restrained?

As a creature of words, Lucy lives in the space of these ambiguities, inhabiting the curiously timeless interval between literal and figurative, surviving for as long as Nature speaks—however long that is. She dies—for us, at least—at the moment the poet reclaims his voice:

> Thus Nature spake—the work was done—
> How soon my Lucy's race was run!
> She died and left to me
> This heath, this calm and quiet scene,
> The memory of what has been,
> And never more will be.

The poet's words force an immediate reevaluation of what Nature has been saying. Is Lucy's living together with Nature merely a trope for her dying into nature? Could Nature have meant what he said, that Lucy would "live" with him, and is her death the aftermath of this romance and not what Nature has been talking about so subtly all along? Or did she die in the poet's reductive interpretation of Nature's words?

In the poet's presentation, Nature's speech and Lucy's life both go by in an instant. "Thus Nature spake—The work was done— / How soon my Lucy's race was run!" Nature's words, as the poet perceives them, have an almost divine force.[32] Our "narrator" makes do with an impoverished role; he provides the scaffolding for Nature's speech and a contrast with that highly wrought and powerful voice. The "narrator's" version occupies only a few lines and seems, in comparison, starkly literal: "She died" either as a result or a translation of Nature's imperative (for that is what it is, not an invitation or a prophecy).

Compared to Nature, the narrator comes across as the lesser poet. His voice is small, ineffective, helpless before clichés. His few poor phrases ("the work" that "was done," "what has been, / And never more will be") are as vague as they are reductive.

"How soon my Lucy's race was run!" Nothing brings the dead metaphor to life; we had not thought of Lucy running a race (against Nature, against time) before, and we do not think of her that way now; it is the poet, not the girl, who has been running, and so fecklessly that until he introduces himself at the end as an "I" and lets us know that he has lost "my Lucy," we do not even know he is there. The poem makes the poet—who speaks but refuses to use his own language, who borrows clichés and depends upon Nature's words to give his own meaning—extraneous. For the first time in all the Lucy poems, the little the poet has to say is too much. Nature has usurped his voice as fatally as he has Lucy's.

But to say that Nature is the poet's more powerful rival is to pretend to more certainty than is possible. It is not clear whether Nature gets into the poem because he is too powerful for the poet to keep out or because the poet has sponsored his appearance; here as in the other Lucy poems, the distinction between rival and double is not easy to make. The poet presents himself as an ordinary man who sees nature in terms of "sun and shower," "this heath, this calm and quiet scene"—nature demythologized,[33] that is, rather than nature in the tradition of Spenser. Talking Nature seems to intrude here from a different kind of poem and a different kind of literary sensibility; he is not the kind of figure the poet would be apt to see or imagine or be likely to use as a means of expressing what he saw happening to Lucy. His function in the poem is to say the vaguely lulling things that in the other Lucy poems come out of the "slumber" that seals the spirit or the "sweet dreams" that the poet experiences. Elsewhere it is the poet himself, albeit in a half-awake state, whose odd dreaminess figures so ironically; here the responsibility for those sinister intimations of Lucy's mortality belongs to Nature. Nature, then, speaking like a character from the far past of the literary tradition and in the form of the shady, magic-working poet/prophet, speaks from the place formerly occupied, perhaps, by the poet's subconscious but, further back than that, by other poets. The poet's own thoughts, too strange and menacing for him to acknowledge as his own, come out of the mouth of a character apparently as unlike him or any of his own creations as possible.

Even this is an oversimplification, because it forgets about Lucy, who is here and throughout the Lucy poems not merely the victim of some obscure rivalry or ambivalence but in fact the rival's double just as she is the poet's. She is an aspect of the poet's soul—"an intermediate modality of consciousness," as Hartman calls her, whose death "brings a new consciousness to birth."[34] She represents the paradoxes of romantic self-consciousness, with its unnerving suggestions of a split in consciousness and language. The ambiguities of Lucy's otherness engender anxieties about the poet's identity: she symbolizes both his integrity and his division, his comforting wholeness and his possible fragmentation. Her existence both confirms and undermines what it doubles, hence the effect of simultaneous splitting and convergence. Like Geraldine, Lucy allegorizes the problems of allegory, language that has become subversive of what it is supposed to represent. Her presence in the poems is the effect of shifting and unnarratable rivalries among representations and their ostensible objects. Her life is ambiguity, double voicing, and uncertain reference; nomination and interpretation kill her. The poet's dreams of her death—dreams he typically denies having dreamed—reflect both his wishes and his fears, for she is both vulnerable and vaguely sinister, both threatened and threatening; to possess her is to possess a rival, and to lose her is to lose oneself. Subject and symbol of fragmentation, she is dispersed among rocks and stones and trees, a violet and a star, plains and glades and bowers and storms. Subject and symbol of identification, she converges with the powers—the moon, Nature—that disperse her.[35]

The Lucy poems reveal the uncanny potential of the language Wordsworth praised in his Preface to the *Lyrical Ballads:*[36] the real language of real men, language that, in theory, derives its propriety from the beautiful and permanent forms of nature and the similarly beautiful and permanent forms of human character. Wordsworth needed no special linguistic resources to bring Lucy into being or to create in these deliberately unsensational poems an effect as sensational as that of the gothic works he abhorred. All he had to do was *not* show his heroine dying, *not* grieve wildly over her grave, *not* give way to extravagance of language. Refusing to give voice to impropriety, he finds his voice stolen from him and used to express meanings he cannot own. The repressed power of improper or unowned language speaks through his reticence, haunting his language and shattering his character.

To find Wordsworth involved through the most orthodox of Wordsworthian principles in an autoventriloquism evidently Coleridgean raises a question or two about the presence and necessity of Coleridge in Wordsworth's program. If ventriloquism is truly a mark of Coleridgean influence, why did it manifest itself just now, when, as we noted earlier, Wordsworth was living apart from Coleridge in what amounted to linguistic isolation? What literary ether need we hypothesize in order to explain the transmission of a Coleridgean disturbance through the vacuum?

If what disturbed Wordsworth was not Coleridge himself exactly but rather his absence, we wouldn't need any ether at all. While I do not go so far as seriously to propose Coleridge as the secret original of the "Violet by a mossy stone / Half-hidden from the Eye," I would suggest that the terrible baffled ambivalence Wordsworth expresses in these poems—the sense of betrayal, uneasy yearning, jealous confusion, and guilty vocal impotence—is what one might expect him to feel at finding himself separated from the friend whose imagination, ear, and voice he had become accustomed to using almost (but this, we have seen, could be a problem) as if they were his own. The Coleridgean quality of the Lucy poems, their ventriloquial likeness particularly to *The Rime of the Ancient Mariner* and "Christabel," might be explicable in part at least as evidence of a precisely Coleridgean bereavement,[37] an attempt to recover through internalization that ideal uncanny other who functioned simultaneously as rival, as object, and as second self.

In fact, however, it was Coleridge who languished (poetically speaking) in Germany, while Wordsworth thrived. In the Goslar poetry—including the beginnings of what would become *The Prelude*—Wordsworth began to create a myth of autonomous imaginative self-generation and to repudiate his dependence on Coleridge.[38] Although not quite happy at being so far from his friend, Wordsworth discovered in himself a source of inspiration that might compensate for what he missed. He learned to distinguish between Coleridge and the abstract position or possibility Coleridge happened to embody in Wordsworth's imaginative life, an imaginative potential that would continue to function regardless of its external realization, representation, occupation, or even vacation by another. Apart from Coleridge, Wordsworth began to apprehend the impersonality of the imagination and its usurpations, which represent no necessarily external disturbance but rather its endlessly self-bereaving and self-recovering nativity.

Goslar was not the end of the Wordsworth-Coleridge collaboration. The poets would return from Germany and to one another. The publication of the *Lyrical Ballads* (1800) was still before them; so were the odes, the failure of the *Recluse* scheme, the trip to Malta, the growing mutual disappointments and disillusionments. There was still over a decade to go before the bitter quarrel over Wordsworth's betrayal of Coleridge to Basil Montague and the long estrangement that never quite healed again. Goslar was only a brief and friendly interval in a still strong and productive friendship. But it prepares us to understand how the poets would work later on, when their isolation from one another was real, enforced by resentments and not merely by geography. The Lucy poems give us a foretaste of the genuine mutual bereavement to come and an indication of how that loss would revise the poets' understanding of the place and function of imagination when its impersonality and abstraction were no longer mere speculative hypotheses but painful social realities.

II

Afterwards: Imaginations in Division

6

The Heterogeneity of the *Biographia Literaria*

The *Biographia Literaria* represents Coleridge's fullest response to questions about the nature of identity, the nature of imagination, and the nature of the relationship between one man's voice and another's. Such questions had been critical seventeen years before, when he and Wordsworth still worked together, and for Coleridge they were still urgent; but Wordsworth no longer cared what his former friend thought about it all. Had Wordsworth had the patience to read the great unwieldy mess of a book that straggled into print so long after their friendship had ended, he might not have known what he was looking at.[1] For the *Biographia*'s method—if it can be called that—is indirect, even hysterical: its diseases are more eloquent than its arguments.

The *Biographia Literaria* flouts the ideal it expounds. This exposition of the freedom and integrity of the self and the poetic voice is a magpie's nest of topics and a Babel of voices. Despite its proclamation of aesthetic organicism, the *Biographia* is not itself an organic growth.[2] Or, if it is one, it resembles "a mushroom growth in which toughness of fibre is scarcely to be expected"[3] or that Freudian mushroom of dreaming whose mycelium reaches down into the unknowable.[4] The book's incoherence can be attributed in part to the multiplicity of purposes it had to serve. The *Biographia* was an attempt to do perhaps too many things at once: raise money, satisfy the printer's demand for more pages than Coleridge had planned to write, defend the freedom of the self from the attacks of Hartley and the mechanistic school of philosophy, respond to *The Prelude* and the prefaces to the *Lyrical*

Ballads and the 1815 *Poems,*[5] examine what it means to write one's own life, and discuss what distinguishes a false voice from a true one. Few have stood up for its integrity,[6] and defenders labor under the disadvantage of knowing that for many readers the lack of apparent coherence does not much matter—they prefer to regard the book as a warehouse of oddities and treasures to be picked over and carried away piece by piece.

The problem is not so vexing in Volume II, which, devoted mostly to a reading of Wordsworth's poetry, stands on its own as a coherent work. But Volume I, the work of a man by all appearances demonically possessed, a metaphysically inclined Ancient Mariner, is another matter. Self-interrupting, digressive, plagiarized, and full of discussion about plagiarism, false voices, imitations, and vocal possession, the *Biographia* suffers the problem that is its theme: the impossible need for identity, the irremediable compromising of the self by the other.

In the ungainly middle of this "remarkable failure"[7] of a work that feels as if it were "put together with a pitchfork. . . . without form or proportion"[8] appears a passage that resists with even more stubbornness than usual logical assimilation into the surrounding material. For a preceding chapter and a half—chapters 5 and 6, that is—Coleridge has been discussing the invidious implications of the law of association, particularly Hartley's formulation of it. He objects principally, it seems, to the implication

> that the will, the reason, the judgement, and the understanding, instead of being the determining causes of association, must needs be represented as its *creatures,* and among its mechanical *effects*. . . . Had this really been the case, the consequence would have been, that our whole life would be divided between the despotism of outward impressions, and that of senseless and passive memory.[9]

If the will and reason are the passive effects of impinging sensations, they can play no role in shaping the data of experience. This would mean, in practical terms, delirium, a chaos of impressions controlled not by will or reason but by the accident of contiguity. For Coleridge, the Hartleyan theory is useless except possibly as a description of the pathological state of "complete lightheadedness." Then, as if presenting an example of lightheadedness—or perhaps as an example of the absurdity of Hartley's ideas—Coleridge tells the story of the girl apparently possessed by a polyglot devil.

> A young woman of four or five, and twenty, who could neither read, nor write, was seized with a nervous fever; during which, according to the asseverations of all the priests and monks of the neighbourhood, she became *possessed,* and, as it appeared, by a very learned devil. She continued incessantly talking Latin, Greek, and Hebrew, in very pompous tones and with most distinct enunciation.

Her ravings "were found to consist of sentences, coherent and intelligible each for itself, but with little or no connection with each other." Doctors investigated, and eventually a physician, searching out the niece of a pastor who had taken the girl in as a charity boarder for several years, discovered an explanation:

> It appeared, that it had been the old man's custom, for years, to walk up and down a passage of his house into which the kitchen door opened, and to read to himself with a loud voice, out of his favorite books. A considerable number of these were still in the niece's possession. She added, that he was a very learned man and a great Hebraist. Among the books were found a collection of rabbinical writings, together with several of the Greek and Latin fathers; and the physician succeeded in identifying so many passages with those taken down at the young woman's bedside, that no doubt could remain in any rational mind concerning the true origin of the impressions made on her nervous system.[10]

The tale has an urgency of interest out of proportion to its humble position in the dry argument about the restricted applicability of a lame theory. The possessed girl is better than Hartley deserves, the story of her ravings more engaging than Hartley's reasonings or Coleridge's refutation of them. Indeed, the story is itself like an interrupting voice, so at odds with its occasion that it is hard to see exactly what it is meant to illustrate, whether Coleridge offers it as evidence of the mind's ascendancy over sensations or as a concession to the view that sensations dominate over a passive mind.[11] It is certainly no typical tale of delirium. Although she manifestly has no understanding of what she is saying, the girl's words are, phrase by phrase at least, "coherent and intelligible" to others, as if a ventriloquistic intelligence worked through her fever and ignorance. She mixes no vulgar English with her scholarly languages. Context alone proves her speech to be nonsensical. "Complete light-headedness" does not usually abide by such strict decorum.

Neither does the story seem to support the interpretation Coleridge places upon it. For him, "This authenticated case furnishes both proof and instance, that reliques of sensation may exist for an indefinite time in a latent state, in the very same order in which they were originally impressed." In other words it is "probable, that all thoughts are in themselves imperishable."[12] The grudging concession to Hartley seems momentarily to have run away with the argument. The sensations whose importance Coleridge has strived to minimize have returned in strength, invulnerable to modification and apparently indistinguishable from the thoughts whose independence they threaten. Their fixed memory counts as evidence even of the immortality of the soul:

> And this, this, perchance, is the dread book of judgement, in whose mysterious hieroglyphics every idle word is recorded! Yea, in the very nature of a living spirit, it may be more possible that heaven and earth should pass away, than that a single act, a single thought, should be loosened or lost from that living chain of causes, to all whose links, conscious or unconscious, the free-will, our only absolute *self,* is co-extensive and co-present.[13]

Somehow the "despotism of outward impressions, and that of passive memory" have come to serve as evidence of free will and the absolute and innermost self, although it is difficult to recognize in the sketch of a girl mouthing phrases she never comprehended an illustration of any "absolute *self.*" Self, in the sense at least of motivated consciousness, seems to be precisely what she lacks. Her words are fully accidental, meaning more than, or other than, she knows; they fail to reflect any aspect of her conscious will. The excellence of her mimicry is the result of the absence of those elements of the self that might interfere with the literalness of her memory.

"Why has Coleridge bothered to tell a story," Jerome Christensen asks, "which, if it performs any function, reinforces the position of his adversary, albeit in a pathological extreme? Has the impulse to give a good rhetorical example been interrupted by Coleridge's desire to tell one of *his* stories?"[14] Coleridge seems to be using the story to exemplify both the passive memory at the mercy of delirious fever and free will asserting itself through a "living chain of causes." Perhaps, like the girl's ravings, not meant at all, it enacts the text's possession by the very philosophical superstitions Coleridge set out to combat: the argument seems to have been coopted by the associationist position against which Coleridge has been steadily arguing. The breakdown of the anti-associationist argument occurs when remote theoretical concerns threaten to become immediately relevant. In the story of the possessed girl nature takes the form of a library and the threat of overwhelming sensations is displaced by the threat of learning—"truth's simulacrum," as Christensen calls it.[15] Coleridge would clearly like to assert the power of the mind over nature, the power of the scholar over his materials. But instead the materials assert their power over him.

After absorbing the story of the girl, incongruously, into an ecstatic assertion of the immortality of the soul, Coleridge gives up his attempt to regain control of the story's implications. Perhaps feeling himself out of his depth,[16] he dismisses the theme, pronouncing his readership unworthy of hearing more:

> But not now dare I longer discourse of this, waiting for a loftier mood, and a nobler subject, warned from within and from without, that it is profanation to speak of these mysteries "To those to whose imagination it has never been presented, how beautiful is the countenance of justice and wisdom; and that neither the morning nor the evening star are so fair. For in order to direct the view aright, it behoves that the beholder should have made himself congenerous and similar to the object beheld. Never could the eye have beheld the sun, had not its own essence been soliform," (*i.e. pre-configured to light by a similarity of essence with that of light*) "neither can a soul not beautiful attain to an intuition of beauty."[17]

According to this sublime put-down, Coleridge's readers are unworthy of hearing wisdom because they are not yet wise. Knowledge depends upon a "similarity of essence" shared between the knower and the known; it is impossible for the perceiver to perceive anything truly alien to himself. The juxtaposition of the myth of the soliform man and the story of the possessed girl raises disturbing questions, however. Does the transformation of being into knowing imply the transformation of knowing into being as well? If one knows only by resembling the objects of one's knowledge, does one come to resemble what one knows? Will the objects of one's attention take one over?[18]

The possessed girl is the *reductio ad absurdum* of the principle that the soliform man epitomizes. Helplessly mimicking the source of a wisdom that is no wisdom to her, she mimics as well the man whose wisdom really is immanent to his being. Her grotesque position subverts the sublimity of the soliform man. If the soliform man is what Coleridge wished to be, the possessed girl is what he feared he might become. Her will paralyzed, uttering words of whose sense she was unconscious, her false inspiration inspiring wonder in others, attended in her illness by an amanuensis, she must have seemed to Coleridge (deeply implicated in plagiarisms even as he wrote this passage) a sinister reflection of himself. The diasparactive[19] nature of her utterance, the failure of her learned quotations to form coherent sense, seems to mock the chaotic work in which the story is embedded. Even the doctors seeking the solution of the phenomenon have real analogues in critics who would interpret Coleridge by finding the sources of his words and thoughts in Kant, Fichte, Schelling, Jacobi, Maass, and others, as if source were meaning.

Coleridge anticipates his critics in the accusation that his memory has usurped the place of his will, repeating rather than thinking. For the demon possessing the girl is her own too-persistent memory. What gives her memory its demonic cast is its disjunction from her will and her understanding; a faculty ordinarily passive has assumed independence.[20] Perhaps the ambiguity of the place of the story in the argument about the laws of association and the activity of the soul makes a little more sense in the light of the complexity of emotion she must have aroused in Coleridge. Her treatment in the chapter may spring from Coleridge's ambivalence toward associationism. Indeed, I. A. Richards has conjectured that one of the reasons for Coleridge's rejection of Locke and the mechanistic school of psychology of which Hartley was a member was that their theory "was too painfully true. It was the intellectual equivalent of his uncreative moods, and the temper of an uncreative century."[21] The story of the girl was perhaps too painfully true as well. After absorbing it into wild speculations about the nature of immortality, Coleridge decides enough is enough. The abrupt Plotinian conclusion to the chapter reflects a need to erase the uncanny image of idiotic mimicry and substitute a new and nobler image of intelligent imitation.

It is characteristic of Coleridge and the *Biographia* that an image so emotionally charged should be so casually shuffled away. *Biographia Literaria, or Biographical Sketches of My Literary Life and Opinions* reveals as little about its subject as an autobiography can. Coleridge seems to present himself more as an occasion for literary reflections and anecdotes than as a topic. Personality is largely eclipsed by learning. The only periods of his life he describes in any detail are his childhood and his attempts to find subscribers to his newspapers. Jean-Pierre Mileur writes of this peculiar personal reticence, "Coleridge succeeds in all but eliminating the 'auto-' element from *Biographia Literaria,* determining that what he has read is as important as what he has written (indeed, is sometimes identical with it) or whom he has married or when he was born."[22] He reduces himself to a writer writing about himself as a reader reading in order to become a writer. Almost everything else is extraneous. Coleridge acknowledges from the beginning that this book will not be an autobiography in the conventional sense:

> It will be found, that the least of what I have written concerns myself personally. I have used the narration chiefly for the purpose of giving a continuity to the work, in part for the sake of the miscellaneous reflections suggested to me by particular events, but still more as introductory to the statement of my principles in Politics, Religion, and Philosophy, and the application of the rules, deduced from philosophical principles, to poetry and criticism. But of the objects, which I proposed to myself, it was not the least important to effect, as far as possible, a settlement of the long continued controversy concerning the true nature of poetic diction: and at the same time to define with the utmost partiality the real *poetic* character of the poet, by whose writings this controversy was first kindled, and has since fuelled and fanned.[23]

He seems to suggest that, in the *Biographia* at least, autobiographical identity is a convenient but artificial means of unifying what would otherwise seem unconnected. Identity—even Coleridge's identity—is less real than the questions it raises. The topic of Coleridge's own life is not absent because of being crowded out. Coleridge is less concerned to present himself to his readers as a man contending with the accidents of family, psychology, and historical circumstance than to discuss the philosophical basis of identity generally. As early as the autumn of 1803 he had considered pulling together his metaphysics and his autobiography: "Seem to have made up my mind to write my metaphysical works, as *my Life, & in* my Life—intermixed with all the other events / or history of the mind & fortunes of S. T. Coleridge."[24] The notebook entry suggests that the notorious chapters of associationism and German idealism were not included as an afterthought in an attempt to have more pages to present to the printer, as some have thought.[25] The form of the *Biographia* was therefore no accident. Nevertheless, the mixture of the personal and the philosophical has been a source of unhappiness to readers since the beginning.

The earliest objections had to do not with the impropriety of the combination but with the sheer bother of drudging through the philosophical portions:

> Had we met with the metaphysical disquisitions to which we now allude, in an anonymous publication, we should unquestionably have laid them aside, as the production of a very ordinary writer indeed, with respect to talents; and supposing we had given ourselves the trouble of thinking farther about them, should probably have concluded that some doubts might be entertained respecting the perfect sanity of the mind in which they were engendered.[26]

When less than twenty years later a more serious objection to the philosophy arose, it took the same tone of amused contempt. Thomas De Quincey first publicly voiced the complaint that the essay on the relationship between knowing and being had no right to be printed under Coleridge's name, for it was "a *verbatim* translation from Schelling, with no attempt in a single instance to appropriate the paper, by developing the arguments or by diversifying the illustrations!"[27] De Quincey presents Coleridge as a kleptomaniac, denies that he could have been motivated by need, and compares his plagiarisms to the contents of a child's pockets:

> stones remarkable only for weight, old rusty hinges, nails, crooked skewers, stolen when the cook had turned her back, rags, broken glass, tea-cups having the bottom knocked out, and loads of similar jewels, were the prevailing articles in this *proces verbal.* Yet doubtless, much labour had been incurred, and some sense of danger had been faced, and the anxieties of a conscious robber endured, in order to amass this splendid treasure. Such in value were the robberies of Coleridge; such their usefulness to himself or anybody else; and such the circumstances of uneasiness under which he had committed them.[28]

Perhaps divided in his reaction to a species of behavior he knew only too well himself, De Quincey cannot make up his mind in this essay whether to condemn the plagiarism as an act of seriously meant deception ("a barefaced plagiarism, which would in prudence have been risked only by relying too much upon the slight knowledge of German literature in this country")[29] or excuse it as one of the eccentricities of genius ("with the riches of El Dorado lying about him, he would condescend to filch a handful of gold from any man whose purse he fancied").[30] Neither can he make up his mind whether the stolen goods are worth the fuss or not.

Everyone agreed upon the facts of the matter, but apologists and critics fought over their significance. James Gillman answered De Quincey's charge that Coleridge had committed "petty larceny" thus:

> With equal justice might we accuse the bee which flies from flower to flower in quest of food, and which, by means of the instinct bestowed upon it by the all-wise Creator, extracts its nourishment from the field and the garden, but *digests* and *elaborates* it by its own *native* powers.[31]

But the question is not simply how to defend the honeybee against the advocates of the spider. A considerable amount of the material Coleridge took from others cannot by any standard be considered digested. While Coleridge did transform or at least elaborate the materials he took from Shelvocke and from Brun, the thefts from Schelling were plain.

Coleridge may have been too careless to hide his thefts; he may have been too guilty. His disclaimers of obligation to Schelling, his professions of delight in acknowledging a literary debt, his morbid fascination with the possibility that he or another should be guilty of unacknowledged literary appropriations all serve to plant in the reader's mind a suspicion that all is not as it should be. Everyone is familiar with his incriminating protestations of innocence: he writes, scrupulously careful about preserving small truths in the midst of major prevarications,

> While I in part translate the following observations from a contemporary writer of the Continent, let me be permitted to premise, that I might have transcribed the substance from memoranda of my own, which were written many years before his pamphlet was given to the world; and that I prefer another's words to my own, partly as a tribute due to priority of publication; but still more from the pleasure of sympathy in a case where *coincidence* only was possible.[32]

Humility alternates with a fiercer defensiveness:

> In Schelling's "NATUR-PHILOSOPHIE," and the "SYSTEM DES TRANSCENDENTALEN IDEALISMUS," I first found a genial coincidence with much that I had toiled out for myself, and a powerful assistance in what I had yet to do.
>
> I have introduced this statement, as appropriate to the narrative nature of this sketch; yet rather in reference to the work which I have announced in a preceding page [the *Logosophia*], than to my present subject. It would be but a mere act of justice to myself, were I to warn my future readers, that an identity of thought, or even similarity of phrase will not be at all times a certain proof that the passage has been borrowed from Schelling, or that the conceptions were originally learnt from him. In this instance, as in the dramatic lectures of Schlegel to which I have before alluded, from the same motive of self-defense against the charge of plagiarism, many of the most striking resemblances, indeed all the main and fundamental ideas, were born and matured in my mind before I had ever seen a single page of the German Philosopher; and I might indeed affirm with truth, before the more important works of Schelling had been written, or at least made public.[33]

He explains the uncanny similarity between his own thoughts and style and Schelling's as the result of their both having studied Kant, Bruno, and Boehme, and goes so far as to reproach Schelling for his failure to acknowledge, as Coleridge does, his "debt of gratitude" to them.[34]

The strategy is typical of the way Coleridge works to defend against the evidence of his own iniquity; he hints at a truth and then tries to draw his reader's attention towards some other, safer topic. Coleridge's praise of Kant is loud and long, but this particular work owes relatively little to that philosopher; Coleridge can extol him safely here, aware that no suspicious critic will be able to fault him for too-extensive borrowing from Kant's work and secure in the knowledge that his gestures of humble obeisance give him the creditable appearance of honest and uncomplicated gratitude. Coleridge dissembles not so much the fact of his dependence as the details of how much and from whom he borrowed. His defensive anticipations of the charges that would soon enough be brought against his writings argue a consciousness of wrongdoing.

It is sufficiently clear that Coleridge wanted credit for ideas not his own, that he coveted the intellectual property of other men. It is also sufficiently clear that, despite his earlier aspheteristic leanings,[35] he held instinctively with the position that literature is the product and property of individuals. Trying to rebut the mechanistic theory of mind that would deny free will, he insists jealously upon the fact, or at least the ideal, of personal authorship: "According to this hypothesis [of Hartley's] the disquisition, to which I am at present soliciting the reader's attention, may be as truly said to be written by Saint Paul's church, as by *me*"[36]—the absurd consequence of absurd reasoning. The "distinction, made by the public itself between *literary,* and other property" is "partial and unjust," he remarks.[37] He urges his readers to take up writing as an amusement for their odd hours, but "NEVER PURSUE LITERATURE AS A TRADE,"[38] not because literature exists in a realm apart from monetary considerations but because it does not pay very well.

Coleridge's inconsistency on the issue of literary property affords him no stable position from which to defend himself from the attacks of his harshest critics. René Wellek and Norman Fruman find that Coleridge has disgraced himself by stealing material that he is not sophisticated enough to use intelligently once he has stolen it. From their perspective, the plagiarisms lead to trouble because Coleridge is incapable of making the material he borrows his own;

the plagiarized material remains unassimilated, and the resulting work is a muddle from which no coherent voice emerges.[39]

Thomas McFarland and Richard Haven disagree, arguing that if plagiarism is to be regarded as a failure of assimilation, Coleridge is no plagiarist. Deeming Coleridge to have been successful in assimilating his sources and keeping the unity of his voice intact, they are unwilling to condemn his work or his method. Haven regards Coleridge as one who borrowed passages in the way another man might borrow a word or a symbol.[40] Taking Haven's rationalization several steps further, McFarland denies that such a genius as Coleridge can properly be called a plagiarist at all:

> The very multiplicity of instances—far more than at first charged, and by no means as yet all identified—suggests the explanation, bizarre though it may seem, that we are faced not with plagiarism, but with nothing less than a mode of composition—composition by mosaic organization rather than by painting on an empty canvas.[41]

Although McFarland and Haven do well to shift the terms of the discussion away from the treacherous ground of moral and intellectual worth that Fruman and Wellek patrol, their insistence upon Coleridge's success in writing works with which a New Critic might learn to feel comfortable makes it difficult to understand why, to achieve a conventional end, Coleridge should have employed such unconventional means. If Coleridge had been motivated solely by the desire to appropriate what he had no right to, he might have gone about his thefts more discreetly. But, as McFarland remarks, he behaves like "a burglar who seems more intent on setting off the alarm than on robbing the safe."[42] The clumsiness Coleridge shows in his plagiarisms suggests that he cared about the borders he violated, that he needed to maintain the distinction between what was his and what was not his.

Walter Jackson Bate and Jerome Christensen consider the possibility that Coleridge may have aimed neither at assimilating others' words to his own voice nor at creating a work in obedience to his own organic prescriptions. Looking at Coleridge's life as a whole, Bate finds a consistent pattern of indirection. Coleridge used the voices of others both to disclaim responsibility for saying what he dared not say in his own words and to draw upon as sources of moral and intellectual authority.[43] Bate argues that Coleridge did not want to identify himself with those from whose work he plagiarized but that, on the contrary, he used plagiarism as a means of maintaining a safe distance from positions about which he was ambivalent. For Bate, the plagiarisms have psychological significance and can help direct our attention to issues that Coleridge felt were somehow dangerous. Where Coleridge plagiarizes, look for uneasiness and ambivalence—not so much about the fact of verbal theft as about its content.

Elaborating upon a hint from McFarland while repudiating the result of McFarland's diagnosis, Christensen argues that

> What Coleridge practices is not mosaic composition but marginal exegesis, not philosophy but commentary. . . . Once added to the margins of the text the comment makes it uncertain what the text *is*. The original text may presume inalienable authority, but the marginal comment always threatens the reduction of the original text to a pretext for commentary—commentary, however, which could not be where it "is" were it not for the margins provided. The marginalium is, thus, both enrichment and deprivation of its host, just as it is, equivocally, neither inside nor outside the text.[44]

Picking apart the integrity of the host text, the marginal text need not develop any coherent identity for itself. Indeed, the basis of its meaning lies outside itself; it depends for its existence upon its secondary position.

Christensen's analysis approaches more closely than any other to the puzzle at the heart of the relationship between language and identity. Christensen enables us to see Coleridge's marginal method as the expression of a consciousness aware not only of its inability to define its own independent position but also of the failure of any position entirely to coincide with or speak for itself. But, despite Fruman, Wellek, McFarland, Haven, Bate, and even Christensen, what makes trouble is not the boundaries between mine and thine or between inside and outside but the absence of any such boundaries. The difficulty is not that a writer has laid claim to what does not properly belong to him but that a body of material has taken possession of him and threatens his selfhood. Property is beside the point; the difficulty lies in the absence of an appropriating selfhood. Coleridge is not so much a thief or even a parasite as a demonized intellect, sharing his identity with strangers.[45]

Of all the major writings Coleridge himself was responsible for having published, in only the *Biographia* is plagiarism a serious problem. Here the plagiarisms are confined to those chapters concerned with the relationship between the self and the nonself, concerned in particular with how anything not consubstantial with the self can influence it or even be known by it. Plagiarism in such a context is necessarily a special case. However plausible the reasoning that it was the "fierce pressure" from Coleridge's printers to speed the writing "that forced Coleridge to plunder Schelling's *Abhandlungen,*" as Fogel suggests,[46] it cannot be accepted as anything near a full explanation. This sort of thing cannot happen simply through careless haste; the method of composition reflects too ironically upon the material to be accidental. Here if anywhere one would expect the author to speak from his own authority and to want to distinguish himself from other men; here one would expect to find even a habitual plagiarist using his own words. What can be the meaning of an autobiography (for that is how Coleridge thought of it, describing it in letters as his "Autobiographia literaria") written, at least in part, in the voices of other men?[47] What is an autobiography if through large stretches of it the word "I" does not refer to the man whose name is on the title page, if there is nothing to indicate where the subject of the author's literary life and opinions leaves off and that of another man's begins? The *Biographia* resembles anonymous autobiography: we have the name but not the man. Perhaps a more appropriate title for it would have been *Allographia Literaria.* Coleridge takes autobiography back to its first principles in his attempt to discover the first principles of the self.

That alien voices should figure so large in such a work calls into question the meaning of autobiography as a form, but in this, perhaps, it remains in the mainstream of serious autobiography, which, as Avrom Fleishman points out, always tends to displace its proper subject, the self, and put something in its stead. Language substitutes for self in autobiography: "If there is inescapable alteration in the act of writing autobiography, it is an alchemy comparable with the Freudian injunction to displace id with ego: there where living was, let writing be."[48] In being written, the self is both the same as and different from itself, actual and ideal, transient and permanent at once, writing being both self-creation and self-destruction.[49] In uttering oneself, one becomes other. What is extraordinary, then, is not the absence of Coleridge as theme, but the absences of Coleridge as writing subject, the lapses of his own voice, the interpolations of others' words among his own.

Writing an autobiography might be regarded as a fulfillment of one of Coleridge's favorite injunctions: Know thyself. From early on, however, the idea of self-knowledge took on for Coleridge the form of a revelation of otherness. "If I die," he wrote in March, 1801, to William Godwin, "and the Booksellers will give you any thing for my Life, be sure to say—'Wordsworth descended on him, like the γνῶθι σεαυτόν from Heaven; by shewing to him what true Poetry was, he made him know, that he himself was no Poet.' "[50] That self-knowledge should come in the form of another person suggests, even in this humorous context, that Coleridge recognized in Wordsworth the self he wished he had.[51] But instead of responding to this ego-ideal with emulation, Coleridge feels himself cut off by it from his desires and alienated from himself; showing another man already occupying his place, self-knowledge has exiled him to the periphery of his own existence. So it is not inappropriate that when the time came for Coleridge to write his life, the attempt should have produced a volume-long critical appreciation of the *authentic* poet from whom he had by that time been estranged for five years.[52]

"Know thyself" meant not only "Contemplate Wordsworth's superiority" but also "Study metaphysics:"

> The postulate of philosophy and at the same time the test of philosophic capacity is no other than the heaven-descended KNOW THYSELF! (E coelo descendit, Γνῶθι σεαυτόν). And this at once practically and speculatively. For as philosophy is neither a science of the reason or understanding only, nor merely a science of morals, but the science of BEING altogether, its primary ground can be neither merely speculative or merely practical, but both in one. All knowledge rests on the coincidence of an object with a subject.[53]

It is paradoxical but not really surprising, given Coleridge's propensity to know himself in terms of others, that this injunction should appear in the midst of the chapter most heavily indebted to other writers.[54] Nor is it surprising that the matter Coleridge reoriginates here should tend toward the conclusion that the self and the other are inextricably implicated in one another. The chapter could be its own apologia, demonstrating "at once practically and speculatively" the impossibility of preserving a self untouched by others, the necessity of absorbing the external or alien into the identical.

Coleridge's plagiarism is transcendental idealism in action. The relationship between his voice and Schelling's is analogous to the relationship between subject and object that Coleridge/Schelling describe. The philosophical chapters, taken together, constitute an attempt to formulate a relationship between nature and consciousness, or otherness and identity, in which consciousness preserves its freedom. This relationship would serve as the basis of sane knowledge, spontaneous but rational thought, a way of perceiving nature without allowing external sensations to tyrannize over the mind. Toward the end of Volume I, the problem is recast in terms of representation and imagination, and in Volume II in terms of poetics. Personal concerns underlie these perhaps apparently unrelated discussions: How can one acknowledge the authority of others without forfeiting one's own strength? How can one become learned without becoming a parrot? How can influence be effective without being absolute? How is reorigination possible?[55] For Coleridge these questions may have had no answers. "If you are what you read," as Frances Ferguson observes, "plagiarism (in a more or less obvious form) becomes inevitable; and if insufficient knowledge or reading is the cause of moral inadequacy, then nothing less than all knowledge—everything—will suffice."[56]

In the system Coleridge presents, self-knowledge or self-consciousness, the unmediated coincidence of subject and object, is the only basis of certain knowledge. Directed inwardly and subject to no external power, self-knowledge would seem at first glance an act of freedom and a condition of perfect presence in which representation and the object represented are one—the paradise Derrida says never was.

As the discussion progresses it becomes apparent that the real question is not how to develop self-knowledge—that, it turns out, comes naturally not only to man but to the entire universe—but how to know anything other than the self. The sense of our own conciousness, the consciousness of self-knowledge,

> not only claims but necessitates the admission of its immediate certainty, equally for the scientific reason of the philosopher as for the common sense of mankind at large. . . . It is groundless; but only because it is itself the ground of all other certainty.[57]

The other "prejudice," as Coleridge calls it, is no more groundless and no less necessary but more mysterious:

> THAT THERE EXIST THINGS WITHOUT US. As this on the one hand originates, neither in ground or arguments, and yet on the other hand remains proof against all attempts to remove it by grounds or arguments (*naturam furca expellas tamen usque redibit;*) on the one hand lays claim to IMMEDIATE certainty as a position at once indemonstrable and irresistible, and yet on the other hand, inasmuch as it refers to something essentially different from ourselves, nay even in opposition to ourselves, leaves it inconceivable how it could possibly become a part of our immediate consciousness; (in other words how that, which ex hypothesi is and continues to be extrinsic and alien to our being, should become a modification of our being) the philosopher therefore compels himself to treat this faith as nothing more than a prejudice, innate indeed and connatural, but still a prejudice.[58]

Much of this is Schelling. Coleridge intrudes only in the parenthesis to stress the almost inconceivable nature of what is proposed: not simply that we should become conscious of what is not ourselves, but that it "should become a modification of our being," that it should change into us and be absorbed into us while it "continues to be extrinsic and alien to our being."

The problem Schelling/Coleridge takes on, that of reconciling the prejudice that "I am" with the prejudice that "it is," looks back to the problem concerning the establishment of a basis for synthetic truth, truth that is not mere tautology. Coleridge's theses reflect this.

THESIS I

> Truth is correlative to being. Knowledge without a correspondent reality is no knowledge; if we know, there must be somewhat known by us. To know is in its very essence a verb active.

THESIS II

> All truth is either mediate, that is, derived from some other truth or truths; or immediate and original. The latter is absolute, and its formula A.A.; the former is dependent or conditional certainty, and presented in the formula B.A. The certainty, which inheres in A, is attributable to B.[59]

The second thesis distinguishes between two forms of propositions: the analytic, which is certain but empty because it tells us only about the language we have used and not about extralinguistic reality; and the synthetic, which gives us information about the world but whose truth is precarious because dependent upon its correspondence to reality.[60] Coleridge and Schelling seek a basis for synthetic knowledge, a point at which identity and difference coincide. Schelling enlarges on the desired possibility of synthetic truth in the *System of Transcendental Idealism,* from which Coleridge borrowed heavily:

> If there is to be certainty in synthetic propositions—and thereby in all our knowledge—the synthetic propositions must be traced back to an *unconditional certainty,* that is, to the *identity of thinking as such,* which is, however, a contradiction.
>
> This contradiction would be soluble only *if some point could be found in which the identical and the synthetic are one, or some proposition which, in being identical, is at once synthetic,* and *in being synthetic, is at once identical.*[61]

or, more plainly,

> If an identical proposition is one in which concept is compared only with concept, while a synthetic proposition is one in which the concept is compared with an object distinct from itself, the task of finding a point at which identical knowledge is at the same time synthetic

> amounts to this: *to find a point at which the object and its concept, the thing and its representation,* are *originally, absolutely and immediately one.*[62]

Schelling seeks the full symbol, the place where, so to speak, no bar divides S from s. At this point analogy is natural because it springs from identity.

I have been quoting from Schelling as if he were interchangeable with Coleridge, as if voice were continuous with voice and text continuous with text. But the presenter does not here completely coincide with the presented. In the *Biographia* Schelling's words do not mean quite what they mean in Schelling's own text. Coleridge veers away from Schelling's subtle insistence upon the otherness of the object. The *Biographia* leaves one with the comfortable impression that the object is not really all that different from the subject, that there is really not much difficulty assimilating one into the other—this despite Coleridge's occasional moments of doubt. The subjective position, though nominally on the same level as the objective, retains the upper hand as the object is seen to be an aspect of the subject but not the other way around. His ten theses are made to follow as if subordinate to the analysis of the possibility that "THE SUBJECTIVE IS TAKEN AS THE FIRST, AND THE PROBLEM THEN IS, HOW THERE SUPERVENES TO IT A COINCIDENT OBJECTIVE."[63] The principle chosen to generate this new philosophy is not the dubious and slightly sinister prejudice "THAT THERE EXIST THINGS WITHOUT US" but that "I AM." By the time we reach the theses, of course, the two contenders have been subordinated each to the other and been declared identical, so that in acknowledging one, Coleridge seems to be acknowledging both:

> Now the apparent contradiction, that the former position, namely, the existence of things without us, which from its nature cannot be immediately certain should be received as blindly and as independently of all grounds as the existence of our own being, the transcendental philosopher can solve only by the supposition, that the former is unconsciously involved in the latter; that it is not only coherent but identical, and one and the same thing with our own immediate self-consciousness. To demonstrate this identity is the office and object of his philosophy.[64]

There are hints scattered through Coleridge's text that the subject is not as fully present to itself as it might be, but these are played down. As Coleridge describes the principle from which he will develop a dynamic transcendental philosophy, the principle of "the SUM or I AM,"[65] the self is remarkable for its ability to create itself out of nothing by free action. In the self,

> object and subject, being and knowing, are identical, each involving and supposing the other. In other words, it is a subject which becomes a subject by the act of constructing itself objectively to itself; but which never is an object except for itself, and only so far as by the very same act it becomes a subject. It may be described therefore as a perpetual self-duplication of one and the same power into object and subject, which presuppose each other, and can exist only as antitheses.[66]

The provision that subject and object are positions defined and brought into being by their relationship to one another and not instances of absolute entities saves the self, this first principle of the dynamic philosophy, from involvement in an infinite regress of representation. Subject and object are perpetual self-duplications, but not for that reason deferred from their origins. Self-representation carries no stigma because it suffers no falling-off from authenticity.

Nevertheless, mutuality briefly departs from the relationship of subject and object in self-consciousness: "The spirit (originally the identity of object and subject) must in some sense dissolve this identity, in order to be conscious of it: fit alter et idem."[67] Self-consciousness, then, is not the consciousness of identity. Identity departs the moment one tries to look at it directly. Instead of seeing a reflection of itself, the conscious subject beholds an unconscious object. Coleridge brushes past this disconcerting notion quickly and rushes towards his goal, the affirmation of freedom:

> But this [movement of self-consciousness] implies an act, and it follows therefore that intelligence or self-consciousness is impossible, except by and in a will. The self-conscious spirit therefore is a will; and freedom must be assumed as a *ground* of philosophy, and can never be deduced from it.[68]

Schelling too talks about the miraculous origin, bootstrap-style, of the self-producing self, a synthesis that is also an identity. For

Schelling more obviously than for Coleridge, the self is an act of knowledge that creates the truth of its own content: "since the self (as object) is nothing else but the very *knowledge of itself,* it arises simply out of the fact *that* it knows of itself; the *self itself* is thus a knowing that simultaneously produces itself (as object)."[69] But he concedes that this self cannot be self-identical in the act of self-consciousness. The otherness it confronts is more radical than the otherness Coleridge hints at, which seems almost more a function of grammatical categories than anything else—for Coleridge, what is known differs from the knower simply by being the object of knowledge rather than the subject. The otherness Schelling suggests the subject confronts in the act of self-consciousness is something supplementary to the self, lying on the other side of its boundaries. The self, says Schelling, is "originally infinite activity." In order to become an object to itself, to become knowable, it must limit itself, become finite. It does this by producing something to oppose to itself. Limitation implies otherness. So the self produces the nonself in the process of becoming an object to itself.[70]

The self, however, is the union of the action that limits and the action that suffers limitation.

> Beyond self-consciousness the self is *pure* objectivity. This pure objective (nonobjective originally, precisely because an objective without a subjective is impossible) is the one and only *in-itself* there is. Only through self-consciousness is subjectivity first added thereto. To this original, *purely* objective activity, that is limited in consciousness, there stands opposed the limiting activity, which cannot, on that very account, itself become an object.—To come to consciousness, and to be limited, are one and the same. Only that which is limited me-ward, so to speak, comes to consciousness: the limiting activity falls outside all consciousness, just because it is the cause of all limitation. . . . The *limiting* activity does not come to consciousness, or become an object, and is therefore the activity of the pure subject.[71]

The original difficulty, that of understanding how the subject can ever come to know the object, has been stood on its head. Now the object is knowable but the subject is not. This subject and object are not equivalent terms for self and nature, Schelling points out; he has not made nature knowable at the expense of the possibility of self-knowledge. The subject and object he discusses here are both components of the self. It is important to understand that consciousness does not necessarily include self-consciousness in its strictest sense: the subject is never conscious of itself as subject. It can be conscious only of the object. One might compare this model with that of a mirror which reflects only the back of the viewer and is unable to reflect his face. The subject cannot see itself in the act of watching.

As Schelling describes the process of self-consciousness, we begin with the unknown and unknowable and then limit it.

> If the limit be unposited, the self contains pure identity, in which nothing can be distinguished. If the limit be posited, it contains two activities, the limiting and the limited, the subjective and the objective. The two have therefore one thing at least in common, that originally *both* are absolutely nonobjective, that is, since we are as yet acquainted with no other characteristic of the ideal, both are equally ideal.[72]

In intuiting itself by means of ideal activity, the subject makes an object of itself. Paradoxically, because it recognizes itself, it cannot recognize itself, for the subject is by definition what cannot be an object:

> The self cannot intuit the real activity as identical with itself, without at once finding the *negative element* therein, which makes it nonideal, as something alien to itself. . . . The finder is the absolutely illimitable and unlimited; it is the limited that is found. . . . The limit . . . can appear only as something found, *i.e.*, foreign to the self and opposed to its nature.[73]

The self does not recognize the objective as its reflection because, being unconscious of its activities, it does not know that it is the source of the limitation that marks the objective.

> Intuiting and limiting are originally one. But the self cannot simultaneously intuit and intuit itself as intuiting, and so cannot intuit itself as limiting, either. It is therefore necessary that the intuitant, which seeks only itself in the objective, should find the negative element therein to be something not posited by itself.[74]

Seeing itself, it sees a stranger. The consequences of this, for us, are twofold. First, and more important for Schelling, through ignorance of its own activities the intuiting self disappropriates the world. Second, the intuiting self, failing to be identical to that which it knows, is unknowable. At the core of identity, then, is an alien that knows nothing of Schelling's prime original "I am"; it is an other that knows the self.

For Schelling[75] the figure of the other behaves like a piece of repressed knowledge; the problem he banished from the larger world (that of the unknowable thing in itself, the absolute other) and tried to refigure as alienated and forgotten self uncannily reappears as a problem of the internal structure of the self. Coleridge omits to mention that self-knowledge has unconsciousness at its core, that knowledge of the self can never, by its very nature, be complete. This forms part of the repressed knowledge of his autobiography, although surely Coleridge himself must have been aware of it. It has the same status as the fact that in this autobiography, in this fulfillment of the imperative to Know Thyself! where presenter and presentation genially coincide, the subject is not himself, and another voice substitutes for his own. Although the printed words let slip few hints that self-knowledge is not the property of the self, the form and the history of the text enact the message.

Interrupting the Schellingian argument of chapter 13, the letter Coleridge writes to himself uses the mechanism of plagiarism, but uses it backwards. Instead of claiming as his own the words of another, Coleridge disowns a piece of his own writing, projecting its authorship onto an anonymous "friend, whose practical judgement I have had ample reason to estimate and revere."[76] He presents as quoted what is in fact original; he represents his own speech as foreign, irruptive,[77] which indeed, in its context, is how it appears.[78]

The uneasy consciousness that expresses its wonder and its doubt in the letter remarks particularly upon the way the *Biographia*'s perspective defamiliarizes things. The book presents "images of great men, with whose *names* I was familiar, but which looked upon me with countenances and an expression, the most dissimilar to all I had been in the habit of connecting with those names."[79] Strange faces, strange voices now answer or refuse to answer to the old names. The letter's remark applies with especial aptness to its immediate context; the letter itself is an instance of the alienation about which it complains.

As the letter continues, what is supposed to be a description of the *Biographia* begins to resemble a description of another work. Comparing Coleridge's book to "one of our largest Gothic cathedrals," the letter-writer echoes Wordsworth's elaborate comparison of his own writings to a cathedral.[80] The comparison implicit within the comparison becomes more apparent when the letter-writer quotes from Coleridge's "To William Wordsworth," a poem written in ambivalent celebration of *The Prelude.* Coleridge goes out of his way to call attention to the strangeness of what he is writing, first drawing upon terms originally associated with another man's autobiography and then altering those terms to emphasize the difference his work suffers not only from the other piece but also from itself. Wordsworth's poem was "A song divine"; Coleridge's prose piece is "A tale *obscure.*" Wordsworth's thoughts were "To their own music chaunted"; Coleridge's are "To *a strange* music chaunted." Had he wanted simply to talk about the weaknesses of his work, he need not have chosen *The Prelude* as his standard of evaluation. Indeed, to most of his readers the allusion would be meaningless, since *The Prelude* had not yet been published and would not be available for another thirty-odd years. Why then did Coleridge choose this particular stick to beat himself with?

Concerned, like the *Biographia,* to "seek the origin" of sensations and the imagination, *The Prelude* begins with an attempt to conjure a poem out of thin air, an inspiration out of the

> blessing in this gentle breeze,
> That blows from the green fields and from the clouds
> And from the sky
>
> [1–3]

but that blows also within his mind with the force of analogy. Having naturalized and then internalized his intended source of inspiration, Wordsworth proceeds to displace it once again, revealing this inspired passage to be a self-quotation and its poetic virtue to inhere in its repeatability:

> Thus far, O friend, did I, not used to make
> A present joy the matter of my song,
> Pour out that day my soul in measured strains,
> Even in the very words which I have here
> Recorded.
> . . . .
> My own voice cheered me, and, far more, the mind's
> Internal echo of the imperfect sound—
> To both I listened, drawing from them both
> A chearful confidence in things to come.
>
> [55–59, 64–67][81]

It is the Ancient Mariner come again, inspired by an ambiguous wind and a paradoxical incorporation. The internal echoes of Wordsworth's own voice celebrating his self-inspiration inspire him.[82] On the one hand this process stresses the nativity of the inspiration,[83] which is purified of its association with external winds. The words that the writer of epic traditionally begged from his muse Wordsworth discovers in his own memory. On the other hand, the process insists, first by analogy, then by repetition, upon the displacement original voice has suffered. The poem comes into being in the turn from inspiration to narrative, in that moment when what seemed immediate or original is revealed to be the recalling of an earlier failed utterance. As in the *Biographia,* the distinction between original and representation is elided; a poet creates by remembering, by sending his voice elsewhere—into the past, into the landscape—in order that it might be recalled.[84] In both works the passages of self-quotation are associated with real or apparent castings-out and reverberations of voices. Wordsworth, letting his natural inspiration lapse, substitutes an inspiration by mental echo. Coleridge, casting out his heavy philosophical muse, turns his attention, too, to originary echoes.

Although critics are inclined to represent the end of chapter 13 as a turning away from the philosophical system that has absorbed Coleridge off and on for the last few chapters,[85] the anonymous letter Coleridge writes to himself and the gnomic definitions of Imagination and Fancy that immediately follow realize the implications of his version of transcendental idealism. The impression of discontinuity results from a change of voice rather than a change of mind: the letter-writer speaks in accents of self-mocking confusion rather than in the impersonal tones of intellectual authority, making playful similes rather than philosophical theses, and the definitions of Imagination and Fancy, though less casually constructed than the letter, hover between epistemological exactness and poetic sublimity. Although once again the tone is more human than bookish, these passages follow from what has come before.

Coleridge's definitions are the culmination of his discussion of the relationship between "I am" and "It is":

> The IMAGINATION then I consider either as primary, or secondary. The primary IMAGINATION I hold to be the living Power and prime Agent of all human Perception, and as a repetition in the finite mind of the eternal act of creation in the infinite I AM. The secondary I consider as an echo of the former, co-existing with the conscious will, yet still as identical with the primary in the *kind* of its agency, and differing only in *degree,* and in the *mode* of its operation. It dissolves, diffuses, dissipates, in order to re-create; or where this process is rendered impossible, yet still at all events it struggles to idealize and to unify. It is essentially *vital,* even as all objects (as objects) are essentially fixed and dead. FANCY, on the contrary, has no other counters to play with, but fixities and definites. The Fancy is indeed no other than a mode of Memory emancipated from the order of time and space; and blended with, and modified by that empirical phenomenon of the will, which we express by the word CHOICE. But equally with the ordinary memory it must receive all its materials ready made from the law of association.[86]

In this passage matters of perception and representation are reinterpreted as matters of identity and voice. Representation, not of external reality but of the self, is the issue.

The first hints that the concept of the self might not be easily extricable from the problematics of representation appear in chapter 12. From the moment Coleridge defines his terms, the boundary between original and representation is in danger of being lost. Coleridge defines the "subject" as "equivalent to mind or sentient being and as the necessary correlative of object or *quicquid objicitur menti.*"[87] The sum of everything subjective "we may comprehend in the name of the SELF or INTELLIGENCE."[88] On the other hand, "the sum of all that is merely OBJECTIVE, we will henceforth call NATURE, confining the term to its passive and material sense, as comprising all the phaenomena by which its existence is made known to us."[89] Ambiguity lies on both sides of this double definition. Both "self" and "nature" do double duty, denoting not only absolute positions but also the "phaenomena" or representations of those positions. Thus the inaccessibility of the thing in itself is mediated by the knowability of "the phaenomena by which its existence is made known to us," and the inconceivability of the subject is figured and domesticated in its knowable contents. Only a shifting of the boundaries Kant so carefully drew between things in themselves and their phenomena permits Coleridge to say that "the truth is universally placed in the coincidence of the thought with the thing, of the representation with the object represented."[90] If this statement does no more than rephrase "all knowledge rests on the coincidence of an object with a subject," one can infer that the subject is not only self or intelligence but also a thought or a representation. The subject consists of the mind as container and its contents.[91] The object is both the thing in itself and its mental representation. At the poles, subject and object are distinct concepts, but they blend into one another at the edges—thoughts blending into mental representations, ideas into phenomena. They do, that is, if "coincidence" means "identity." The antithesis in that case would be alarmingly elastic.

But what does "coincidence" mean here? How can two distinct things coincide? Coleridge has translated the word from Schelling's term *Übereinstimmung*—agreement, concurrence, harmony, or unison[92]—a word whose root is derived from *Stimme,* or voice. While thoughts may take the form of voice, objective phenomena, insofar as they are objective, are voiceless—unless[93] of course they are the phenomena of the mystics rather than of the Kantian school and speak the language of the book of nature. "Coincidence," no less than *Übereinstimmung,* glosses over the difficulty, the problem of mediation or how the different can become identical or even capable of comparison. Who or what judges whether coincidence has occurred or not? Is coincidence an identity or merely a resemblance, and if the latter, what provides the ground of analogy? Coleridge here seems to assume what he does not explicate, a natural bridge between objects and significances, signs and meanings. The world is always already spoken.

The epistemological question necessarily involves the mimetic.

"Intelligence is conceived of as exclusively representative, nature as exclusively represented; the one conscious, the other as without consciousness." Intelligence or self, then, is essentially imagination, but imagination absolved of the charges Plato brought against it. Its creations, though "repetitions in the finite mind of the eternal act of creation in the infinite I AM," are not poor copies of a distant reality; they are as real as anything else. "There is here no first, and no second; both are coinstantaneous and one."[94]

When the self is described as self-representing, present only through representation, an epistemological problem is translated into aesthetic terms and the self can be renamed imagination. Ironically enough, however, behind Coleridge's distinction between Fancy and Imagination (which led him to begin writing the *Biographia*) lies a desire to evade the bruteness of the brute fact of representation, to allow the imagination freedom from the literalness of sensations. The *Biographia* is a defense against the secondariness of consciousness that page by page concedes belatedness. But in his definition of imagination Coleridge chooses a form of secondariness that is no humiliation, no tyranny. He chooses the sublimest of precursors.

For Coleridge, God is the sole origin of reality. Everything and everyone else is a synecdoche or a metonymy of that original reality. Seeing is like imagining is like creating. Thus not just the poet but the ordinary man as well shares in the divinity of cosmopoiesis when he looks at the world. And just as the creation of the world was a reflex of God's self-definition, so (as Coleridge has been arguing) perception is a reflex of human self-consciousness. The ability to say "It is" is bound up with the ability to say "I am," and the ability to say "I am" depends upon God's "I am that I am"—the original and originary tautology. Human consciousness images divine consciousness; the human definitions of self and other derive from God's creative act and His revelation of Himself to Moses.[95] In erasing the boundary between representation and represented, Coleridge allows no place for originality or identity. Human identity can never be literal identity, original and independent; it is inevitably because originally a figure, a synecdoche or repetition of a greater, earlier tautology. As man's perception of the world depends upon or reflects his consciousness of himself, his consciousness of the world and of himself reflects

God. No man can say "I am" in his own voice. His identity is a quotation, even, presumably, if he is an atheist, a plagiarism. He can do no more than echo the original "I am," itself an echo of "It is" or, rather, "Let there be."

The *Biographia* is something the Ancient Mariner might have produced had he been philosophically inclined. Like the *Rime* an autobiography that undoes identity, the *Biographia* defends its own undoing. The *Biographia* rationalizes its ventriloquism, not (this time) as a curse to be expiated by reenactment but rather as the condition of consciousness in language. There are moments when the book, like the earlier poem, seems to frighten itself, half horrified at the sound of its own voice (which is also not its own voice) and at the implications of its production, insisting upon its difference from the delirious mimics whose stories it tells. And the horror is real in a way it was not before, for the strangeness of these compulsive quotations is a fact and not a fiction. But what appalls the writer, the sense of being overwhelmed by influence and becoming what he reads, also cheers him: the curse of ventriloquy is also a blessing and a reassurance. That taint of vocal alienation, the othering or uttering of voice from self, is imagination. In Volume II he claims it, this power analogous to the echo of a quotation, not for himself but for Wordsworth.

7

The Impropriety of the Imagination

If Volume I of the *Biographia* reads at times like a confusion of voices, Volume II, focusing upon literary heterogeneity and homogeneity, can be read as both a critique and a purification of vocal confusion. The discussion of the basis of "a *legitimate* poem," the analysis of Wordsworth's theory of poetic language, and the description of the characteristics of Wordsworth's poetry all reflect Coleridge's desire to protect literary virtue from contamination by the arbitrary, the unconnected, and the uninterpretable. As in Volume I, Coleridge is trying to understand the relationship between the mind and the external world or (not necessarily the same thing) between meaning and necessity. At the same time that they express his delight in the freedom of the mind, Coleridge's remarks express a horror of the merely accidental or arbitrary, and this horror extends to the heterogeneous, the casually related, and the strange. But—lest it appear that Coleridge feels the same way as Wordsworth, whose attitudes might be similarly summarized—the reader must understand that for Coleridge it is the familiar, matter-of-fact, and insignificant rather than the out-of-the-way or the overly portentious that threaten poetry with strangeness of the unmeaning or the incoherent.

Reclaiming the theoretical ground the Preface to the *Lyrical Ballads* had staked out fifteen years earlier, the second volume of the *Biographia* is not primarily an explication or even a correction of Wordsworth's ideas. Wordsworth's poems and prose serve rather as the pretext for Coleridge's discussion than the object of respectful scrutiny. The relation between Coleridge and Wordsworth resembles that of a parasite to a host but resembles even more that of a cannibal to his captive. Once Coleridge has digested what he needs, the formerly Wordsworthian matter is no longer quite what it had been. Nevertheless, despite the distance Coleridge puts between his views and Wordsworth's, fundamentally they are closer than they appear to be.

Imagining a poetry in which meanings would speak for themselves in their native tongue,[1] Coleridge and Wordsworth sought to describe the form that ideal poetic language might take. They agreed upon its natural purity but could not agree upon the signs from which natural purity might be inferred, or even upon what was meant by "natural." Nature according to the Preface and nature according to the *Biographia* are very different things. For Coleridge, as the first volume of the *Biographia* makes clear, nature is what is opposed to or outside of the mind; it is the not-self whose relation to the self has always puzzled the philosophers. But nature is also associated with a commonsensical dismissal of those problems and paradoxes that nature in its other sense raises: as a growing plant triumphs over the logical difficulty of its condition, imagery of organic wholeness supplies the place of rigorous argument about how a form or faculty "assimilates to its own substance the alien and diverse."[2] Both senses have to do with the complex relationship between sameness and difference or the intrinsic and the extrinsic.

Wordsworth, on the other hand, while recognizing in principle a distinction between inner and outer nature, prefers in practice to overlook it and concentrate instead on the opposition between town and country, rural nature and urban unnaturalness. His interest lying in the direction of human rather than inhuman nature, metaphysical problems become in his hands pastoral problems.[3] The natural poetic language he would like to recover (and whose recovery belongs properly to the long history of attempts to return to the wellsprings of English undefiled[4]) owes something to the conversational ideal, the traditional notion, examined in Chapter 1, that the best or most proper poetic language is derived from the language spoken by a certain class of men in social conversation. But Wordsworth's notion of the constituency of that certain class—uneducated rustics rather than educated Londoners—puts him on the other side of the fence from Coleridge.

If Wordsworth chooses characters and settings from rural life, he does so because, first, he says, people living in the country feel their emotions more simply and strongly and express what they feel more plainly than other people, and, second, "because such men communicate with the best objects from which the best part of language is originally derived." Country people are closer to the sources of human behavior and language; they are more nearly original and more nearly natural than the rest of us. Their language seems natural because it refers largely to natural as opposed to artificial objects and because the changelessness of its referents enables the language to share the apparent permanence of nature.[5] It is ironic that his identification of the natural with the rural—his desire to attach poetic propriety to the irrefutably solid reality of the countryside—should so nearly have eclipsed his meaning and laid his theory open to charges of arbitrariness, capriciousness, and peculiarity: precisely those failings the natural language he prescribed (common, necessary, and lasting) would avoid.

Wordsworth's insouciant treatment of the relationship between internal and external nature allows him to pass unpuzzled and unalarmed the theoretical problems of perception and representation that would so intrigue Coleridge. The poet, Wordsworth says, "considers man and nature as essentially adapted to each other, and the mind of man as naturally the mirror of the fairest and most interesting properties of nature."[6] The nature of this doubly natural mirroring does not interest him here. He is concerned instead with reproducing the emotional source of language. As W. J. B. Owen observes, the Preface, especially in its 1802 revision, turns from a mimetic toward an expressive theory of poetry.[7] The shift is not completed, however. Wordsworth presents a theory based upon imitation of the motivation for poetic language rather than imitation of language itself or extralinguistic objects.

It has been said that Wordsworth mistrusted language and tried to avoid its mediation, wishing to write verse as plain and artless, as close to a transcript of real speech, as possible.[8] The argument of the Preface does sometimes seem to say that a poem can have the same ontological status as a natural object. But at the same time Wordsworth insists upon the difference between real passion (and the language it naturally produces) and the poet's sympathetic passion (and the language it *almost* naturally produces). The poet has

> an ability of conjuring up in himself passions, which are indeed far from being the same as those produced by real events, yet (especially in those parts of the general sympathy which are pleasing and delightful) do more nearly resemble the passions produced by real events, than anything which, from the motions of their own minds merely, other men are accustomed to feel in themselves:—whence, and from practice, he has acquired a greater readiness and power in expressing what he thinks and feels, and especially those thoughts and feelings which, by his own choice, or from the structure of his mind, arise in him without immediate excitement.
>
> But whatever portion of this faculty we may suppose even the greatest Poet to possess, there cannot be a doubt that the language which it will suggest to him, must often, in liveliness and truth, fall short of that which is uttered by men in real life, under the actual pressure of those passions, certain shadows of which the Poet thus produces, or feels to be produced, in himself.[9]

It sounds as if imitation, though necessary, is regrettable: real passion produces truer language than imitated passion. But the formula for producing poetry out of one's own passions involves a mimetic stance similar to the one Wordsworth recommends for making poetry out of another's passions. One alienates the original passion in order to reproduce it later. Articulating a position surprisingly close to that which Coleridge develops with so much anxiety in Volume I of the *Biographia,* Wordsworth seems to suggest that the poet must regard his own passions precisely as though they belonged to someone else:

> Poetry is the spontaneous overflow of powerful feelings: it takes its origin from emotion recollected in tranquility: the emotion is contemplated till, by a species of reaction, the tranquility gradually disappears, and an emotion, kindred to that which was before the subject of contemplation, is gradually produced, and does itself actually exist in the mind. In this mood successful composition gradually begins, and in a mood similar to this it is carried on.[10]

Wordsworth turns what one might assume to be a lyric utterance into what amounts to a dramatic one: the poet treats himself as a character whose passions and voice he sympathetically recreates within himself.

Stephen Parrish has argued that the subject of disagreement between Wordsworth and Coleridge is dramatic method—the question of whose voice a poem should represent, the poet's or his character's:

> The passion that Wordsworth expressed in poetry was likely to be that of his characters; the passion that Coleridge looked for was mainly that of the poet. For Wordsworth, the passion could appear only if the poet maintained strict dramatic propriety; for Coleridge, the passion was obscured unless the poet spoke in his own voice. As against Wordsworth's dramatic propriety, Coleridge cited what he might have called poetic propriety.[11]

The distinctions Parrish draws make enormous sense. Surely this is the heart of the quarrel over diction. One thinks of Wordsworth's own remarks on the subject of dramatic propriety. About "those parts of composition where the Poet speaks through the mouths of his characters" he argues that "the dramatic parts of composition are defective, in proportion as they deviate from the real language of nature, and are coloured by a diction of the Poet's own, either peculiar to him as an individual Poet or belonging simply to Poets in general."[12]

But that is as far as we get before Coleridgean doubts overtake us: What is the poet's voice? Does he have a character of his own? If there is a difference between the dramatic and the poetic, what is the content of the poetic? To these questions, which, as we saw in Chapter 1, are implicit in traditional conceptions of propriety, Wordsworth provides no direct answers. But his evasions are telling. He refuses to allow a distinction between the poet and his characters or between the poet's voice (when he is a true poet) and his characters' voices. Even in poetry "where the Poet speaks to us in his own person and character," Wordsworth writes, he is not allowed a diction "either peculiar to him as an individual Poet or belonging simply to Poets in general." His passions being the same as other men's, his language should be, too. If it is not, he must remember that "Poets do not write for Poets alone, but for men," for the poet is a man speaking to men. He is remarkable only for his capacity for almost limitless sympathy for the passions of others, for feeling like other men only more so.[13]

Coleridge's criticism of Wordsworth's prescriptions for poetry is in part a critique of the other man's conceptions of nature and natural language.[14] But his skepticism towards the kind of language Wordsworth almost accidentally seized upon as his model must be regarded in the context of his uneasiness about language and consciousness generally. It becomes increasingly clear that when Coleridge talks about Wordsworth's writings and ideas he has in mind not simply his old unphilosophical colleague with his brilliance and his weakness for the commonplace, but the abstract poetic imagination that no man fully embodies.

Coleridge's discussion of poetry in Volume II of the *Biographia* parallels his discussion of perception and knowledge in Volume I, the themes of nature and mechanism giving way to those of language and ventriloquy. The problem in both volumes is the same: how to bring into connection ideas with no common basis and provide a ground for the meaningful distinction of differences. But in Volume II Coleridge is concerned more with internal coherence, harmony, and purity than with fidelity of representation. As he sees it, a good poem harmonizes part with part and part with whole so perfectly as to seem ordered by strict necessity. Coleridge defines "a *legitimate* poem" as

> one, the parts of which mutually support and explain each another. . . . The philosophic critics of all ages coincide with the ultimate judgement of all countries, in equally denying the praises of a just poem, on the one hand, to a series of striking lines or distichs, each of which absorbing the whole attention of the reader to itself disjoins it from its context, and makes it into a separate whole, instead of an harmonizing part; and on the other hand, to an unsustained composition, from which the reader collects rapidly the general result unattracted by the component parts.[15]

In bad poetry either the parts, too different from one another, do not cohere or else, too much the same, they cannot be distinguished. On the one hand disjunction, on the other hand indistinctness—the danger in either case is failure of articulate relationship. Coleridge insists upon the need for the harmonious, the connected, the commensurate—qualities on a human scale and adapted to the human mind. The connection and the commensurability he seeks, however, are as tenuous in his aesthetic as in his epistemological theories.

Neither the presence of sheep nor the isolation of shepherd from urban manners suffices to establish to Coleridge's satisfaction the naturalness or purity of the rural language Wordsworth recommended. It is not essentially different from other languages. Its basis is common English; accidents of vocabulary, impure admixtures, and awkwardness alone distinguish it from other kinds of speech. It is the language not of our visionary forefathers but of our country cousins, no more ancient and no less impoverished than the speech of our own neighbours. Wordsworth's contention that rustic language, "purified indeed from what appears to be its real defects, from all lasting and rational causes of dislike or disgust," is the best or truest language, makes no sense to Coleridge, who observes:

> A rustic's language, purified from all provincialism and grossness, and so far re-constructed as to be made consistent with the rules of grammar (which are in essence no other than the laws of universal logic, applied to Psychological materials) will not differ from the language of any other man of common-sense, however learned or refined he may be, except as far as the notions, which the rustic has to convey, are fewer and more indiscriminate.[16]

No mountain can teach the arts of speaking and writing pure English as well as the Bible can. Coleridge praises the language of those whose "unambitious, but solid and religious EDUCATION, . . . has rendered few books familiar, but the bible, and the liturgy or hymn book."[17] To the extent that Wordsworth's rustics speak this language, they speak purely and poetically, but Coleridge is careful to distinguish between this style and its "*accidental*" association with rustic speech.

Denying that rustic language is more primary, pure, or literal than the language of other men, Coleridge points out that in certain ways it is even more heavily derivative than the language of polite discourse:

> In civilized society, by imitation and passive remembrance of what they hear from their religious instructors and other superiors, the most

> uneducated share in the harvest which they neither sowed nor reaped. If the history of the phrases in hourly commerce among our peasants were traced, a person not previously aware of the fact would be surprized at finding so large a number, which three or four centuries ago were the exclusive property of the universities and the schools; and at the commencement of the Reformation had been transferred from the school to the pulpit, and thus gradually passed into common life.[18]

The rustic speech that results from this unconscious accretion is neither divine language nor natural Adamic language but something nearer to Babelistic catachresis. Parthenogenesis would be the source of Coleridge's divine language; bastardy is the apparent condition of Wordsworth's. Its heterogeneity—in every sense of the word—makes it unsuitable for poetry. Purified, rustic language retains no special virtue; it is ordinary language with a somewhat narrower vocabulary.

Although Coleridge is concerned to show rustic speech to be unoriginal and impure, he attacks Wordsworth's theory of the purity of rustic language not so much for the sake of revealing its degeneracy or derivativeness as to counter Wordsworth's implication that rustic language yields unmediated representation of external and internal nature. He disallows Wordsworth's argument for the purifying and ennobling effects of rustic living. The source of the best part of language is internal, he says, not external; it is generated by mental self-reflection, not by mountain-gazing. Men who live closest to nature do not on that account speak the most natural or real language. If, leading a narrow existence, their minds are impoverished, so will be their language. The poet must regulate his style not according to the conventions of rustic speech but

> by principles, the ignorance or neglect of which would convict him of being no *poet,* but a silly or presumptuous usurper of the name! By the principles of grammar, logic, psychology! In one word by such a knowledge of the facts, material and spiritual, that most pertain to his art, as if it have been governed and applied by *good sense,* and rendered instinctive by habit, becomes the representative and reward of our past conscious reasonings, insights, and conclusions, and acquires the name of TASTE.[19]

To some extent Coleridge knew his strictures on the impurities of rustic language were beside the point. The real language of men, rustic or not, is appropriate for certain kinds of poetry, and Wordsworth had the good sense, in practice, to reserve it for his less important poems.[20] Nevertheless, what motivates Coleridge's criticisms of Wordsworth's theory motivates also his criticisms of Wordsworth's poetry.

Describing what he calls the "characteristic defects" of the poems, Coleridge nowhere makes explicit the general theme of his particular complaints. He lists, as unrelated perceptions, (1) "the INCONSTANCY of the style," (2) "*matter-of-factness*" or "accidentality," (3) "an undue predilection for the *dramatic* form" with its resulting evils of "incongruity of style" and "ventriloquism," (4) "an intensity of feeling disproportionate to *such* knowledge and value of the objects described, as can be fairly anticipated of men in general," and (5) "thoughts and images too great for the subject," or "*mental* bombast."[21] Common to these complaints is the observation that the language is inappropriate to its context, occasion, or speaker, that it represents a breach of decorum or propriety. Wordsworth commits outrages against every object of rhetoric: character, decorum, intelligibility. Each "characteristic defect," each violation of propriety, is the product of alien voice resistant to the harmonizing power of imagination, language lacking natural connection to its surroundings and emanating from elsewhere than its apparent source. For the convenient space of a brief misreading, Coleridge seems to suggest that Wordsworth is not responsible for those surprising passages of bad writing in his work, that some other voice, speaking through him, pronounced those disturbing lines. "He was not himself when he said that"—such, momentarily, seems to be Coleridge's explanation of his friend's offenses.

But while some such implication may lie buried there, these complaints are less concerned with the uncanny than with the boring, the disappointing, and the insignificant—perhaps one could say with the uncanny in the form of the arbitrary. Coleridge stresses that the exceptionable passages are not exceptional; "*characteristic* defects," these incongruities have to do with the nature of his genius.

As Coleridge presents the matter, the interruptions and incongruities reflect lapses of poetic power and represent Wordsworth's capitulation to the insignificant and the obvious. They are distressing because unassimilable; they add nothing to the poetry, and they frustrate the reader's legitimate expectations. The first two charges Coleridge brings against Wordsworth's poetry concern passages of unsuitable writing. By the first, "the INCONSTANCY of the *style,*" Coleridge means either anticlimax or hyperclimax, an abrupt descent into the drearily commonplace meanness or a startling elevation of the mean into the splendid.[22]

The second complaint on Coleridge's list, matter-of-factness, concerns impropriety of subject rather than of language. It serves to rally a little crowd of doubts about Wordsworth's excessive (because distracting) attention to details, his dependence upon fancy, his "*anxiety* of explanation," and his didacticism—all reflections of what Keats would see as the poet's manipulative designs upon the reader. Coleridge explains that matter-of-factness is irrelevant to the purpose of true poetry, which is pleasure and not persuasion. Produced by an act of intention rather than imagination, the matter-of-fact combines aspects of both the unintended and the overly intended. The accidental quality of these passages is the effect partly of the single-mindedness of their purpose, their recalcitrance to full relationship with their context. As a result, they appear either extraneous to the poem or insufficiently condensed. The particulars do not pull their own weight; the machinery of signification is out of proportion to the significance produced.

The third class of defects, "an undue predilection for the *dramatic* form in certain poems," is produced by what Coleridge sees as yet another kind of incongruity, this time between the speaker and his language. The relation between the self and its utterances is not inherently more natural than that between an object and its name or that between a word and the one following it. In Wordsworth's dramatic poems, Coleridge remarks,

> Either the thoughts and diction are different from that of the poet, and then arises an incongruity of style; or they are the same and indistinguishable, and then it presents a species of ventriloquism, where two are represented as talking, while in truth one man only speaks.[23]

It seems Coleridge has made up his mind to be displeased. Undoubtedly his grievance against characters who speak differently from Wordsworth arises in part from his prejudices against both rustic language and Wordsworth's fondness for what Coleridge regarded as unnecessarily prosaic characters. Shepherds who speak like shepherds are as little suited to poetry as shepherds who speak like Cambridge-educated poets. But, *pace* Parrish, Coleridge is not talking about Wordsworth's choice of characters;[24] social delicacy is not the problem. The very symmetry of his objections suggests a deeper uneasiness than that of the snob.

The last two objections treat more explicitly than the others the incongruity between sign and significance. Coleridge reprehends the "prolixity, repetition, and an eddying instead of progression of thought" that result from the disproportion between emotion and its object, and the "mental bombast" that results from "thoughts and images too great for the subject."[25] He describes the uncanniness of language whose motivation is invisible, whose force is greater than the reader can account for.

Coleridge calls all these qualities defects, and indeed that is how they sometimes appear: Wordsworth was notoriously deaf to the sound of his own poetry, unable to distinguish between his best and his worst work, and liable to lapse unwittingly into tedious verse. But surely to demonstrate the unevenness of his style does not require this elaborate analysis into multitudinous categories and subcategories. Each separate complaint approaches the same puzzle from a slightly different angle, as if Coleridge were not satisfied that he had yet quite defined the problem and wanted to try again:[26] if the voice does not belong to its apparent speaker, if it does not belong to the poet, then where does it come from? Repeatedly he encounters the element of the extraneous in Wordsworth's poetry: irrational, inexplicable, and inextricable from the source of Wordsworth's imaginative power, it acts as a Derridean supplement. That other voice, the one that, oblivious to literary proprieties, uttered inanities and burdened the reader with details he did not want to hear, could upon occasion generate sublimities.[27] What Coleridge identifies as Wordsworth's characteristic defects are also his characteristic strengths.

Coleridge feels toward this quality as Aylmer did toward his wife's birthmark. His attempt to remove it, no less disastrous in the *Biographia* than in the Hawthorne story, comes in his perversely commonsensical criticism of the "Intimations" ode. The arbitrariness Coleridge notices elsewhere becomes particularly threatening here, as Wordsworth attempts to interpret infancy and speak for the unspeaking, finding a significance which its subject is unable to articulate.[28] What especially disturbs Coleridge is Wordsworth's claim to be the mouthpiece for otherwise unconscious and mute prophecy, his suggestion that as the children are to their unconscious wisdom, so he is to the children. Critical of both forms of prophecy or "speaking for," Coleridge cavils at the apostrophe to a six-year-old:

Thou best philosopher who yet dost keep
Thy heritage! Thou eye among the blind,
That, deaf and silent, read'st the eternal deep,
Haunted for ever by the Eternal Mind—
  Mighty Prophet! Seer blest!
  On whom those truths do rest,
Which we are toiling all our lives to find!
Thou, over whom thy immortality
Broods like the day, a master o'er the slave.
A presence that is not to be put by!

The megalomanic aphasia that Wordsworth finds wonderful in children Coleridge finds absurd in Wordsworth—the poet able to make no better sense of childhood sensations of omniscience than the children themselves. Coleridge refuses to credit either the children or Wordsworth. He denies the possibility of inexpressible knowledge or unconscious wisdom. Insisting, for the moment, that language is adequate to thought, he confronts the ineffable with the skepticism of a positivist:

> We will merely ask, what does all this mean? In what sense is a child of that age a *philosopher?* In what sense does he *read* "the eternal deep?" In what sense is he declared to be "*for ever haunted* by the Supreme Being? or so inspired as to deserve the splendid titles of a *mighty prophet,* a *blessed seer?* By reflection? by knowledge? by conscious intuition? or by *any* form or modification of consciousness?" These would be tidings indeed; but such as would pre-suppose an immediate revelation to the inspired communicator, and require miracles to authenticate his inspiration. Children at this age give us no such information of themselves; and at what time were we dipt in the Lethe, which has produced such utter oblivion of a state so godlike?[29]

Coleridge asks how something that eludes consciousness, memory, and language can be recognized. He does not wait to hear Wordsworth's answer: by

> those obstinate questionings
> Of sense and outward things,
> Fallings from us, vanishings;
> Blank misgivings of a Creature
> Moving about in worlds not realised,
> High instincts before which our mortal Nature
> Did tremble like a guilty thing surprised:

—by, that is, a sense of incongruity that implies the loss of something. This sense of incongruity, of the disjunction between things and their significances, is the basis of the sublime Wordsworth constructs in the poem. But at this point Coleridge finds it mere nonsense.

Coleridge's critique of the Ode, particularly his complaint that Wordsworth's choice of subject is arbitrary, not naturally connected to the significance he tries to draw from it, turns upon his critique of identity:

> If these mysterious gifts, faculties, and operations, are *not* accompanied with consciousness; who *else* is conscious of them? or how can it be called the child, if it be no part of the child's conscious being? For aught I know, the thinking Spirit within me may be *substantially* one with the principle of life, and of vital operation. For aught I know, it may be employed as a secondary agent in the marvellous organization and organic movements of my body. But, surely, it would be strange language to say, that *I* construct my *heart!* or that *I* propel the finer influences through my *nerves!* or that *I* compress my brain, and draw the curtains of sleep round my own eyes![30]

Emphasizing the distinction between the conscious self and the unconscious forces that work through it, Coleridge insists that only the conscious counts as part of human identity; what one is unaware of is no proper part of the self. Unconscious knowledge is no knowledge because it has no knower:

> In what sense can the magnificent attributes, above quoted, be appropriated to a *child,* which would not make them equally suitable to a

> *bee,* or a *dog,* or a *field of corn;* or even to a ship, or to the wind and waves that propel it? The omnipresent Spirit works equally in *them,* as in the child; and the child is equally unconscious of it as they.[31]

Coleridge's criticism of the Immortality Ode is often taken to be a surprisingly obtuse and eccentric misinterpretation of the poem. Yet it is of a piece with the rest. It exhibits the workings of the ambivalence Coleridge feels toward the character of Wordsworth's poetry; only now, confronting greater poetry, his uneasiness is greater. (A few pages further on Coleridge will be quoting a different passage from the same poem as an example of poetic excellence.) Although Coleridge assures his readers that the defects he finds in Wordsworth's poetry occur only occasionally and affect only a very small part of his writing, they are not merely incidental. The "excellencies" Coleridge finds are frequently the defects regarded from a different perspective.[32] The discontinuities and incongruities between significance and object are also signs of the power of the poet's imagination to generate poetry independent of external sensations. The imbalance between significance or passion and object demonstrates that the source of the significance apparently drawn from the external world is really the poet's mind, its power to invest the meaningless with meaning. If Wordsworth's weakness is incongruity, his strength is propriety. That Coleridge should tell us this at such length tells as much about Coleridge as about Wordsworth: reading the second volume of the *Biographia,* we learn not only Wordsworth's strong and weak points but also the qualities that most interested Coleridge.[33]

The first characteristic excellence Coleridge discovers in Wordsworth's poetry is also the most surprising. It is "an austere purity of language both grammatically and logically; in short a perfect appropriateness of the words to the meaning."[34] Coleridge's test for purity is

> untranslatableness in words of the same language without injury to the meaning. Be it observed, however, that I include in the *meaning* of a word not only its correspondent object, but likewise all the associations which it recalls. For language is framed to convey not the object alone, but likewise the character, mood and intentions of the person who is representing it.[35]

Thus purity is perfect verbal propriety, the right naming, the freedom from tropical "abuses or rather trespasses in speach" we discussed earlier. It recognizes no substitutions and no synonyms. It depends upon the strict exclusion of the arbitrary and the accidental. It guarantees what impure language threatens: the natural and necessary relations both between the mind and language and between language and the external world.

The second and fourth on the list of Wordsworth's excellences have to do with naturalness and freshness, or, in Coleridge's words, "a correspondent weight and sanity of the Thoughts and Sentiments,—won, not from books; but—from the poet's own meditative observation," and "the perfect truth of nature in his images and descriptions as taken immediately from nature."[36] One observation elaborates upon the other; both present Wordsworth as a writer who writes directly from nature and from his own experience—the poet every freshman knows and (precisely because of what Coleridge's list of defects reveals) every senior English major suspects.

By a generous change of the critic's heart, stylistic unevenness is permitted to become the third excellence on the list, "the sinewy strength and originality of single lines and paragraphs."[37] And the fifth excellence, "a meditative pathos, a union of deep and subtle thought with sensibility," seems to reply to the earlier charge of ventriloquism; it is an effect of the perfect unity of Wordsworth with his voice: "Here the man and the poet lose and find themselves in each other, the one as glorified, the latter as substantiated."[38]

Finally, for Coleridge, Wordsworth is the poet of imagination: "I challenge for this poet the gift of IMAGINATION in the highest and strictest sense of the word." Indeed, one may wonder whether the collection of qualities Coleridge lauds belong as absolutely to the real Wordsworth as to the abstract imagination. Despite the samples of poetry Coleridge appeals from, he seems often to be describing rather his ideal of poetry than the work of any particular writer[39]—even the defects are those of an ideally bad poet. The substitution of the ideal for the man seems to have occurred just as Coleridge turns from his grievances to his appreciations. Coleridge describes an inimitable poet: "WORDSWORTH, where he is indeed Wordsworth, may be mimicked by Copyists, he may be plundered by Plagiarists; but he can not be imitated, except by those who are not born to be imitators."[40] Inimitable except by those incapable of imitation, Wordsworth would seem to embody the principle of originality. Coleridge describes him—or his work[41]—as if it were a source, something which cannot be uncreatively copied, as opposed to a product, which is liable to being copied. To imitate Wordsworth truly is to be genuinely creative.[42]

Jerome Christensen has described Coleridge's interrogation of the concepts "property" and "propriety" as "part of a genealogical and genial strategy that will insist on the retrieval not only of their likenesses but their essential identity," a strategy that, when applied to the "sovereign genius" of Wordsworth, results in Coleridge's anxious recognition that he "must risk impropriety by challenging Wordsworth's sole property in his own work":

> One explanation of the *Biographia*—both its overall autobiographical disposition and its local *ad hominem* diversions—is that propriety cannot, without the most reckless impropriety, be neatly abstracted for analysis, however much that would pacify the querulous understanding, because propriety belongs to the man, it *is* his self-possession; to transfer propriety from the person to the arid discourse of the understanding would be, regardless of the benevolence of one's intentions, to assist in that dispossession that reason and imagination would reverse.[43]

That the *Biographia* produces evidence of impropriety is indisputable. That the impropriety is Coleridge's and the result of his analytical method, is not. Although perhaps Coleridge might have prefered to exclude the alien, the arbitrary, and the artificial from his descriptions of Wordsworth's work and the imagination, he is incapable of doing so. His feeble attempts to blame the defects of the poetry on Wordsworth's dependence upon the fancy and credit the excellences to Wordsworth's imagination fail.[44] The defects and the excellences are too closely related, sinister and benevolent aspects of the same creative or signifying force. The reservations Coleridge expresses about Wordsworth's poetry are the reservations he feels about the imagination.

If, as it appears, the defects Coleridge sees in Wordsworth's poetry are integral to the excellent qualities that he regarded as signs of the power of Wordsworth's imagination, it follows that Coleridge's theory of imagination, at least as he puts it into practice, is not a theory of homogeneity, purity, and continuity. Despite the ascetic drive behind Coleridge's remarks, his discussion of what constitutes literary propriety acknowledges sanely and explicitly the difference between homogeneity and harmony.[45] The function of imaginative art is dialectical. Instead of denying or annihilating differences, it brings them into significant relation.[46] Imaginative power

> reveals itself in the balance or reconciliation of opposite or discordant qualities: of sameness, with difference; of the general, with the concrete; the idea, with the image; the individual, with the representative; the sense of novelty and freshness, with old and familiar objects; a more than usual state of emotion, with more than usual order; judgement ever awake and steady self-possession, with enthusiasm and feeling profound or vehement; and while it blends and harmonizes the natural and the artificial, still subordinates art to nature; the manner to the matter; and our admiration for the poet to our sympathy with the poetry.[47]

The list that begins with antitheses ends with complements. At what point do the qualities cease to be compatible and their reconciliation cease to be miraculous? Is the reconciliation between sameness and difference an organized heterogeneity like the supper Milton's Eve served Raphael, "Taste after taste upheld with kindliest change," or is it the simultaneous identity and difference that is the paradoxical condition of figuration?

At issue is the question of whether the elements are different only from each other or also from themselves. The answer depends in part upon how one decides to define the elements: a whole volume of poetry contains, as it were, more difference than a single word. But the answer depends also upon the possibility of an absolutely same or identical element, no matter how small.[48] Coleridge always suspects internal differences: "The composition of a poem is among the *imitative* arts; and . . . imitation, as opposed to copying, consists either in the interfusion of the SAME throughout the radically DIFFERENT, or of the different throughout a base radically the same."[49] The hypothesis of an aesthetic relationship between the same and the different is comparable to the first volume's hypothesis of a metaphysical and epistemological relationship between the self and nature. The slide that Coleridge's list performs, slipping from the difficult reconciliation of sameness with difference to the easy reconciliation of admiration for the poet to sympathy with his poetry, suggests his desire that harmony might be reduced to homogeneity. Nevertheless, Coleridge insists that the artistic purity he values is not homogeneity.

In bold letters the *Biographia* upholds the purity, naturalness, and propriety of poetic language; the fine print, however, subverts the very notions of purity, naturalness, and propriety.[50] The distinction Coleridge wants to draw between appropriate and inappropriate language simply will not let itself be drawn. When in the following two passages he calls upon the rhetoric of property to bolster his arguments for propriety, his words, forgetting his purpose, mock the coherence of the system of thought from which they are taken. Having, as Jerome Christensen points out, figured linguistic propriety in terms of property,[51] Coleridge's language proceeds, by apparent inadvertence, to show that property is theft:

> The best part of human language, properly so called, is derived from reflection on the acts of the mind itself. It is formed by a voluntary appropriation of fixed symbols to internal acts, to processes and results of imagination, the greater part of which have no place in the consciousness of uneducated men; though in civilized society, by imitation and passive remembrance of what they hear from their religious instructors and other superiors, the most uneducated share in the harvest which they neither sowed nor reaped.[52]

Coleridge assigns this best part of language first an internal and then an external source. It is first the product of mental self-reflection, then what the mind appropriates from the external world. Coleridge places the two incompatible accounts side by side as if in apposition or mutual explanation. The "voluntary appropriation" that he says characterizes the formation of appropriate language looks puzzlingly like the thievery that characterizes the formation of the language of the uneducated. There are other disturbing features here as well. Coleridge confuses the educated class with its ancestors, the men whose acts of self-reflection generated the language he praises. Although according to Coleridge's theory of education every member of the educated class repeats these originary acts,[53] education is only partly the development of self-consciousness; it is in greater measure the inheritance of that product of one's ancestors' reflections—the same "imitation and passive remembrance" Coleridge condemns in the uneducated. The oppositions he sets up are unravelled. Mental generation runs into appropriation and thence into imitation. Far from demonstrating the purity and propriety of language at its best, the passage suggests precisely its impropriety.

The second passage subverts its proprieties more elaborately. In the course of his remarks on Wordsworth's "INCONSTANCY of . . . style," Coleridge observes that

> Even in real life, the difference is great and evident between words used as the *arbitrary marks* of thought, our smooth market-coin of intercourse with the image and superscription worn out by currency; and those which convey pictures either borrowed from *one* outward object to enliven and particularize some *other;* or used allegorically to body forth the inward state of the person speaking; or such as are at least the exponents of his peculiar turn and unusual extent of faculty. So much so indeed, that in the social circles of private life we often find a striking use of the latter put a stop to the general flow of conversation, and by the excitement arising from concentrated attention produce a sort of damp and interruption for some minutes after.[54]

Although Coleridge seems to invite us to hear the exposition of a "great and evident" contrast between two kinds of language, he offers us riddles instead: How is a worn coin like an arbitrary mark of thought? And: When is a borrowing not a market transaction? Since Coleridge sets forth examples of concepts he does not fully name, we cannot be sure what his examples are meant to exemplify. What is the opposite of arbitrary language? For that matter, in what precisely does the arbitrariness of arbitrary language consist?

First a simple reading. Coleridge is contrasting two kinds or functions of language. If the first kind of language facilitates the economy of speech, the second, commanding silent attention, momentarily halts conversational exchange. The first, like coins whose images are no longer distinct, is exchanged in the marketplace of speech for meaning or for reply before it is noticed. This kind of language is made up of words and images so familiar as to seem natural or literal. The users of dead metaphors are unaware that they are using figures of speech; they seem to themselves to be speaking plainly. The arbitrariness of this kind of speech is a function of amnesia. But if common, undistinguished language is arbitrary, then, presumably, poetic or obviously figurative language must be unarbitrary. The images of the second kind of language are so new as to make it impossible for speaker or auditor to remain unaware of their figurative status. The metaphors are still alive, and one apprehends them as figures of speech, products of thought.

One must ask whether this recognition preserves a part of language from the threat of the arbitrary. Instead of contrasting arbitrary language with natural language, the passage contrasts unconsciously arbitrary language with manifestly arbitrary language. The difference between them is that the second kind of language makes no bones about its condition. Furthermore, the arbitrariness suggested by the imagery Coleridge uses for one kind of language is different from the arbitrariness suggested by the terms used for the other kind of language. In the interpretation offered above, arbitrariness is figured by the effacement of the coin's image. But the description of the second kind of language directs our attention to the arbitrariness inherent in any image, effaced or not, contrived or not. Words used to "convey pictures . . . borrowed from *one* outward object to enliven and particularize some *other*"—such could stand as a description of what a coin is, the realization of metaphor, and it describes aptly enough the arbitrariness of the relation between the lump of metal and what is stamped upon its surface.[55] But what has this to do with words "used . . . to body forth the inward state of the person speaking"? This kind of speech would seem to be free from the first kind of arbitrariness; the bodying forth suggests a natural relationship between the sign and what it refers to—suggests, indeed, an index. Nevertheless, Coleridge characterizes this relation as allegorical. He is apparently untroubled by the differences between a metaphor and a self-representation and between either of them and self-expression (words used as "the exponents of [the speaker's] turn and unusual extent of faculty"). The passage ignores the difference between levels of figuration, even the difference between figuration and its apparent absence.[56]

By lumping together the sign that originates from its referent and the sign that originates elsewhere than from its referent, Coleridge may be suggesting either that the kind of arbitrariness he associates with the worn coin has little to do with the arbitrariness of the relationship between sign and referent, or else that arbitrary signs are more closely related to nonarbitrary signs than it is comfortable to contemplate, that neither commonplace nor poetic language is natural.

One might have expected that if Coleridge meant to illustrate the arbitrariness of language, he might have chosen—if from the monetary realm at all—the image of a new coin,[57] one whose stamp is clearly visible and clearly arbitrary. On a disk of precious metal one might see the outline of a king, his titles, the arms of Great Britain and Ireland. The relationship between the stamped image and the material into which it is stamped is arbitrary rather than natural, as is made abundantly clear by the variety of characters one finds stamped upon disks of identical substance and comparable weight. The stamp becomes more important than the substance, whose real value is forgotten in its nominal value. Instead of this, Coleridge presents us with a "smooth market-coin of intercourse with the image and superscription worn out by currency," an artificial object returning, apparently, to its natural state. Its artificially imposed design having largely worn off, one might expect it, a simple, unembossed lump of silver or copper, to revert to its natural significance, to be worth whatever such a weight of metal might be valued at.

But is this its natural state? Is there any return to innocence for an old shilling? Most likely the old coin remains a coin,[58] its stamp gone but its function the same, the sign of a now-erased sign, even more highly arbitrary than before, since the outward evidence of its function is gone. The arbitrariness of the worn coin derives from the confusion between its apparently natural state and its cultural significance. Even worn smooth, a coin remains a coin, representing not itself but a certain value measurable in other coins or in objects or in work.

A notebook entry made at about the same time as the writing of the *Biographia* uses similar terms and poses similar problems:

> Homogeneous Languages favorable to Metaphysics—exemplified in the Greek and in the German. And why? the Words, as percipere, i.e. capere per census; concipere, i.e. capere aliquid *cum* alio vel aliis—

> Einbildung, i.e. formatio in unum—bedingt, bedingung, i.e. what presupposes some thing as the condition of its existence, i.e. *be-thinged*—all are like a series of historical medals—the stamps remain—while in derivative Languages they are mere *Coins,* current for so much, by a *credit,* without any distinct knowledge or reference. It was given One—& *it goes* in our Market.—Hence Indistinctness—& as the human mind still craves for distinctness, thence the turning to & resting wholly in *imagible* things / but as there must be likewise a sense of indefiniteness (or all activity would cease) this is wasted on what is called common sense—i.e. the Shells, or the Wampum, or the Minted Coin, or the Bank, or Country, or Town Notes, which happen at *the moment* to be current & in credit, tho' the month after a Bankruptcy shews the hollowness of the Foundation.[59]

The relation between homogeneous and derivative language is figured in the contrast between historical medals and money, between, that is, an object presented as art and an object whose aesthetic and referential values are incidental to its function as counter. If not only the two relationships but the terms within them are analogous, then we find what the *Biographia* calls "arbitrary" the notebooks label "derivative," and the indistinctness of the *Biographia*'s effaced coin is a function not of its physical effacement but of its economic use as an open signifier "without any distinct knowledge or reference." It is arbitrary because of the failure of derivation to coincide with reference. Curiously enough, Coleridge does not distinguish between coins and other forms of money such as bank notes and wampum. He lumps all these kinds of payment together as forms of credit, symbols of value stored elsewhere. The distinction between coin and paper money vanishes; indeed, Coleridge seems to regard coin as the embodiment of the principle that animates paper money.[60] So in May of 1811 he describes money as

> whatever has value among men according to what it *represents,* rather than to what it *is.* The high expedience that some part of this representative medium should possess an intrinsic, and universally acknowledged, value, in order to be a common measure of the rest, is admitted, but yet forms a distinct and subordinate question. Among nations at all civilized, the latter, though general, is not universal, or in an *absolute* sense necessary; the former is strictly both universal and necessary.[61]

From this perspective there is little real difference between paper money or clipped coin and coin of full weight. The relationship between money as representation of value, and the value represented, is artificial even when the two, inhabiting the same material, seem to coincide. Coleridge insists upon an absolute split between the representation and what is represented. Material is not function:

> The distinction between money and commodity, the representative and the thing represented, is not verbal or arbitrary, but real and of practical importance. As soon as a commodity becomes money, it ceases to be a commodity; even as a bag of guineas sold by its weight at Paris or Pekin loses the nature, as well as the name, of money.[62]

Self-representation is never simple, not even for a gold coin.[63]

The coin is so traditional an emblem of the word[64] that Coleridge may not have been thinking of the real coins in his pocket as he wrote these passages. Nevertheless, the status of the coin was a particular problem at the time of Coleridge's writing, and his concern for the issue resulted in a number of short essays on the subject.[65] The relationship between a coin and the value it stood for was clear to no one; during the suspension of aural redemption, questions arose concerning whether money worked by simple representation of transcendent value (gold) or by virtue of a network of forces—the two approaches roughly analogous to a classical view of language and a Saussurian view.

In the context of Coleridge's underargument about the arbitrariness of language, the effacement of the coin's character is significant because it ultimately does not matter. Originally the stamp (the *character*) was a guarantee of authentic identity, a guarantee of equivalence between the intrinsic value of the substance and the conventional value indicated by its size and design; paradoxically, this guarantee indicates by its very presence the arbitrary nature of its significance. In a worn coin there is no visible guarantee of this identity; indeed, the intrinsic value is visibly less than the conventional. The wearing smooth does not remove a false surface masking and disguising the nature of the underlying material, however; the extrinsic has become intrinsic. The relationship of the metal to its new nonsurface is no less arbitrary than that to its old impression. The smoothness is blank but not transparent.

As Marc Shell reminds us, "A coin is both a proposition and a thing. It is an inscription and a thing on which the inscription is stamped, to which it refers, and together with which it becomes legal tender."[66] As an instance of writing whose material circumstances vouch for its validity, a word that is also a thing, a happy coincidence of representation with represented, a coin may be said to embody that condition of absolute propriety to which autobiography, or perhaps all writing, aspires but from which, Paul de Man reminds us, autobiography, representative of all signed writing, is debarred.[67]

What of the propriety of effacement? Rubbed smooth, its stamp of origin and authenticity effaced in the iterated economic transactions its original character made possible,[68] a coin is made anonymous, technically characterless, and therefore one might assume improper. But its very effacement serves as a character, and one more proper than that of any sovereign, for the blankness expresses the proper anonymity of the coin's function as universal signifier, appropriable (like words) by anyone, exchangeable (like tropes) for anything.

If a coin is like a word, then the coin image is like a whole text. The effaced coin serves as a mirror in whose blankness the text of the *Biographia,* that anonymous autobiographical meditation on self-as-other, seeks its proper or improper identity. But it mirrors other texts as well, including perhaps the partly blank title pages of the *Lyrical Ballads* (1798 and 1800). And it introduces the problem that will be the subject of the final chapter, the desire to realize propriety in substantial property and words in inscribed things, to make money do what imagination, however powerful, cannot.

8

Mortal Pages: Wordsworth and the Reform of Copyright

> Oh! why hath not the Mind
> Some element to stamp her image on
> In nature somewhat nearer to her own?
> Why, gifted with such powers to send abroad
> Her spirit, must it lodge in shrines so frail?
>
> *THE PRELUDE* (1850), V, 45–49

The acts and objects of literary acquisition, dispossession, borrowing, and theft on which we have thus far concentrated our attention are not the sort of thing that would much interest a tax collector or a policeman. In worldly terms, the values at issue have ranged between the exiguous and the imaginary. Even when, as in the "Poems on the Naming of Places," tangible objects have been involved that would be capable in other contexts of being bought and sold, they have been implicated in an economics essentially literary, self-referential: their value has been measurable in texts, tropes, and figures but not, except metaphorically, in money or labor or market goods. But these economic figures have all along, as we have noted, demonstrated a tendency to realize their own economic implications—to enact their own fictions and so create facts of material significance. This tendency, particularly strong in Wordsworth's poetry, laid the basis for literary-political action late in that poet's career.

Always concerned with the acquisition and significance of property, Wordsworth developed a fascination with the laws governing the property a writer has in his writings. He believed that the current system of copyright cheated him and other serious writers of their due reward, and his resentment was extreme. "The wrongs of literary men are crying out for redress on all sides," he declared in 1819. "It appears to me that towards no class of his Majesty's Subjects are the laws so unjust and oppressive."[1] To right these wrongs, to improve the writer's lot and put him in a better position to write what would be worth owning, he lobbied for reform of the copyright system, urging in particular an extension of the term of copyright.

His efforts were extraordinary. "No other man of letters had exerted himself to anything like the same extent in 'the cause,' "[2] Mary Moorman notes. His complaints, which began quietly in 1808, grew louder and more eloquent over the course of the next three and a half decades, and by 1837 the matter had begun to absorb considerable amounts of his time and energy. He went to London to lobby the House of Commons and enlist Thomas Noon Talfourd as his Parliamentary champion.[3] As Talfourd began his efforts to extend the term of copyright from twenty-eight to sixty years, Wordsworth began a gigantic effort of his own. There was an outpouring of letters—fifty that he admitted to, plus anonymous letters to newspapers. He ran after members of Parliament. He supplied Talfourd with material for speeches and John Lockhart with material for the *Quarterly Review*. He composed hortatory sonnets on the subject.[4] And he permitted Talfourd to turn him into a public example of the kind of worthy genius that copyright reform would most fitly reward—an opportunity for the nation to make up for its sins against Shakespeare and Milton. Parliament was slow to respond to Wordsworth's heroics, and it was 1842 before it finally acted to lengthen the term of copyright—not to the sixty years Wordsworth had demanded or the eternity he desired but to forty-two years or, if the author survived that period, his life plus seven years. For a little while afterward Wordsworth continued to fuss, taking obvious delight in admonishing those who seemed likely to infringe on his new rights; but the necessity of contenting himself with the moderation of the legal adjustment seems to have deprived him of one of the pleasures of his life.

Although a writer's interest in copyright would seem to be the most natural thing in the world, a reflection of his concern for his legitimate literary interests, Wordsworth's interest in the matter verged upon the excessive. He seems to have invested the problem with a significance for which practical considerations cannot altogether account.

Wordsworth's active involvement in the politics of copyright reform was motivated partly by his altruistic belief that the law should recognize the right of genius to receive the fullness of its reward, partly by his belief that an extension of the term of copyright might improve his family's finances. Attempting to rescue Wordsworth from the unfortunate appearance of vulgar self-interest that his activities created, P. M. Zall has argued that the poet cared as much about the improvement of the general lot of serious writers as about the prospect of personal gain. There is evidence for Zall's contention that Wordsworth's interest in copyright had "its roots in what was, in effect, a struggle for survival of literature of quality in an age demanding quantity."[5] Wordsworth presented himself as a defender of beleaguered genius, writing on behalf of those who wrote for the ages. By limiting the term of copyright, he contended, the law recognized the right of a writer to profit only from immediate, brief popularity; if he had the misfortune to be neglected by his contemporaries, no later recognition could help him. Failing to distinguish between the genius and the hack, the current copyright arrangements acted, Wordsworth believed, "as a premium upon mediocracy,"[6] encouraging the proliferation of potboilers at the expense of masterpieces. In 1808, when the term was fourteen years, he wrote:

> The law, as it now stands, merely consults the interest of the useful drudges of Literature, or of flimsy and shallow writers, whose works are upon a level with the taste and knowledge of the age; while men of real power, who go before their age, are deprived of all hope of their families being benefited by their exertions.[7]

The doubling of the term of copyright from fourteen to twenty-eight years in 1814 did nothing to appease him:

> Many of my Poems have been upwards of 30 years subject to criticism, and are disputed about as keenly as ever, and appear to be read much

> more. In fact thirty years are no adequate test for works of Imagination, even from second or third-rate writers, much less from those of the first order, as we see in the instances of Shakespeare and Milton.[8]

But despite these complaints, it is not clear whether the state of contemporary literary taste or the state of his pocketbook bothered the poet more. He suspected that readers sometimes confused market price with literary value.[9] Although he wanted people to read his books and sometimes wished that he could arrange for them to be sold more cheaply, he cared as much about the buying of his books as about the reading of them, going so far as to prohibit one friend from lending a volume of his poems to anyone who could afford to go to a bookshop and buy a copy for himself.[10]

Wordsworth's writings had just begun to produce considerable income when the issue of copyright first caught his attention, and he feared that by the time his greatness was at last fully recognized, neither he nor his family would be able to profit by it. He was not, presumably, aiming at opulence; his poems never brought in much money, and he seems to have cared for his few pounds precisely because they were so few. The 1798 *Lyrical Ballads,* which he privately professed to have published for money,[11] brought thirty guineas,[12] and his publisher made him a present of the copyright, which was valued at nothing. In 1812 Wordsworth told a friend he was earning less than £140 a year from the sale of his poems.[13] But by 1835 his annual literary income had apparently risen to about £220,[14] and in 1838 he was able to complain to Gladstone

> that within the last three years or so my poetical writings have produced for me nearly 1,500 pounds, and that [under the present system of copyright] much the greatest part of them either would be public property to-morrow, if I should die, or would become so in a very few years.[15]

In consequence of having written

> with a view to interest and benefit society, though remotely, yet permanently. . . . [h]is works, though never out out of demand, have made their way slowly into general circulation . . . within the last four years [he wrote that same year] these works have brought the author a larger

pecuniary emolument than during the whole of the preceding years in which they have been before the public.[16]

Such being the pattern of his profits, his family would lose greatly, he said, if he were then to die.[17]

Wordsworth's literary politics appear to express simultaneously ordinary greed and extraordinary idealism. Certainly the money he stood to gain from any amendment in the copyright laws was not great,[18] and, had money been his sole object, he could have found more effective ways to secure it. In fact, he concentrated his energies on a measure whose effects would be felt most only after his death, while the most immediate threat to his authorial profits, international piracy, interested him comparatively little.[19] True greed would have behaved differently. But so, on the other hand, would disinterested benevolence. His attitude toward copyright was not merely reasonable. To hear his appeals at their most grandiloquent, one would have no idea that the problem was the assignment of profits; his rhetoric, so wildly in excess of its apparent object, suggests a desperation more nearly eschatological than financial. For Wordsworth, the solution of legal and financial problems stood for the solution of poetic and even metaphysical ones. Complaining "that the duration of copyright, as the law now stands, is far from being co-extensive with the claims of natural affection,"[20] begging Parliament "to relieve men of letters from the thraldom of being forced to court the living generation,"[21] he addressed the government as if it had jurisdiction over the border between the dead and the living and could repair by legal means the damage death wreaks upon human bonds.

In 1819 Wordsworth received a letter asking him to contribute toward a monument for Robert Burns. He lost no time in refusing. Burns required no monuments, Wordsworth said; his name lived in the hearts of his countrymen, and he "has raised for himself a monument so conspicuous, and of such imperishable materials, as to render a local fabric of stone superfluous, and, therefore, comparatively insignificant."[22]

> Let the Gallant Defenders of our Country be liberally rewarded with Monuments; their noble Actions cannot speak for themselves as the Writings of Men of genius are able to do; gratitude in respect to them

> stands in need of admonition. . . . Let our great Statesmen and eminent Lawyers, our learned and eloquent Divines, and they who have successfully devoted themselves to the abstruser Sciences, be rewarded in like manner; but towards departed Genius, exerted in the fine Arts and more especially in Poetry, I humbly think, in the present state of things, the sense of obligation to it may more satisfactorily be expressed by means pointing directly to the general benefit of Literature.[23]

What Wordsworth had in mind as the proper tribute to the dead poet was a reform of copyright laws: no monuments, just money. "Showy Tributes to Genius," he wrote, are liable to distract people from what they ought to be doing to promote "the interests of Literature." It is an extraordinary response, and its implications are puzzling. For the tirade encloses a riddle: How is copyright like a tombstone? One seems to be but a grander version of the other, properer for the dead than for the living. As he presents it here, copyright is something due to the memory of the dead, a symbolic refutation of the material facts it confirms, and the money it brings a poet's heirs does the cause of literature more good than all the sculpted marble in the world. He seems to forget the use living writers make of copyright. His amnesia, whatever its origin, serves the purposes of tactful persuasion: a quiet dead genius may seem more deserving than noisy living ones, and one rarely accuses the departed of greed. Represented thus, the money that copyright produces loses its materialistic associations and becomes spiritualized, after a fashion; offered to the dead, it comes to resemble an oblation.

The letter is something only an obsessed man would write, and Wordsworth was indeed obsessed. But although one of the strangest things about this strange letter is the way it seizes upon the request for a contribution as a pretext for a tirade upon a favorite subject, the analogy Wordsworth ends up making between a monument and the remuneration copyright would bring in is not unsuggestive. It reminds us of the material aspect of writing: not only the materials of inscription or the mortal physicality of the men who engage in it, but also the materiality of the remuneration it brings. The two issues brought so crazily together, money and monuments, are really one. Etymology reminds us that money and monuments are close verbal cousins, both descendents of *monere,* to warn or to remind. In Wordsworth's mind, copyright has then everything to do with epitaph, the writing due to the memory of the dead.

We may be disturbed by the spectacle of a poet in furious pursuit of shillings and pence, the altitude of his rhetoric rising with his income. Poets have never seriously renounced the material world, and the reading public cannot renounce it for them. Yet the sale of a poem for a price affected Wordsworth's contemporaries and may affect us still as an act of hypocrisy or a breach of contract. Literature that traffics in the world looks suspicious, its participation in material concerns liable to be read as evidence of a lack of genuine literary substance. The reluctance to acknowledge that writers sometimes must write in order to eat is as exploitative as it is ancient, but the uneasiness it expresses is real, deriving as it does from a sense that the remuneration of what readers prefer to think of as genius threatens the boundary between the verbal and the material.

For Wordsworth, that boundary was much less well defined and much more ambiguous than it tends to be for his readers. "In Wordsworth," writes Thomas Weiskel, "the imagination is the faculty which transforms everything into the money of the mind."[24] At the height of his powers Wordsworth's writing was, as we have seen, self-consciously economic in theme and style. He treated property and dispossession, those major themes of the early poetry, in language that reflected the anxiety of an unstable fortune: his style, borrowed in part (so he said) from the rural poor, was designed to produce the greatest poetic effect by means of the least verbal expenditure. His texts were conditioned by their frugality. Words were not to be spent extravagantly; poems were to be valued and defended from trespassers. In this extraordinary economy of language, poetic production seemed to hedge the danger of a greater loss or absence that it brought into being.

The money of Wordsworth's mind had a way of becoming money in his pocket—which was fitting, given his propensity toward literalness.[25] He liked the value of his inspirations to be bankable, to be realized in terms of real property. As we saw in the "Poems on the Naming of Places" and in "Michael," his attitude toward his poems sometimes resembled that of a landowner towards his lands. Something, indeed, about Wordsworth's poetry—its jealous territoriality, its strong identification of poetry with place[26]—had the power to inspire wealthy readers with the desire to make him presents of land. His patrons were good readers; the financial gesture was an appropriate response to this aspect of his poetry.

Under another aspect, however—under the dread of an originating calamity—he sometimes wrote almost as one of the dispossessed. Frustration over the long blockage of his paternal legacy and an awareness that his literary career had been made possible by the death of a generous friend must have complicated his attitude toward the property he had in his writings. I have been arguing that the publication of the *Lyrical Ballads* was an economically ambiguous act,[27] simultaneously a claim and a renunciation. In the Preface to the 1800 edition the poet declared that his attempt to "look steadily at my subject" had "necessarily cut me off from a large portion of phrases and figures of speech which from father to son have long been regarded as the common inheritance of Poets."[28] Despite his efforts to create his own patrimony, Wordsworth sensed that his poetry did not really belong to him, or that, if it did, it came at a deadly cost.[29] From very early on in his career, creation was attended by loss; to talk about poetic imagination was to talk about loss and recompense. Although Wordsworth may originally have chosen to write about the loss of sheep and lands because they evoked the intense passions he claimed were his real subject, he must very soon have felt the intrinsic fascination of poverty. The radical impoverishment so feared in "Tintern Abbey," "Resolution and Independence," and the "Intimations" ode is hard to connect with Simon Lee's simple destitution, but the anxious cry that sounds through these lyrics is still a question about livelihood: "How is it that you live, and what is it you do?"

For a man whose poetics were inextricable from his economics, however, Wordsworth displays surprising doubts about the compatibility of literary and financial values. In the midst of hard work to persuade the government that writers deserved to be paid for their labor, he noted with approval William Gomm's remarks on the folly of assuming that literature and money were commensurable:

> "Burke says," as in a letter was lately observed to me by a much esteemed friend, "that between certain services that he had rendered to the State & money, there was no common measure of comparison—that they are qualities incommensurable"—this applies with tenfold force my friend goes on to say, in the case of sound literature in as much as the services here rendered [are] for all states & for all time. Still there has always appeared to me, something monstrous in the existing relation between Author & Bookseller or Publisher, as regards remuneration of this sort—a positive reversing of the natural order of things, as we find it obtains in all matters else—a subservience (pro tanto) of the spiritual to the material.[30]

Was the problem that booksellers offered too little money or that they offered money when they should have been offering homage instead? What is the just price for a poetry founded upon economic analogy, generated in the attempt to overcome or internalize the incommensurability between the written and the material, between words and things?

For Wordsworth the distinction between the verbal and the material was never as clear or as absolute as it was for the average reader. Words and things seemed to him very nearly alike, and the possibilities for their confusion filled him with both yearning and alarm.[31] From the beginning of his career Wordsworth regarded writing and language in strikingly physical or material terms. As early as 1800, when he wrote the Preface to *Lyrical Ballads,* he announced his desire that his words might share the materiality and permanence of the rocks that formed the landscape around him and that informed the rustic language he idealized; in 1810 the "Essays upon Epitaphs" reaffirmed his belief in language that acknowledged its connection with materiality; in 1815, writing of the similarity of poetry to religion in the "Essay, Supplementary to the Preface," he distinguished the former as "ethereal and transcendent, yet incapable to sustain her existence without sensuous incarnation." But language could be too material for even Wordsworth to bear. The act of writing—pushing a pen across a sheet of paper—was for him a sickeningly physical labor that he preferred to leave to others,[32] and the product of such labor partook of its grossness: De Quincey tells us that Wordsworth buttered the books he read along with the toast he ate at tea.[33]

Wordsworth's own uneasiness about the materiality of his writing transmitted itself to his critics. To many readers, Wordsworth's poetry presents itself as somehow infused with the materiality of the objects it so ostentatiously depends upon. It is as if the "nostalgia for the object" that de Man says motivates romantic poetry generally[34] had achieved in Wordsworth's case unwonted, inexplicable success and the poems that common sense tells us can be made of nothing more substantial than words had succeeded in becoming as palpable as what they represented. The suspicion that with his "matter-of-factness" Wordsworth has either transcended or perhaps fallen short of the literary prompts not only Geoffrey Durrant's description of Wordsworth's art as "partly pre-verbal" and Robert Gleckner's characterization of Wordsworth's words as "palpable and intransigent, 'things' that . . . resist total transmutation" but also Thomas McFarland's observation that "in refusing to deliver a golden world, that is, restricting himself to 'substantial things,' Wordsworth in some paradoxical way seems almost to be refusing to be a poet" and Thomas Weiskel's perception that Wordsworth's imagination is that power which, refusing to read the signified in the signifier, "occludes the symbol."[35] The poetry is mute to questioning, intractable in the face of efforts to read it, thinglike in its radical dumbness. But the elusiveness that manifests itself sometimes as opacity shows itself at other times as what Geoffrey Hartman, following Wordsworth, calls "ghostly language":

> At times . . . Wordsworth's poetry almost transcends representation, and thus reality-testing. It seems to exist . . . without the material density of poetic texture—without imagistic or narrative detail. The presence it continues to evoke becomes 'untouchable.'[36]

Is the disagreement among the critics a reflection of the poet's inconsistency or of our confusion? Something about Wordsworth's poetic materialism or matter-of-factness—the quality that assimilates the condition of his words to the condition of their referents and that makes it impossible for critics consistently to distinguish between his poems and their subjects—works against itself. Maurice Blanchot describes "this wish to be a thing" exhibited by literature that says, "I no longer represent, I am; I do not signify, I present," as a "refusal to mean anything, a refusal immersed in words turned to salt . . . [an] insane effort to bury itself in itself, to hide itself behind the fact that it is visible": "If it were to become as mute as stone, as passive as the corpse enclosed behind that stone, its decision to lose the capacity for speech would still be legible on the stone and would be enough to wake that bogus corpse."[37] Figuring the uncanniness of language, "that bogus corpse," literary materiality recreates the incommensurability it sought to resolve.

Wordsworth was not alone in his interest in the problems of copyright. Other writers echoed his concerns. A small but vocal group—including Thomas Carlyle, Hartley Coleridge,[38] and a number of minor academics who feared that their copyrights might expire before their laborious scholarship began to return a profit[39]—joined Wordsworth in his efforts to reform copyright, believing, with him, that they were fighting in defense of their books, their children, and the English reading public. They believed that in asking for an extension of the term of copyright they were asking for the partial restoration of a right long acknowledged by common law, which, according to their version of history, allowed writers a perpetual property in their works. "This right I hold to be more deeply inherent in that species of property than in any other,"[40] Wordsworth wrote.

This argument from common law—which Wordsworth and his allies regarded as their strongest—was based upon a falsehood, or, at least, upon a confusion. Copyright was never the property a writer had in his intellectual productions; it had, in its origins, everything to do with booksellers and nothing to do with authors, involving manufacturing and selling rights rather than the ownership of particular texts as texts.[41] Until 1709 it was legally available only to printers and publishers, who regarded their copyrights as perpetual investments. The 1709 Statute of Anne first made it legal for anyone—even a writer—to own a copyright, but only for fourteen years (or twenty-eight if the author survived the first fourteen).[42] The century was three-quarters over before it was possible for a writer to make practical use of this opportunity or to speak seriously of copyright as if it were an *author's* right. What brought this idea into circulation was a dispute among the booksellers, who had fallen to squabbling over copyrights that had lapsed according to the Statute—but not according to what the

London faction now called their traditional common-law right of perpetual copy, which right they insisted remained unaffected by statutory restrictions.

The common-law copyright the booksellers talked about had a fabulous origin. In their struggles to preserve their traditional powers, the booksellers tried to show that common-law copyright was grounded in what they now spoke of as the author's natural right in his works. This maneuver required the conscientious confusion of copyright with authorial property.[43] Writers had little to say in the debates occupying the courts because the issues simply did not affect their interests.[44] That authors' rights were merely a stalking horse for booksellers' privileges was a fact apparent to authors[45] but not generally acknowledged until 1774, when the House of Lords affirmed the distinction between authorial rights and copyright and held that the term of copyright was indeed limited by the Statute of Anne.

By the 1830s, authorial interest in the reform of copyright was not regarded as anything extraordinary. It was no longer, as it had been in the 1770s, absurd to speak of an author's legal and financial interests in his writings; authors might now profit for as long as the copyrights to their works lasted. Booksellers, meanwhile, many of whom now specialized in works whose copyrights had lapsed, had a sometimes considerable stake in their expiration.[46] Clearly, the situation had changed greatly since 1774. What had not significantly changed were the terms of the debate. In appealing to the notion that a common-law copyright embodied the author's property in his works and in representing his cause as the "restoration" of a right of which the Statute of Anne and then the rulings of 1774 had unjustly deprived writers, Wordsworth revived a fiction that had been created and exploded more than half a century earlier. The arguments that had supported the eighteenth-century booksellers' defense of authorial rights became, ironically enough, the chief weapons against the booksellers' descendents in the authors' struggle for what writers regarded as their rightful property. In the battle over literary property, the writers ended up annexing the words of their antagonists.

There was poetic justice in this turning of the tables: how fitting that a writer should appropriate the arguments that had once been offered in his name for the purpose of exploiting him! Wordsworth and his allies seem to have been ignorant of the history of the arguments they used[47] and certainly never consciously intended either to disclaim poetic originality or to deny the intangibility of words. Nevertheless, the effect of their adoption of the topoi of the booksellers was just that. Agitating for their creative rights, they spoke rather as purveyors of books than as authors of texts. In putting themselves in the place of members of that industry for whose benefit the copyright laws had originally been instituted, manufacturers of material goods made of paper and boards, the petitioning writers seem to have confused the production of words with the production of their material embodiment.[48] Nor would most of them have resented the inference. For Wordsworth's allies, the enemy were those who urged them to aspire to things higher than money, admonishing them, in the words of an anonymous journalist, to "look up at the stars of Futurity, while the Present picks your pocket."[49] The idealization of the literary having often proved hazardous to their finances, these writers were inclined to represent themselves as working men and their writings as the products of their industry. It was their object to claim the same property in their writings as other men had in their farms and grocery stores.

It was an object with Wordsworth, too, but not the ultimate one. Although Wordsworth was as earnest as his contemporaries in his desire for financial security, literary property was not for him quite the same thing as agricultural property. Any man could own a plot of vegetables; only a writer could own a plot of words. Most kinds of property—even most kinds of intellectual property—were fundamentally anonymous: if one man failed to invent a particular mechanical device or cultivate a particular patch of land, someone else would invent or appropriate it instead. The ownership of a patent or a grocery was a matter of almost accidental circumstances. But, wrote Wordsworth, "who will suggest that if Shakespeare had not written *Lear,* or Richardson *Clarissa,* other poets or novelists would have invented them?"[50] Literary property, unlike any other kind of property, embodied an aspect of essential character; a function of individual identity, it was inalienable.

Although from any other writer such a piece of argument would be unsurprising, how strange it sounds coming from Wordsworth. Dramatic and novelistic plots may, perhaps, need to wait for their

Shakespeares and Richardsons to call them into being. But Wordsworth had long before proclaimed that the stuff of lyric poetry was common to us all, declared that the poet was only a man speaking to men in the language really used by men, and hinted that the primordial language of poetry had almost more to do with the dead, who have no voices with which to speak for themselves, than with the living, who found both property and identity upon their power to name. The works he is concerned with here bear little apparent resemblance to those nearly anonymous, partially unowned utterances he described in the Preface to *Lyrical Ballads* and in the "Essays upon Epitaphs."

There are other problems as well. Even as he argues for the naturalness and necessity of verbal property, Wordsworth gives us words whose doubtful provenance call their own validity into question. Wordsworth's logic is and is not his own. He reveals the passage quoted above to be a quotation from Talfourd, whose words he has borrowed for the occasion. But Talfourd did not own the words, either; as Wordsworth tells us, "I have had the honour of hearing them adopted from suggestions of my own."[51] Each man is a borrower from the other; the argument for the absoluteness of a writer's property in his writings is owned absolutely by neither one. And although Wordsworth clearly thinks of himself as its ultimate source, he is wrong. The argument's history has no authentic source at all; as we have seen, it has always had quotation marks around it. Wordsworth's presentation of his apparently reasonable argument unwittingly undercuts its own credibility; disclaiming possession, the words disclaim their connection with any earthly marketplace.

For Wordsworth, copyright is not just a market mechanism but a means of judgment in which life and death—eternal life, eternal death—are at stake. Like his contemporaries, Wordsworth saw copyright in terms of life insurance, something that might help protect a family's finances after the author's death. But his description of how this "posthumous remuneration" would work, developed in a letter he sent anonymously to the editor of the Kendal *Mercury,* uses a logic only ostensibly financial:

> A conscientious author, who had a family to maintain, and a prospect of descendants, would regard the additional labour bestowed upon any

> considerable work he might have in hand, in the light of an insurance of money upon his own life for the benefit of his issue; and he would be animated in his efforts accordingly, and would cheerfully undergo present privations for such future recompense.[52]

Realistically, immediate critical appreciation need not preclude continuing success. But Wordsworth, who was touchy about his early obscurity, preferred to think in terms of a Christian economics: you can have glory now on earth or you can have glory later in heaven, but you can't have both.

The context of the passage further complicates matters. Although life insurance returns a reward at the death of the one whose life is insured, Wordsworth says less about the dead writer than about the "dead letter," by which he means work out of print and unread. Books usurp the place of the poet's progeny as the beneficiaries of this "life insurance" and as the bearers of his name after his death. As he talks about it, copyright begins to sound like a policy a writer might take out on his book to ensure that it will continue to live, not in the uncertain afterlife of its readers' memories but in its natural physical body.[53]

If copyright has the power to overleap the problematic distinction between mortal materiality and immortal immateriality—perhaps even to stave off death itself—then by this measure of legal reform Wordsworth can be said to have realized, for his works if not for himself, an early wish. Commenting on the "Intimations" ode, he told Isabella Fenwick, "I used to brood over the stories of Enoch and Elijah, and almost to persuade myself that, whatever might become of others, I should be translated in something of the same way to heaven." The copyright reform measure he advocated would provide for worthy books a heaven on earth—or, at least, an immortality that required no sacrifice of either material being on the part of the book or material reward on the part of the author.[54]

In linking his mortal fate with that of his writings, Wordsworth was responding to an aspect of copyright that probably everyone felt. The law established a connection between the length of copyright and the length of life that gave a morbid aspect to the question of how long copyright ought to run. The twenty-eight-year term provided for by the Copyright Act of 1814 applied only if the author died; if he survived, the copyright survived with him and expired only when he did, regardless of the continuing popularity and sale of his works. There would undoubtedly have been discontent had the term been eighteen years or eighty instead of twenty-eight; the number of years may have mattered less than the fact that the term was finite. For many of the writers who addressed themselves to Parliament, to think of the end of copyright must have been to think of the end of life; the legal limitation of copyright must have come to signify death. When to leave one's body behind was also to leave one's books, fears for one's writings must have taken a tinge of dread from fears for one's abandoned corpse. Thomas Hood was hardly joking when in a petition judged too facetious to present before Parliament he said, "When your petitioner shall be dead and buried, he might with as much propriety and decency have his body snatched as his literary remains."[55]

Wordsworth seems to have taken more seriously than most the feeling behind Hood's little joke about the literary corpse he expected to leave behind. He seems to have thought of his literary corpus as a second self.[56] As Wordsworth saw it, the fate of his poems was involved with the fate of his person. Many of his works (he says in his petition to Parliament) are at least twenty-eight years old, and most will have reached that age within a few years; the copyrights on these writings (which he has retained) are thus largely "contingent upon the duration of his life." Unless he survives, within four years his major work, *The Excursion,* will have become public property.[57] At that time, not only will his family cease to profit from his writings but those writings will themselves be endangered. The dispossessed heirs can no more provide for the maintenance of the poet's writings than the writings can provide for the maintenance of the heirs. Bad, uncaring editors will "seize upon expiring copyrights," and with none of the author's "representatives" able "to secure copies correctly printed," the body of his literary works will suffer corruption; the corpus will decay.[58]

Wordsworth's strange talk of poetry as life insurance—or, perhaps more accurately, as what Jacques Derrida calls "life-after-life insurance"[59]—suggests he had a superstitious belief in the convention that poetry itself, if it was good enough, possessed, or perhaps conferred, immortality. Poetry serves as a symbolic guarantor of immortality because it is the poet's double; but precisely because it is his double, it signifies not only immortality but also death.

Perhaps it was an intuition of such a possibility that prevented Wordsworth from publishing his autobiography during his lifetime. At the beginning, of course, *The Prelude* had been meant as an appendage to *The Recluse*. But *The Recluse,* which alone of all his works would be "of sufficient importance to justify me in giving my own history to the world,"[60] proved unwritable, as Wordsworth seems to have known all along it would be. Although literary immortality could be the only excuse for offering to the reading public such an exercise in egotism as he suspected *The Prelude* to be, he seemed to think that giving proof of his personal mortality might serve almost as well. There is a curious ambiguity about Wordsworth's early indications of when the poem might be published. Thus on 6 March 1804 he wrote to De Quincey, "This Poem will not be published these many years, and never during my lifetime, till I have finished a larger and more important work to which it is tributary."[61] Six weeks later, in a letter to Richard Sharp, the ambiguity remains: "[*The Prelude*] will never be published (during my lifetime, I mean), till another work has been written and published."[62] Later he and his friends dropped all reference to *The Recluse* and admitted that it was his own death the poem waited for. "Had it been published as soon as it was finished," Wordsworth wrote Talfourd in 1839, "the copyright would long ago have expired in the case of my decease."[63] He kept the poem alive by postponing its birth to his death. *The Prelude* "is to appear when he ceases to be," wrote Isabella Fenwick in 1838,[64] as if its publication were to be a sort of ghostly afterimage of its author, the poem deriving its vitality from his dissolution.[65] As the poet's nephew noted in his *Memoirs,* "The Poem remained anonymous till his death."[66] To have published *The Prelude* during his lifetime would have been a breach not only of modesty but also of psychic security.

Surely Freud's observations are relevant here:

> the "double" was originally an insurance against the destruction of the ego, an "energetic denial of the power of death", as Rank says; and probably the "immortal" soul was the first "double" of the body. . . . But when this stage has been surmounted, the "double" reverses its

> aspect. From having been an assurance of immortality, it becomes the uncanny harbinger of death.[67]

Or, as Blanchot puts it, "The cadaver is its own image."[68] When we multiply what we fear to lose, our copies remind us of our fear. If Wordsworth's literary corpus is such a multiplication—its life signifying his own—it makes sense that he should be especially anxious about its preservation. Just as a book doubles the body, so copyright doubles the book. Insuring the insurer, it multiplies the chances of survival; at the same time, it multiplies the signs of death. By rendering immortality as materiality, copyright acts not only like a life insurance policy but also like a tombstone.

But how can a poet ensure the survival of his poem? One way might be, like the Arab in the *Prelude* fleeing the waters of a drowning world, to hide it in a place past harm: to prevent death by prevenient burial. Another way might be to en*grave* it somewhat differently in stone. Wordsworth gave serious consideration to this latter possibility in his "Essays upon Epitaphs," in which he develops another aspect of the concern with the material circumstances of writing that shows itself in his fondness for inscription[69] as well as in his devotion to copyright reform. In many respects a typical poetic form, the epitaph is distinguished by its inscription upon some durable material and its proximity to a dead body. Although epitaphs can, of course—like those that Wordsworth transcribes in the course of these essays—be copied onto paper and printed, the poet begins his discussion of the form with an analysis of the more usual physical circumstances of the verse:

> It needs scarcely be said, that an Epitaph presupposes a Monument, upon which it is to be engraven. Almost all Nations have wished that certain external signs should point out the places where their dead are interred. Among savage tribes unacquainted with letters this has mostly been done either by rude stones placed near the graves, or by mounds of earth raised over them. This custom proceeded obviously from a twofold desire; first, to guard the remains of the deceased from irreverent approach or from savage violation; and, secondly, to preserve their memory.[70]

Indeed, the epitaphic verse itself is something of an afterthought, an epi-epitaph. The stone is of primary importance, revealing the place of the hidden body, protecting it from being forgotten faster than it need be.

What is to be engraved in the granite ought to be as much like that granite—"matter of fact in its intensity"[71]—as possible. Although Wordsworth does not stipulate that the stone be hard, he does require that the language and the sentiments expressed upon it be worth eternal inscription. Ideally, the marmoreal changelessness of the survivors' affections and the conventional changelessness of their expression figure the durability of their objects. Despite Wordsworth's attempt to link language with immortality, however, his words turn against him to reveal their own deathliness. Although Wordsworth associates poetic language with the changeless universal human passions and the "permanent forms of nature," he associates it also with what will ultimately decay. In relation to thought, poetic language is "not what the garb is to the body but what the body is to the soul,"[72] vital yet somehow inessential, involved in the corruptible materiality it was meant to transcend.[73] To incarnate thought is to render it mortal; language is no safer than the body itself. Writing, devoted at its invention to the commemoration of death, falls victim to the very force its artificial memory seeks to deny.

One can only speculate that Wordsworth's insistence upon the stone (he repeats in italics the necessity of placing the "sepulchral monument . . . in *close connection with the bodily remains of the deceased*")[74] derives its force from his perception that the physical solidity of the stone must compensate for the corruptibility of both the body itself and language—and that the immortality of the soul is propped ultimately upon the everlastingness of the monument. Maintaining the physical integrity that the body cannot, the stone may be more important than its inscription; the fact of its permanence may be more important than what (in theory if not in fact) is rendered thus permanent. But even stone will wear away with time; the words ceasing to be legible, only the memorial intention will remain.[75] The stone then reveals itself as a sign of signs now lost, the mere material stump of narrative, comparable to the effaced coin of Coleridge's *Biographia*. Shedding inscription, materiality becomes metonymy.

The analogy between copyright and monumentality that Wordsworth had pointed up in his letter on the proposed memorial to

Burns continued to exert an implicit influence over his thinking. As that branch of the law that takes as its subject the relation between writing and materiality, copyright is the legal counterpart to epitaph, that form of writing most conscious of its relation to materiality and, as Paul Fry has pointed out, a prime "figure for poetry itself."[76] Copyright assumes not only the functions of epitaph but its ambiguities as well. It serves as a memorial to the work whose immortality it asserts. Attempting to compensate for the corruptibility of writing, it makes tacit admission of the frailty of words.

A younger Wordsworth would have recognized in the older Wordsworth's involvement in the politics of copyright reform a story well suited to his poetic purposes. Wordsworth the politician behaves very much like one of his own early characters: a man driven by what appear to be motives of economy into extravagant passion. The disproportion between emotion and object that characterizes Wordsworth's poetry, the sublime as well as the humble, also characterizes this episode of his life. Wordsworth exerts himself mightily in the pursuit of what might in worldly terms be thought not worth the effort. It is this apparently inappropriate investment in material accident that most firmly links the political writings with the poetic ones.

There is something disquieting in the literal-mindedness of Wordsworth's attempts to make copyright answer, in terms of pounds, years, and legal obligations, questions about how much a book is worth, how long it will endure, and who takes ultimate responsibility for it. Wordsworth could not have been happy with the particular answers copyright gave these questions—that, for example, the *Lyrical Ballads* were worth nothing, or that Scott was a more valuable writer than he was—but the very materialism of the terms of response given by copyright seems to have satisfied his need to find a substantial ground and a literal equivalent for his poetry. Copyright insists upon the substance promised by the words—in this case, the material ink and paper that produce material wealth for the poet. It legislates the translation of the verbal into the material: the reality of payment stands for the substantiality of the poet's words. Substituting incarnation for representation, the operations of copyright embody the material facts to which the words can only refer; copyright puts things in the place of the words that can only refer to things. Copyright thus reifies what the words only stand for; the materiality with which it is involved is made to figure truth. It proves that, in the deepest sense of the word, writing *matters*.

In the late political writings as in the early poems, Wordsworth's matter-of-factness may be seen as a development of the impulse that drove him in childhood to clutch at trees and walls—evidence, perhaps, rather of doubt than of belief in the ultimate reality of the material, which remains seductively, intractably, mute. The real object of Wordsworth's efforts to reform copyright was to secure a refuge from oblivion, a means to enable writing to transcend itself. Ostensibly concerned with worldly realities such as wages, inheritance, and merit, his arguments use financial realism as a cover for what looks like a primitive fear of annihilation. The attempt to extend the term of copyright was an attempt to back the ephemerality of words with the durability of substances—but also, paradoxically, to rescue the material from the death that the finite term figures. In seeking a way around the limitation on copyright the poet sought to pronounce from beyond the grave a controversion of his own mortality. The campaign to extend the term of copyright—Wordsworth wanted it extended not to forty-two or to sixty years but forever[77]—may have been, for him at least, an attempt to realize his intimations of immortality in legal form.

Conclusion

By the time of their falling out, Wordsworth and Coleridge had long realized their independence from one another. The genial coincidence that had brought them so fruitfully together, the shared fantasy of vocal influence, had revealed that its power derived as much from an abstract configuration of roles—self to second self, voice to usurping voice—as from the particular characters of the poets who happened to take up those roles within it. The structure of appropriation and possession, the idea of collaboration, remained after its temporary occupants had abandoned one another.

The double nature of this structure of doubling, at once particular and generic, was responsible in part for the paradoxes of the *Lyrical Ballads,* which I have read as interpretations, variously defensive and eager, of the configuration that they generated and that generated them. The congruence between the vital particulars and the generic fantasy was not perfect, however, and their divergence revealed implications both exhilarating and terrifying. If the second self who, receiving one's voice, returns it, still one's own and yet one's own no longer—if that second self is not Coleridge (for Wordsworth) or Wordsworth (for Coleridge), then who or what is it?

The ideally convenient and reassuring Wordsworthian answer, of course, might be that it is oneself. If one can manage to convince oneself that the voice in one's ear is one's own, troublesome obligations are much simplified. And traditionally literary history cooperates to a surprising extent with the poet's wish to owe his generative powers to himself alone, erasing the names of his literary creditors. But if literary propriety founds itself upon what is rendered common or anonymous, it keeps the taint of what, despite its appropriation, remains common or anonymous still. In spite of Wordsworth's gestures of appropriation in the *Lyrical Ballads,* he cannot make that ground securely enough his own. He can exclude Coleridge's voice, suppress Coleridge's name, but he cannot altogether repress an uneasy awareness of the radical anonymity in himself that Coleridge has come to represent to him. Nor is his clutching either at matters of fact or at the facts of materiality sufficient to reassure him of the wholeness and integrity of his imagination.

Coleridge, like Wordsworth, makes attempts to cast the strange out of his work and (through his criticism) out of Wordsworth's. But his attempts are sabotaged by his own ambivalence or even hopelessness toward the project; there could be no casting out of something that he seemed to sense was intrinsic to the project of writing. In spite of his evident desire to be persuaded by his own arguments about the ideal propriety of imaginative poetry, he is troubled by evidence of an irreducible impropriety not only in Wordsworth's most deeply imaginative poems but also in his own. I believe that Coleridge saw steadily though unwillingly what Wordsworth saw by glimpses only—that because the imagination is itself uncanny, to oust strangeness from writing is to undo writing itself. It proved, in Coleridge's case, a debilitating rather than a liberating perception. Although intellectually right, perhaps, it was poetically wrong: the imagination will not readily answer a summons issued from such a premise.

It was for the treatment of just this problem that the muse was invented. Unfortunately, our poets came too late to call upon her. But they might profitably have observed the example of another poet who turned to his advantage the requirements of a vocal power that, demanding proper invocation, eluded those who succumbed to the temptation of the proper name.

> Descend from Heav'n *Urania,* by that name
> If rightly thou art call'd, whose Voice divine
> Following, above th' *Olympian* Hill I soar,
> Above the flight of *Pegasean* wing.
> The meaning, not the Name I call:
>
> [*Paradise Lost,* VII, 1–5]

It had always been important in an invocation to get the name of the muse just right, and so it is for Milton. Yet he lets an error—if that is what it is—stand. It is important in this invocation, which is as much an unnaming as a naming, to name aright by naming wrong and then by refusing to name at all. To call upon the imagination is to call upon something that cannot be named without error. The turning of recognition upon itself as misrecognition, the identification of misidentification, brings to presence what the poet cannot otherwise summon. For Milton—as, I have been arguing, for Wordsworth and Coleridge—it is important, rather than perhaps merely inevitable, to substitute for the name a blank, a pseudonym, an evasion, a stutter, a divagation, an excuse about trouble with names or bad eyesight or albatrosses.

I would offer the invocation as a pattern for the workings of the Romantic imagination, whose characteristic manifestation I am not the first to locate in misrecognition and misnaming.[1] The imagination that has been the subject of this book is the relationship between a poet and what he takes to be his second or other self, a relationship of mistake: the mistaking of one's own voice for another's, or another's for one's own. It is an uncomfortable phenomenon, unsettling properties, proprieties, and identities. Although it manifests itself as an othering of voice, a writer can inhabit the structure of imagination in solitude, language or self-consciousness or even inanimate things supplying the absence of a separate human other. For as Coleridge suggested, imagination is in part a consequence of the nature of language itself and that psychic division that is fundamental to consciousness. Every identity, being a self-representation, participates in the condition of imaginative language; Coleridge had an intuition of this a century before Freud, a century and a half before Lacan. Occupied by ourselves, beings unknown to us, how can we help but allow strange voices to speak through us? Confronting the failure of language to coincide with what it represents and the failure of consciousness to coincide with identity, how can we prevent words from stealing our meanings? The relationship between Coleridge and Wordsworth offers itself as a social analogue or objective correlative to the configuration of this imagination, which reveals itself to be what the title page of the first *Lyrical Ballads* suggested: the emergence of voice from anonymity.

Notes

Preface

1. Stephen Parrish, *The Art of the Lyrical Ballads* (Cambridge: Harvard University Press, 1973); Thomas McFarland, *Romanticism and the Forms of Ruin: Wordsworth, Coleridge, and Modalities of Fragmentation* (Princeton: Princeton University Press, 1981); Lucy Newlyn, *Coleridge, Wordsworth, and the Language of Allusion* (Oxford: Oxford University Press, 1986); Paul Magnuson, *Coleridge and Wordsworth: A Lyrical Dialogue* (Princeton: Princeton University Press, 1988).

2. *Coleridge and Wordsworth: A Lyrical Dialogue,* p. 26.

3. Particularly *The Anxiety of Influence: A Theory of Poetry* (New York: Oxford University Press, 1973).

4. "Intentional Structure" and "Autobiography As De-Facement" appear in *The Rhetoric of Romanticism* (New York: Columbia University Press, 1984); "The Rhetoric of Temporality" can be found in *Blindness and Insight: Essays in the Rhetoric of Contemporary Criticism* (1971; rpt. Minneapolis: University of Minnesota Press, 1983).

5. In *The Unremarkable Wordsworth* (Minneapolis: University of Minnesota Press, 1987), see especially "A Touching Compulsion," "Inscriptions and Romantic Nature Poetry," and "The Unremarkable Wordsworth"; in *Beyond Formalism: Literary Essays 1958–1970* (New Haven: Yale University Press, 1970), see "Romanticism and Anti-Self-Consciousness" and "Romantic Poetry and the Genius Loci." Hartman's analysis of apocalypse and akedah comes in *Wordworth's Poetry, 1787–1814* (1964; rpt. New Haven: Yale University Press, 1977).

6. Thomas Weiskel, *The Romantic Sublime: Studies in the Structure and Psychology of Transcendence* (Baltimore: The Johns Hopkins University Press, 1976); Frances Ferguson, *Wordsworth: Language as Counter-Spirit* (New Haven: Yale University Press, 1977); Cynthia Chase, "The Accidents of Disfiguration: Limits to Literal and Figurative Reading of Wordsworth's 'Books,'" in *Decomposing Figures: Rhetorical Readings in the Romantic Tradition* (Baltimore: The Johns Hopkins University Press, 1986). See also J. Douglas Kneale, *Monumental Writing: Aspects of Rhetoric in Wordsworth's Poetry* (Lincoln: University of Nebraska Press, 1988).

7. *Coleridge's Blessed Machine of Language* (Ithaca: Cornell University Press, 1981).

8. Jerome McGann, *The Romantic Ideology* (Chicago: University of Chicago Press, 1983); David Simpson, *Wordsworth and the Figurings of the Real* (London: Macmillan, 1982); Marjorie Levinson, *Wordsworth's Great Period Poems: Four Essays* (Cambridge: Cambridge University Press, 1986); Alan Liu, *Wordsworth: The Sense of History* (Stanford: Stanford University Press, 1989). James A. W. Heffernan's *The Re-Creation of Landscape* (Hanover: University Press of New England, 1984), working from rather different premises, treats many of the same problems Liu does.

9. Marc Shell, *The Economy of Literature* (Baltimore: The Johns Hopkins University Press, 1978), and *Money, Language, and Thought: Literary and Philosophic Economies from the Medieval to the Modern Era* (Berkeley: University of California Press, 1982); Kurt Heinzelman, *The Economics of the Imagination* (Amherst: The University of Massachusetts Press, 1980).

Chapter 1: The Propriety of the *Lyrical Ballads*

1. Coleridge was to write about "persons and characters supernatural, or at least romantic; yet so as to transfer from our inward nature a human interest and a semblance of truth sufficient to procure for these shadows of imagination that willing suspension of disbelief for the moment, which constitutes poetic faith. Mr. Wordsworth, on the other hand, was to propose to himself as his object, to give the charm of novelty to things of every day, and to excite a feeling analogous to the supernatural, by awakening the mind's attention from the lethargy of custom, and directing it to the loveliness and the wonders of the world before us" (Samuel Taylor Coleridge, *Biographia Literaria, Or Biographical Sketches of My Literary Life and Opinions,* edited by James Engell and Walter Jackson Bate, Bollingen Series 75 [Princeton: Princeton University Press, 1983], II, 6–7. Hereafter cited as *BL*).

2. Stephen Parrish writes, "It should be clear to any reader of *The Ancient Mariner* that what principally separates Coleridge from Wordsworth is not his theory of diction, or metre, or the management of narrative, but the allegorical bent of his imagination" ("'Leaping and Lingering': Coleridge's lyrical ballads," in Richard Gravil, Lucy Newlyn, and Nicholas Roe, eds., *Coleridge's Imagination: Essays in Memory of Pete Laver* [Cambridge: Cambridge University Press, 1985], p. 116).

3. For Timothy Bahti writing of the *Prelude,* not just Wordsworth's writing but Wordsworth's very self was founded on appropriation of objects rendered as improper or figured. See "Wordsworth's Rhetorical Theft," in Arden Reed, ed., *Romanticism and Language* (Ithaca: Cornell University Press, 1984), pp. 86–124.

4. Coleridge welcomes the uncanny—the intrusion of something which he and his readers regard as truly alien and which represents less a source of authority than a threat to autonomy. Wordsworth shuns it; the voice he achieves gives evidence of his avoidance of something he plainly holds to be threatening. And yet it is Wordsworth's poetry that more closely approximates the workings of the

uncanny, which, writes Freud, represents "nothing new or alien, but something which is familiar and old-established in the mind and which has become alienated from it only through the process of repression"; it is "that class of the frightening which leads back to what is known of old and long familiar" ("The Uncanny," *The Standard Edition of the Complete Psychological Works of Sigmund Freud,* edited and translated by James Strachey [London: Hogarth Press, 1955], vol. 17, pp. 241, 220). In Wordsworth's writings the ordinary behaves as if it were extraordinary. His uncanny is a resurfacing of part of his own consciousness, a recovery of something lost or estranged or denied, a reappropriation or renewed self-possession. The ordinariness he creates is the effect of the un-uncanny.

5. As a result of a disparity in sales—the new second volume of the 1800 edition sold many more copies than the first volume—most contemporary readers would have found the poems of 1800 more familiar than those of 1798. Taken thus out of context, however, the second volume's gestures of retraction, repression, and reappropriation must have been either invisible or incomprehensible. Mary Moorman notes the imbalance in the sales figures in *William Wordsworth: A Biography. The Early Years, 1770–1803* (Oxford: Oxford University Press, 1957), p. 501.

6. In the Middle Ages, when no great value was placed on literary originality, it might reasonably be a matter of indifference whether a work was attributed or not. That minority of writers who chose anonymity did so in accordance with local traditions of decorum, as a defense against *vanitas terrestris,* or out of that proud humility that insists that a particular book is not good enough to sign. Anonymity sometimes took the form of pseudonymity, but medieval pseudonyms tended to function more as nicknames than as disguises. (See Ernst Robert Curtius, *European Literature and the Latin Middle Ages,* translated by Willard R. Trask [Princeton: Princeton University Press, 1953], pp. 515–18; see also Archer Taylor and Frederick J. Mosher, *The Bibliographical History of Anonyma and Pseudonyma* [Chicago: University of Chicago Press, 1951], pp. 80–82.) Attitudes towards the moral and cultural significance of anonymity had shifted by the time of the Renaissance, but practices had not; publication was considered undignified, and aristocrats often preferred either to circulate private copies of their writings or to publish them anonymously or pseudonymously. Speculating on the motives behind Renaissance pseudonymity, one scholar suggests, "The usual incentive was the customary etiquette of publishing in a learned language. Other reasons were a genuine or pretended desire to conceal identity, a delight in mystification, or sheer high spirits" (Franklin B. Williams, Jr., "Renaissance Names in Masquerade," *PMLA* 64 [1954], 314). Some pseudonyms were teasing, but others were meant to be puzzled out. Among the forms pseudonyms could take, Williams mentions translations and transliterations into languages ancient and modern, "facetious renderings" into Latin, "reversed spellings," "camouflage jumbles," "motto anagrams," and other, even wilder, forms of contorted verbal self-creation.

7. John O. Hayden, ed., *Romantic Bards and British Reviewers: A Selected Edition of the Contemporary Reviews of the Works of Wordsworth, Coleridge, Byron, Keats and Shelley* (Lincoln: University of Nebraska Press, 1971), p. xv.

8. William Courtney, reviewing the history of this odd phenomenon but not attempting to explain it, mentions hundreds of instances. Among the more notable

anonymities are Pope (*An Essay on Criticism, An Essay on Man*), Young (*Night-thoughts*), Akenside (*The Pleasures of Imagination*), Johnson (*London*), Gray ("Ode on a Distant Prospect of Eton College," "Elegy Written in a Country Churchyard"), Cowper (*John Gilpin*), Beattie (*The Minstrel*), Darwin (*Loves of the Plants*), Crabbe (*Inebriety, The Candidate, The Library*), Boswell (*Ode to Tragedy*—dedicated to "James Boswell, Esquire"), Samuel Rogers (*The Pleasures of Memory*—"as by the author of *An Ode to Superstition with some other Poems*"—also *Italy* and *Jacqueline*), Byron (*Don Juan* and *Lara*), Blake (Volume 1 of *Poetical Sketches*—"by W. B."), Campbell (*Poems*), Charles Lamb (*Beauty and the Beast, or a Rough Outside with Gentle Heart,* and *Satan in Search of a Wife*), Shelley ("The Necessity of Atheism," *Refutation of Deism, a Dialogue,* and *Oedipus Tyrannus, or Swellfoot the Tyrant*). See William Prideaux Courtney, *The Secrets of Our National Literature: Chapters in the History of Anonymous and Pseudonymous Writings of Our Countrymen* (London: Archibald Constable & Co. Limited, 1908).

9. Thus Wordsworth in letter #84, 6 March 1798, in *The Letters of William and Dorothy Wordsworth: The Early Years* (1787–1805), edited by Ernest De Selincourt, revised by Chester L. Shaver (Oxford: Clarendon Press, 1967), p. 211. Hereafter this work will be cited as *EY*.

10. So Coleridge to Robert Southey in letter #294, 30 September 1799, in *Collected Letters of Samuel Taylor Coleridge,* edited by Earl Leslie Griggs (Oxford: Clarendon Press, 1956), I, p. 535. Hereafter cited as *STCL*.

11. He may have had Robert Southey in mind here, who, having learned through his friend Cottle that Coleridge (then his enemy) and Wordsworth were about to publish their joint volume, obtained an advance copy and prepared a hostile review of it.

12. Letter #250, 28 May 1798, in *STCL,* I, p. 412.

13. Ibid. Emile Legouis believes that political considerations figured largely in Coleridge's and Wordsworth's decision against putting their names on the title page. See "Some Remarks on the Composition of the *Lyrical Ballads* of 1798," in Earl Leslie Griggs, ed., *Wordsworth and Coleridge: Studies in Honor of George McLean Harper* (Princeton: Princeton University Press, 1939), p. 9. Robert Mayo, in "The Contemporaneity of the *Lyrical Ballads*," *PMLA* 69 (1954), 490, 495–506, has shown that the plights of the poor, the abandoned, the imprisoned, and the mad were subjects common in contemporary magazine verse and were treated less as political than as sentimental topics.

14. Two years later we find him complaining to Southey about the difficulty he is having persuading Longman to keep the title page clear of names: "I find resistance which I did not expect to the *anonymousness* of the Publication—Longman seems confident, that a work on such a Subject without a name would not do.—Translations and perhaps Satires, are, he says, the only works that Booksellers now venture on, *without a name*" (Letter #317, 12 February 1800, in *STCL,* I, p. 570.) It is clear enough why translations would be published without the name of the translator, who serves merely as the medium for another man's voice. In this letter Coleridge goes on to propose that Southey join him in writing "a novel, to be published in the name of one of us—or *two,* if that were all—and then christen 'em by lots,"—displaying his characteristic indifference to distinctions

between "mine" and "thine," or perhaps just willing to efface himself behind another in a gesture of obeisance.

15. H. W. Garrod, *The Profession of Poetry and Other Lectures* (Oxford: Oxford University Press, 1929), p. 66.

16. Letter #126, 27 December, 1799, in *EY,* p. 281. As Wordsworth was never one to offer unnecessary encouragement to his friends, we may believe that he wrote this in a spirit of open-eyed pragmatism.

17. Letter #140, to Jane Marshall, 10 or 12 September 1800, in *EY,* p. 297.

18. Though her discussion has nothing explicitly to do with the *Lyrical Ballads,* Peggy Kamuf's Derridean treatment of the questions a signature poses sheds a valuable sidelight on some of the problems discussed here. See *Signature Pieces: On the Institution of Authorship* (Ithaca: Cornell University Press, 1988).

19. *The Poetical Works of William Wordworth,* edited by Ernest De Selincourt (1944; rpt. Oxford: Clarendon Press, 1952), II, 385. Hereafter this work will be cited as *WPW.*

20. Letter #356, 9 October 1800, in *STCL,* I, p. 631. Coleridge then goes on to say, "We mean to publish the Christabel therefore with a long Blank Verse Poem of Wordsworth's entitled the Pedlar—", suggesting that he did not see, or did not care to show that he saw, the rejection of his poem as the end of their joint publishing, which it was. It was also the end of hopes for the poem's ever becoming anything more than an extraordinary fragment. Whether Coleridge really had written 1300 lines by this time or whether he was exaggerating we cannot know; but the poem was never completed, and fewer than 700 lines are known to have survived.

21. *STCL,* I, p. 643, note #2.

22. *WPW,* II, p. 392.

23. See *The Notebooks of Samuel Taylor Coleridge,* ed. Kathleen Coburn, Bollingen Series 50, Vol. I (Princeton: Princeton University Press, 1973), #1336. Hereafter cited as *STCN.* How recent the desynonymization must have been one can judge by a glance at Samuel Johnson's *Dictionary.* The first definition of "propriety" he gives is "peculiarity of possession; exclusive right." Jerome Christensen remarks on the desynonymization and its implications for the relationship between the two poets later in their careers in *Coleridge's Blessed Machine of Language* (Ithaca: Cornell University Press, 1981), pp. 138–41.

24. John Hughes, "Of Style," in Willard Higley Durham, ed., *Critical Essays of the Eighteenth Century, 1700–1725* (1915; rpt. New York: Russell & Russell, 1961), p. 80.

25. *The Works of Aristotle,* translated by W. D. Ross, Vol. XI (Oxford: Oxford University Press, 1959), "Rhetorica," 1408 a. The Greek text I use is from Aristotle, *The "Art" of Rhetoric,* ed. John Henry Freese, the Loeb Classical Library (Cambridge: Harvard University Press, 1959).

26. See Klaus Dockhorn, "Wordsworth und die rhetorische Tradition in England," *Nachrichten von der Akademie der Wissenschaften in Gottingen, Philologisch-Historische Klasse,* 11 (1944), 255–92.

27. Many rhetoricians recognized, however, that it was the nature of language to generate tropes and figures; there being too few proper names for all the objects

and concepts requiring names, some are required to share their names with others. These "deviation[s] from what may be reckoned the most simple form[s] of speech," as Hugh Blair put it, are "both the most natural, and the most common method of uttering our sentiments. . . . [T]hey are to be accounted part of that language which nature dictates to men" (Hugh Blair, *Lectures on Rhetoric and Belles Lettres* [1783], in James L. Golden and Edward P. J. Corbett, eds., *The Rhetoric of Blair, Campbell, and Whately* [New York: Holt, Rinehart and Winston, 1968], pp. 76, 74). See also Derrida's critique of proper naming in "White Mythology: Metaphor in the Text of Philosophy," in *Margins of Philosophy,* translated by Alan Bass (Chicago: University of Chicago Press, 1982), esp. pp. 241–44.

28. George Puttenham, *The Arte of English Poesie* (1589), edited by Edward Arber, English Reprints, Vol. IV (1869; rpt. New York: AMS Press, 1966), p. 166.

29. Puttenham, p. 197.

30. Dramatic propriety was not the only reason a writer might choose to violate decorum. If propriety means "calling things by their right names," Quintilian points out, it "is consequently sometimes to be avoided, for our language must not be obscene, unseemly, or mean" (*The Institutio Oratoria,* translated by H. E. Butler [Cambridge: Harvard University Press, 1953], III, p. 197).

31. Aristotle, "Rhetorica," 1408 b.

32. This is the paradox over which Wordsworth and Coleridge would eventually split. The issue, which we shall discuss later, was not to what extent a poet's voice was his own but rather how far his language might depart from that of common poetic discourse, how far he might go toward adopting the language of the characters he portrayed, one of whom might himself be a poet.

33. John Locke, *An Essay Concerning Human Understanding,* edited by Peter H. Nidditch (1975; rpt. Oxford: Oxford University Press, 1979), p. 479.

34. Adam Smith, *The Theory of Moral Sentiments,* ed. D. D. Raphael and A. L. Macfie (1976; rpt. Indianapolis: Liberty Classics, 1982), particularly Part I, "Of the Propriety of Action." For a particularly good reading of Smith's discussion of sympathy and identification, see David Marshall, *The Figure of Theater: Shaftesbury, Defoe, Adam Smith, and George Eliot* (New York: Columbia University Press, 1986), pp. 167–93.

35. Quintilian, p. 197.

36. Blair, p. 68.

37. Renato Barilli, *Rhetoric,* translated by Giuliana Menozzi, Theory and History of Literature, vol. 63 (Minneapolis: University of Minnesota Press, 1989), p. 3.

38. James Turner, *The Politics of Landscape: Rural Scenery and Society in English Poetry 1630–1660* (Oxford: Basil Blackwell, 1979), pp. 5–6.

39. As C. B. Macpherson observes, from at least the seventeenth century onward the individual is conceived "as essentially the proprietor of his own person or capacities," "as an owner of himself." Identity is self-possession. See *The Political Theory of Possessive Individualism: Hobbes to Locke* (Oxford: Oxford University Press, 1962), p. 3.

40. Puttenham, p. 22.

41. Ibid., pp. 52, 53.

42. Wordsworth, for example, offered Francis Wrangham three sonnets, apparently to be published, if Wrangham so chose, under his own name. Letter #201, late January or early February, 1805, in *EY,* pp. 436–38.

43. Margaret Homans discusses the relationship between Dorothy's respectful refusal to appropriate nature and her brother's appropriation both of nature and of Dorothy's writings. See *Women Writers and Poetic Identity: Dorothy Wordsworth, Emily Brontë, and Emily Dickinson* (Princeton: Princeton University Press, 1980), pp. 41–103. Paul Magnuson points out passages that Coleridge got from Dorothy in *Coleridge and Wordsworth: A Lyrical Dialogue* (Princeton: Princeton University Press, 1988), pp. 120n., 157. Magnuson's study, a fine reading of the fragmented contents of what he calls the "Coleridge-Wordsworth canon" in terms of "a poetic dialogue or poetic dialectic," is the latest and fullest discussion of the relations between the two poets.

44. Stephen Maxfield Parrish, *The Art of the Lyrical Ballads* (Cambridge: Harvard University Press, 1973), p. 210. The context for this remark is a discussion of whose poem "'Tis said, that some have died for love" really is.

45. Magnuson, *Coleridge and Wordsworth,* p. 194.

46. In addition to Parrish and Magnuson, see Mary Jacobus, *Tradition and Experiment in Wordsworth's 'Lyrical Ballads' (1798)* (Oxford: Oxford University Press, 1976), pp. 59–82 and passim., and Thomas McFarland, *Romanticism and the Forms of Ruin: Wordsworth, Coleridge, and Modalities of Fragmentation* (Princeton: Princeton University Press, 1981).

47. Actually Wordsworth rarely wrote anything down himself; he usually had a sister, his wife, or a friend write for him.

48. Entry of 13 March 1802, in *Journals of Dorothy Wordsworth,* edited by E. De Selincourt (London: Macmillan, 1959), I, p. 123.

49. Mary Jacobus, *Tradition and Experiment in Wordsworth's Lyrical Ballads,* p. 6.

50. See Magnuson, *Coleridge and Wordsworth,* esp. pp. 170–71.

51. Letter #194, Wordsworth to Sir Walter Scott, 16 October 1803, in *EY,* p. 413.

52. Letter #208, Wordsworth to Thomas de Quincey, 6 March 1804, in *EY,* p. 455. It is ironic that Wordsworth should have complained of one plagiarist to another and have employed another still, Coleridge, in his cause.

53. Letter #282, Dorothy Wordsworth to Lady Beaumont, 27 October 1805, in *EY,* p. 633.

54. He heard the rumors not from the Wordsworths but from Lady Beaumont. Soon not just Lady Beaumont but many of his friends and even strangers were telling him that he had been wronged. For some time Coleridge replied simply that it was impossible. He did not get around to reading Scott's poem until late in 1807, and when he did what disturbed him was not the idea that Scott might have stolen anything from him, but that others would now suspect him either of having imitated Scott or of holding a grudge against the other poet. This behavior may bespeak either a remarkably anxiety-free or forgiving attitude on Coleridge's or perhaps a

bad conscience about his own plagiarisms. See letter #664, to Wordsworth, 21 May 1808, in *STCL,* III, 111, and letter #1230, to Thomas Allsop, 10 April 1820, in *STCL,* V, p. 40.

55. Letter #845, ca. 15–21 December 1811, in *STCL,* III, p. 355.

56. Letter #845, in *STCL,* III, p. 357. According to Coleridge, true plagiarism, as distinct from honorable participation in the literary tradition, is a guilty thing that seeks to hide itself. Yet Coleridge's own plagiarisms in the *Biographia Literaria* do not attempt to conceal themselves by any means other than their furtive forthrightness.

57. Letter #845 in *STCL,* III, p. 361. This is Coleridge at his most Coleridgean, but the middle of the letter is taken up with an indirect defense of himself against a suspicion voiced at his lecture on *Romeo and Juliet* that he had plagiarized from A. W. Schlegel. Under the circumstances, Coleridge's high-minded generosity appears somewhat suspicious.

58. Sir Joshua Reynolds, *Discourses on Art,* edited by Robert R. Wark (San Marino, CA: The Huntington Library, 1959), Discourse VI, p. 107.

59. *The Prose Works of William Wordsworth,* edited by W. J. B. Owen and Jane Worthington Smyser (Oxford: Oxford University Press, 1974), I, pp. 128, 130. Hereafter cited as *Prose Works.*

60. If Wordsworth regarded Coleridge as a purveyor of improprieties, Coleridge regarded Wordsworth the same way. Years afterward, Coleridge would remark on instances of stylistic "incongruity," even "ventriloquism," in Wordsworth's poems, passages in which the voice seems not to belong to its apparent speaker but to come from elsewhere. See Chapter 7 for a fuller discussion of this problem.

61. Parker discusses the play's "ventriloquistic network" and its reproduction in the relations between the two poets in "'Oh Could You Hear His Voice!': Wordsworth, Coleridge, and Ventriloquism," in Arden Reed, ed. *Romanticism and Language* (Ithaca: Cornell University Press, 1984), pp. 125–43.

62. Ibid., p. 126.

63. Charles J. Rzepka's remarks on Wordsworth's need for acknowledgment, for external confirmation of his own reality, illuminate the poet's desire to reproduce his poetic self in his audience. Fearing "the possibility that his intentions may be 'misread,' he attempts to reeducate his 'reader,' the person he confronts or before whom he enacts his sense of himself. He will preempt the Other's responses to his presence, appropriate the Other in his own scenario, or characterize the Other in such a way as to reassure himself that he is recognized properly." See *The Self as Mind: Vision and Identity in Wordsworth, Coleridge, and Keats* (Cambridge: Harvard University Press, 1986), pp. 31–99. The passage I quote is from p. 71.

64. Turning Coleridge's strictures on Wordsworth against their author, Tilottama Rajan calls the conversation poems "monologues rather than conversations, attempts to create a self-confirming poetry through 'a species of ventriloquism, where two are represented as talking, while in truth one man only speaks'" (*Dark Interpreter: The Discourse of Romanticism* [Ithaca: Cornell University Press, 1980], p. 212). Charles Rzepka argues that "as semidramatic monologues apparently addressed *to* others, they reveal an impulse to enter the very world the poet himself

has uttered, to reembody the self as a *recognized* sharer of perceptions that, as a mind removed and ruminating, it has just transformed" (*Self as Mind,* p. 114).

65. *The Rhetoric of Romanticism,* (New York: Columbia University Press, 1984) pp. 75–76.

66. The text I am using here is from *The Poetical Works of Samuel Taylor Coleridge,* edited by Ernest Hartley Coleridge, 2 vols. (Oxford: The Clarendon Press, 1912), hereafter cited as *CPW.*

67. Tilottama Rajan, who calls this second self an "alter ego" and describes its presence in the poems a "self-duplication," argues that Coleridge's own self-exclusions are self-protective and sentimental. See *Dark Interpreter,* pp. 215, 223, 228–31. Jean-Pierre Mileur develops the implications of Rajan's critique into an analysis of Coleridgean generosity and gift-giving. See his "Deconstruction as Imagination and Method" in Christine Gallant, ed., *Coleridge's Theory of Imagination Today,* Georgia State Literary Studies, No. 4 (New York: AMS Press, 1989), esp. pp. 76 and 77. Walter Jackson Bate notes the significance of the blessings Coleridge utters in these poems, reminding us of the older sense of the word: "a surrender, a giving, which assumes sacrifice (the word 'blessing' is connected with 'blood'—with 'bleeding')." See *Coleridge* (1968; rpt. Cambridge: Harvard University Press, 1987), p. 50.

68. Wordsworth classed the "Intimations" ode with his "Epitaphs and Elegiac Pieces."

69. Letter #172, 14 June 1802, in *EY,* p. 367.

70. John Jones, *The Egotistical Sublime: A History of Wordsworth's Imagination* (London: Chatto & Windus, 1954), p. 15.

71. F. W. Bateson, *Wordsworth: A Re-Interpretation,* 2nd ed. (London: Longman's, 1956), p. 4.

72. *Wordsworth and the Poetry of Encounter* (Urbana: University of Illinois Press, 1971), pp. 35–36.

73. Emile Legouis, *The Early Life of William Wordsworth, 1770–1798: A Study of "The Prelude,"* translated by J. W. Matthews (1897; New York: E. P. Dutton & Co., 1952), pp. 445–46.

74. William Hazlitt, *The Spirit of the Age; or, Contemporary Portraits* (Paris: A. and W. Galignani, 1825), p. 105. M. H. Abrams too remarks that Wordsworth's mean style, his attempt to bring together the lowest and the highest, the base and the sublime, has its roots in the Bible, especially the New Testament. See his "English Romanticism: The Spirit of the Age," in Northrop Frye, ed., *Romanticism Reconsidered: Selected Papers from the English Institute* (New York: Columbia University Press, 1963), pp. 65–66.

75. Hazlitt, p. 104.

76. Freud, "The Uncanny," p. 244.

77. Ibid.

78. Lawrence Kramer interprets the demonic in Wordsworth this way: "The feeling analogous to the supernatural represents the mind's power to defamiliarize and reperceive objects so fully that the borders between mind and nature, nature and supernatural, begin to blur." See "That Other Will: The Daemonic in Coleridge and Wordsworth," *Philological Quarterly* 58 (1979), 312.

79. The uncanniness of Wordsworth's matter-of-factness is thus linked with the structure of the Wordsworthian sublime as Thomas Weiskel analyzes it. See *The Romantic Sublime: Studies in the Structure and Psychology of Transcendence* (Baltimore: The Johns Hopkins University Press, 1976), esp. pp. 174–85.

80. The relevance of the term *uncanny* to Coleridge's poetry is clear enough; whatever produces uncertainty about whether something is real or unreal, alive or dead, may produce an uncanny effect, and Coleridge's greatest poems are filled with uncanny figures and events. It may seem strange, however, to apply the word to Wordsworth's writing, which, although it includes an occasional ghost, is characterized by its devotion to the unremarkable, the matter-of-fact, the familiar. Nevertheless, Wordsworth's very rejection of the sensational and the supernatural—indeed, his rejection of much of his literary inheritance—leads him back into the domain of the uncanny.

It is in the preface of 1800 that Wordsworth writes that his attempt always to look steadily at his subject and employ language that faithfully represents the importance of his ideas "has necessarily cut me off from a large portion of phrases and figures of speech which from father to son have long been regarded as the common inheritance of Poets" (*WPW*, II, p. 390).

81. Wallace Jackson, *The Probable and the Marvelous: Blake, Wordsworth, and the Eighteenth-Century Critical Tradition* (Athens: The University of Georgia Press, 1978), pp. 123–24. Jackson argues that Wordsworth and the other Romantics inherited from Collins, Gray, and the Wartons a literary sublime that had become a system of mechanical abstractions and personifications and that they subordinated it to a concern with the ordinary surface of life. The agents of the sublime were no longer Fear and Melancholy but familiar domestic or rural objects.

Chapter 2: Voice and Ventriloquy in *The Rime of the Ancient Mariner*

1. "The difficulty of the poem," writes Frances Ferguson, "is that the possibility of learning from the Mariner's experience depends upon sorting that experience into a more linear and complete pattern than the poem ever agrees to do. For the poem seems almost as thorough a work of backwardness—or hysteron proteron—as we have." See "Coleridge and the Deluded Reader: 'The Rime of the Ancient Mariner,'" *Georgia Review* 31 (1977), 617–35.

2. Wordsworth's remarks can be found in *Lyrical Ballads: The text of the 1798 edition with the additional 1800 poems and the Prefaces,* edited by R. L. Brett and A. R. Jones (London: Methuen, 1963), p. 277. It was the kind of accusation frequently heard at the time. Coleridge himself charged Goethe in just such a fashion. Remarking to Crabb Robinson that Mephistopheles had no character and that "the character of Faust is not *motivirt [sic],*" Coleridge said he wanted to write a new *Faust.* See *The Diary, Reminiscences, and Correspondence of Henry Crabb Robinson,* edited by Thomas Sadler (New York: Hurd and Houghton, 1877), pp. 254–55. The date of the entry is 20 August 1812.

3. If he can be said to have a self, that is; his identity is almost entirely absorbed into its representations. For a discussion of the relationship between the presence

and the representation of self in this poem, see Geoffrey Hartman, "Christopher Smart's *Magnificat:* Toward a Theory of Representation," in *The Fate of Reading and Other Essays* (Chicago: University of Chicago Press, 1975), pp. 74–76.

4. In the best reading of this kind, Lawrence Kramer discusses the poem in terms of demonic imagination, which reveals itself "as a kind of anti-self" or "hostile other," "the personification of an unconscious will to represent whatever aspects of the self that the self chooses to forget—the side of the self we can still call repressed, if we use the term loosely." See "That Other Will: The Daemonic in Coleridge and Wordsworth," *Philological Quarterly* 58 (1979), 298–320. Anya Taylor reads the story as the product of psychological projection or dreams in *Magic and English Romanticism* (Athens: The University of Georgia Press, 1979), p. 115. Richard Haven offers a perceptive reading of this "history of an ego" in *Patterns of Consciousness: An Essay on Coleridge* (Amherst: The University of Massachusetts Press, 1969), pp. 18–36. In a related version, the poem is supposed to be an allegory of epistemological categories. See, for example, Irene Chayes, "A Coleridgean Reading of 'The Ancient Mariner,'" *Studies in Romanticism* 4 (1965), 81–103.

5. The Wedding Guest, whom Paul Magnuson has called "a psychological double of the mariner," is required to suffer (vicariously) what the Mariner suffered in his own person (Magnuson, *Coleridge's Nightmare Poetry* [Charlottesville: University Press of Virginia, 1974], p. 84. See also Ward Pafford, "Coleridge's Wedding Guest," *Studies in Philology* 60 [1963], 618–26, and Arnold E. Davidson, "The Concluding Moral in Coleridge's *The Rime of the Ancient Mariner,*" *Philological Quarterly* 60 [1981], 90). No more than the Mariner is he free to release himself from the story that tells itself through the Mariner; he is transfixed by the Mariner's eye as the ship was transfixed by the tropical sun. As the Mariner begins his confession, the Wedding Guest makes what in another context would be an unmistakable gesture of repentance, breast-beating. Nor is the Wedding Guest the only character who must share the burden of the Mariner's being. It is not until he shoots the albatross that the Mariner distinguishes himself as an "I" from the crew's collective "we" (see Haven, pp. 29–30, and Paul Magnuson, *Coleridge's Nightmare Poetry,* p. 62). It is by shooting the bird and uttering his first "I" that the Mariner brings himself into being as a subject and properly enters language. (For a discussion of the relationships among subjectivity, the first person pronoun, and the appropriation of language, see Emile Benveniste, *Problems in General Linguistics,* translated by Mary Elizabeth Meek [Coral Gables: University of Miami Press, 1971], pp. 218–26.) For his crime the crew are condemned to death, and their bodies remain, after death, intact, monuments to his guilt. The Hermit, the Pilot, and the Pilot's boy, who come to greet the ship, meet him to mirror him, their solitude, praying, trance, and madness repeating crucial moments of his own experience.

In similar fashion, the Mariner experiences the genuine otherness of nature as psychic disorder. Being at the South Pole, where the ice "crack'd and growl'd, and roar'd and howl'd— / Like noises of a swound" (59–60), is like descending conscious into the illogical realm of the unconscious. The terrible heat and stasis at the Equator, the vision of the spectre ship, and the demons behave like manifestations of submerged anxieties. The weather that so troubles him is the weather of his mind.

6. See "Two Aspects of Language and Two Types of Aphasic Disturbances," in Roman Jakobson and Morris Halle, *Fundamentals of Language,* 4th ed. (1956; New York: Mouton, 1980).

7. *Miscellaneous Criticism,* edited by Thomas Middleton Raysor (London: Constable & Co., 1936), p. 99.

8. His exclamation identifies the unnameable "something in the Sky" that, when it "took at last / A certain shape," proves to be not only an image of what the Mariner's ship will become but an emblem of the story they are living through: the very vehicle of contagion, metonymy turned literal.

9. Lines 29–34. Unless otherwise noted, all citations will be from the 1798 edition of the poem printed in *Lyrical Ballads 1798,* edited by W. J. B. Owen, 2nd ed. (Oxford: Oxford University Press, 1969).

10. Arden Reed, *Romantic Weather: The Climates of Coleridge and Baudelaire* (Hanover, NH: University Press of New England, 1983), p. 177.

11. Geoffrey H. Hartman, *Beyond Formalism: Literary Essays, 1958–1970* (New Haven: Yale University Press, 1970), p. 334.

12. Not until the end of the poem does the Mariner attempt to direct the course of his narration, and the resulting moral stanzas strike many readers as the most incredible part of the poem. Gayle Smith's contention that the moral stanzas, though spoken by the Mariner, "are the retrospective sentiments of a 'grey-beard loon,' far removed from his trial in time and space, and once more free of the inner stress which periodically forces him to relive his long ago experience," would be more convincing if the Mariner were in a position to afford easy sentiments. His trials are not over; his "agony" cannot be more than two minutes past. Even now the Mariner is incapable of taking a larger view. The moral he draws is not a lesson but an attempt either to forget or to deny the reality of his experience. The very fact that he continues to repeat the tale suggests that he has not yet mastered it. Nor can I agree with Martin Wallen, who argues that the Mariner repeats his tale "out of recognition that the tale as already told is perfect. He knows that it is in the telling that his understanding of himself consists." Indeed, the Mariner sustains his existence through narration; but the narration need not for that reason be "perfect." Wayne Koestenbaum is more persuasive in locating the motive for the poem's narrative extension in Coleridge himself: "As the Mariner detains the guest, Coleridge's protracted tale keeps the reader of the *Lyrical Ballads* from turning to Wordsworth's poems. Obsessive narration—the Mariner's punishment, and the poem's method—helps Coleridge steal the reader's favor." For Smith's argument see "A Reappraisal of the Moral Stanzas in *The Rime of the Ancient Mariner,*" *Studies in Romanticism* 3 (1963), 42–52. For Wallen's argument see "Return and Representation: The Revisions of 'The Ancient Mariner,'" *Wordsworth Circle* 17 (1986), 148–56. For Koestenbaum's remarks, see *Double Talk: The Erotics of Male Literary Collaboration* (New York: Routledge, 1989), p. 76.

13. Homer Obed Brown, "The Art of Theology and the Theology of Art: Robert Penn Warren's Reading of Coleridge's *The Rime of the Ancient Mariner,*" in William V. Spanos, Paul A. Bové, and Daniel O'Hara, eds., *The Question of Textuality:*

Strategies of Reading in Contemporary American Criticism (Bloomington: Indiana University Press, 1982), p. 254.

14. Jonathan Arac, "Repetition and Exclusion: Coleridge and New Criticism Reconsidered," in Spanos et al., eds., *The Question of Textuality,* p. 269.

15. In this same volume, two of Wordsworth's poems, "Anecdote for Fathers" and "The Mad Mother," contain examples of similar carelessness with regard to closing quotation marks, suggesting that no reader would be greatly surprised by Coleridge's handling of punctuation in the *Rime.* Coleridge himself was habitually careless about closing quotation marks in his informal writing. In his early letters, especially, he is willing to indicate where a quotation begins but liable not to reclaim authority from those he is quoting, so that other men's voices blend into his own. Those who wish to interpret this as an anticipation of his later involvement in plagiarism may do so.

16. For a more detailed examination of this effect and a fuller reading of its implications, see Wallen, pp. 151–56. Arden Reed observes of the first of the two following stanzas that although "it is not difficult to sort out the pronouns' references . . . as one reads straight through the stanza, the diction tends to confuse the interlocutor's [sic] separate identities in one's mind, an effect redoubled thematically over the course of the poem" (*Romantic Weather,* p. 158).

17. It is a curiously shrewd reply, reinterpreting the Wedding Guest's exclamation at the possibility that he might be possessed as a question about the nature of the spirits inhabiting the bodies of others. His reassurance that the spirits are not the original inhabitants of the bodies is not really reassuring, however.

18. I cannot entirely agree with Arden Reed, who believes that the Wedding Guest finds the Mariner ghostly (*Romantic Weather,* p. 153). Although given the Mariner's insistence that he is a living man I cannot convincingly argue that the Mariner is really and literally a zombie, I find him more zombie-like than ghostly: the Wedding Guest is horrifyingly aware of the details of his quite physical appearance. It is telling, however, that he arouses the fears of the Wedding Guest and the men who row out to save him not so much by his appearance as by his speech: he speaks as if it were not himself speaking. And in the world this poem describes, speech seems to be more important than action. It is, after all, for their irresponsible speech that the crew are punished with death.

19. The Mariner is something of a self-portrait of the poet, who was at the time of the poem's composition only slightly less odd than his creation. Coleridge was still a young man when he wrote the poem and, though a great talker, not yet the notorious glittery-eyed monologuist of the Highgate years. He did have a weakness for recycling his words; when the demands of correspondence became too great, he would repeat not only the same bits of news but the same wording, sometimes pages at a time, letter after letter. His penchant for reusing poetry and prose was still probably a matter of efficiency, not pathology. It was only later that Coleridge began drawing parallels between his experience and the Mariner's.

James Averill has pointed out that following immediately upon the "Advertisment" that in 1798 warned its readers to expect a certain "strangeness and awkwardness" in the poems, the *Rime* plunged readers into the strangest and most awkward of poems, in which the protagonist is himself a storyteller with an enviable power over his audience: Coleridge as he would wish to be, perhaps. See "The Shape of *Lyrical Ballads* (1798)," *Philological Quarterly* 60 (1981), 391–94.

20. Brown, "The Art of Theology," p. 249.

21. Walter Jackson Bate, *Coleridge* (1968; rpt. Cambridge: Harvard University Press, 1987), pp. 56–57. What Frances Ferguson says of the gloss is true of any possible remark on the poem: "In assuming that things must be significant and interpretable, [the gloss] finds significance and interpretability, but only by reading ahead of—of beyond—the main text" ("Coleridge and the Deluded Reader," 623).

22. *Critical Review,* October, 1798; in John O. Hayden, ed., *Romantic Bards and British Reviewers: A Selected Edition of the Contemporary Reviews of the Works of Wordsworth, Coleridge, Byron, Keats and Shelley* (Lincoln: University of Nebraska Press, 1971), p. 4. In a letter written a decade later, Coleridge gets Southey's witticism interestingly wrong: " 'over-polished in the diction with *Dutch* industry' " (Letter #762, to Thomas Longman, 27 April 1809, *STCL,* III, p. 203).

23. Richard Payne has demonstrated that "Coleridge was attempting, in the idiom of the *Ancient Mariner,* to recapture the lost natural idiom" of the "elder poets" and that he succeeded in producing "a quite authentic rendition of the idioms of a broad section of the British literary tradition" of the sixteenth and seventeenth centuries" (" 'The Style and Spirit of the Elder Poets': The *Ancient Mariner* and English Literary Tradition," *Modern Philology* 75 [1978], 368–84).

24. "There is . . . enough historical evidence to date the imaginary voyage, very broadly, around 1500, a natural date for a late-medieval ballad, and consistent with the elaborately Catholic and medieval detail," writes George Watson (*Coleridge the Poet* [London: Routledge and Kegan Paul, 1966], p. 90). See also Huntington Brown, "The Gloss to *The Rime of the Ancient Mariner,*" *Modern Language Quarterly* 6 (1945), 319.

25. The purity and simplicity of the minstrel's language mark him as a medieval minstrel, as opposed to one of "the broadside journalists of Shakespeare's London," observes Huntington Brown, p. 319. Coleridge copied this particular ballad form keeping an eye on Percy's *Reliques,* particularly "Sir Cauline" (*STCL* I, p. 379 n.). John Livingston Lowes traces another large portion of the *Ancient Mariner*'s vocabulary to Chaucer, Spenser, William Taylor's translations of Burger's "Lenore," Chatterton, Hakluyt, Purchas, Martens, and Harris (*The Road to Xanadu: A Study in the Ways of the Imagination* [Boston: Houghton Mifflin Company, 1927], pp. 296–308).

26. The writer of the gloss was an inhabitant of the seventeenth century. See Huntington Brown, pp. 322, 320.

27. Quoted in Hayden, p. 4. Southey's position on imitations of literary antiquities was not consistent. About the same time as Coleridge was writing the *Rime,* Southey was planning a preface to *The Works of Thomas Chatterton* and fighting a battle with Sir Herbert Croft in the pages of the *Monthly Magazine* and *The Gentleman's Magazine* over who was the rightful protector of Chatterton's poems. Ironically enough, Coleridge was unable to give Southey much encouragement. In July of 1797 he wrote, "You are acting kindly in your exertions for Chatterton's sister: but I doubt the success. Chatterton's or Rowley's poems were never pop-

ular—the very circumstances which made them so talked of—their *ancientness*—prevented them from being generally read" (Letter #197, ca. 17 July 1797, in *STCL,* I, pp. 332–33). See also letter #331 in the same volume, p. 585 and note.

28. Hayden, p. 6.

29. B. R. McElderry, Jr., "Coleridge's Revision of 'The Ancient Mariner,'" *Studies in Philology* 29 (1932), 71.

30. Albert Friedman, *The Ballad Revival: Studies in the Influence of Popular on Sophisticated Poetry* (Chicago: University of Chicago Press, 1961), p. 269.

31. *The Road to Xanadu,* p. 307.

32. Earl Wasserman explores the neoclassicals' confusion about and ambivalence toward their forebears in *Elizabethan Poetry in the Eighteenth Century,* Illinois Studies in Language and Literature, vol. 32 (Urbana: The University of Illinois Press, 1947).

33. Quoted in J. R. de J. Jackson, ed., *Coleridge: The Critical Heritage* (London: Routledge & Kegan Paul, 1970), p. 55. Burney's attitude was the kind that made writers of pseudo-antique poems into hoaxers. The poetry of Chatterton, for example, was valued, when it *was* valued, largely for being a relic of an earlier age.

34. Despite the similarity of their sources, Coleridge was no Chatterton. Henry A. Beers writes, "It might be hard to prove that the Rowley poems had very much to do with giving shape to Coleridge's own poetic output. Doubtless, without them, 'Christabel,' and 'The Ancient Mariner,' and 'The Dark Ladye' would still have been; and yet it is possible that they might not have been just what they are" (*A History of English Romanticism in the Eighteenth Century* [New York: Henry Holt and Company, 1899], p. 369). Chatterton conscientiously mined Chaucer, Speght's Chaucer glossary, Kersey's dictionary, Spenser, Drayton, Marlowe, Shakespeare, Percy's *Reliques,* as well as Elizabeth Cooper's *Muses' Library,* Ossian, Dryden, and Pope. See Donald S. Taylor, ed., *The Complete Works of Thomas Chatterton* (Oxford: Oxford University Press, 1971), p. xliv, and Bertrand H. Bronson, "Thomas Chatterton," in Frederick W. Hilles, ed., *The Age of Johnson: Essays Presented to Chauncey Brewster Tinker,* (1949; rpt. New York: AMS Press, 1978), pp. 244, 245.

35. "The composition of a poem is among the *imitative* arts; and . . . imitation, as opposed to copying, consists either in the interfusion of the SAME throughout the radically DIFFERENT, or of the different throughout a base radically the same" (*BL,* II, p. 72).

36. *CPW,* II, p. 1139.

37. Letter #225, to William Wordsworth, 23 January 1798, in *STCL,* I, p. 379.

38. *WPW,* I, p. 361.

39. *CPW,* I, pp. 285–87.

40. *Ibid.,* p. 285.

41. Although more fully developed than "Cain," "Salisbury Plain" never entirely freed itself from the structural problems that make the earliest drafts so hard to follow. One may blame the near incoherence of the earliest surviving draft upon the state of the manuscript, which is missing nearly fifty lines. But the poem never achieved a strong narrative organization and was published at last, in 1842, with

its problems still unresolved. I use the text of "Adventures on Salisbury Plain" (1795–1799) established by Stephen Gill in *The Salisbury Plain Poems of William Wordsworth* (Ithaca: Cornell University Press, 1975).

42. Wordsworth himself conceded that "the incidents of this attempt do only in a small degree produce each other, and it deviates accordingly from the general rule by which narrative pieces ought to be governed." Still, he insisted, the poem "is not therefore wanting in continuous hold upon the mind, or in unity." See *The Prose Works of William Wordsworth,* edited by Alexander B. Grosart, 3 vols. (1876; rpt. New York: AMS Press, 1967), 3, p. 11.

43. The sailor is at the point of stepping inside his own door when he comes upon his victim; the Mariner has, presumably, with the rest of the crew, been feeding the albatross crumbs.

44. J. R. Watson recognizes the similarity but not its full extent. He writes, "The vagrant is like the ancient mariner: the retelling of her story seems to be the single, necessary course of action left to her, the one thing that gives meaning to her life. The events which lead up to this state are, of course, very different from those which occur in Coleridge's poem; indeed the printing of the woman's story in the 1798 *Lyrical Ballads* under the title of 'The Female Vagrant' makes a neat contrast with 'The Ancient Mariner', and shows very clearly the working out of the plans [the division of labor] described by Coleridge in *Biographia Literaria*" (*Wordsworth's Vital Soul: The Sacred and Profane in Wordsworth's Poetry* [London: Macmillan, 1982], p. 68). It is possible to make too much of the contrast. The differences between the poems are real, of course, but what is telling is how alike the structures of two such apparently unlike poems turn out to be. Lines 392–96, 427–35, and 546–49 are strikingly similar to passages in the *Rime.*

45. Hartman points out the poem's Spenserian consonance, caesurae, inversion, and "multiplication of monosyllables," in *Wordsworth's Poetry, 1787–1814* (1964; rpt. New Haven: Yale University Press, 1977), p. 119.

46. Samuel Schulman compares Salisbury Plain with the topography of *The Faerie Queene* in "Wordsworth's Spenserian Voice," Ph.D. diss., Yale University 1978, p. 30.

47. Schulman, p. 17.

48. Wasserman points out in *Elizabethan Poetry in the Eighteenth Century,* p. 131, that since Beatty's *The Minstrel,* the Spenserian stanza was independent not only of Spenser but of everything the eighteenth century associated with Spenser.

49. The opening stanzas of the 1793–94 version of the poem express pity for those unhappy men who can remember a time when things were different from the way they are now. But, as Samuel Schulman points out, the poem presents history not so much in terms of a progression or a decline as in terms of repetition: "The Spenserian tones of the Woman's narrative echo the bloody legends of Stonehenge; and collapse the distance between past and present. The style of *Salisbury Plain* forces the reader to recognize a horrible rebirth of ancient barbarism in the political arrangements of the present day" (Schulman, p. 17).

50. In the course of a full and meticulous analysis of the *Rime*'s debt to "Salisbury Plain," Paul Magnuson argues that "'The Ancient Mariner' alters the Salisbury

Plain poems, not only in giving a voice to suffering, but also in characterizing the voice as dissociated from the mariner." Persuasive as Magnuson's reading is, I am not convinced that what Coleridge has done in the *Rime* amounts to "giving a voice" to its protagonist. See *Coleridge and Wordsworth: A Lyrical Dialogue* (Princeton: Princeton University Press, 1988), pp. 68–84.

51. Reed, *Romantic Weather,* p. 150.

52. Presumably now that the crew have absorbed the wind into themselves in the form of singing spirits they no longer need an external wind to sail the ship. The Mariner suggests that a spirit moves the ship from below.

53. From all this a reader bent on finding a certain kind of poetic unity might deduce a kind of poetic justice: as the albatross responds to the ship, so the ship responds to the spirits who administer its doom. The Mariner's perception that the death of the crew was linked to the death of the albatross might support such a reading. But it does not take us far, partly because we see so little into the spirits' motivations, partly because the behavior of a living albatross does not shed much light on the behavior of a skeleton ship.

54. Lines 41–50. I am quoting here from the 1817 version printed in *CPW,* I.

55. Magnuson, *Coleridge's Nightmare Poetry,* p. 58.

56. But see Lawrence Kramer, who argues that the appearance of the albatross means a respite from the nightmare of the ice and that "by killing the albatross, therefore, the Mariner does not initiate his nightmare; he returns to it, and allows it to perpetuate itself" ("That Other Will," 307).

57. See Lawrence Lipking's remarks on the opening "phantom reference" in "The Marginal Gloss," *Critical Inquiry* 3 (1977), 615.

It is curious to note that the first of the two spirits whose voices the Mariner hears in his trance begins in a similar manner: "'Is it he?' quoth one, 'Is this the man?'"

58. The incident recalls a passage in the 1793 version of Wordsworth's *Descriptive Sketches,* in which the unhappy chamois hunter, in an attempt to gain a foothold on the slippery rocks, bleeds his feet. Coleridge would return to the image in 1809 in the course of an essay about the relationship between writerly authority and truth: "The reader, who would follow a close reasoner to the summit and absolute principle of any one important subject, has chosen a Chamois-hunter for his guide. Our guide will, indeed, take us the shortest way, will save us many a wearisome and perilous wandering, and warn us of many a mock road that had formerly led himself to the brink of chasms and precipices, or at best in an idle circle to the spot from whence he started. But he cannot carry us on his shoulders: we must strain our own sinews, as he has strained his; and make firm footing on the smooth rock for ourselves, by the blood of toil from our own feet." See lines 394–97, as well as Wordsworth's note on the practice, in *Descriptive Sketches by William Wordsworth,* edited by Eric Birdsall and Paul M. Zall (Ithaca: Cornell University Press, 1984), p. 76, and *The Friend,* ed. Barbara E. Rooke (Princeton: Princeton University Press, 1969), I, p. 55.

59. Shipwrecked men were known to commit cannibalism in order to survive, however, and maritime law made allowance for the fact.

60. *The Odyssey* offers at different points somewhat different explanations for

the ceremony: that it enables the ghosts to speak, that it forces them to speak truly, and that it rouses them from oblivion. It could well be that the offering of blood derives from the archaic belief in the chthonic divinity of the dead and the necessity to offer sacrifice to them.

61. The very next passage, in which the crew "all at once their breath drew in / As they were drinking all" (ll. 157–58), contributes to the confusion, or identification, of drinking and inhaling, liquid and air.

62. It is linked as well to familial violence, a connection the Hermit makes for us when the sight of the ghastly returning ship leads him to free-associate to "the wolf below / That eats the she-wolf's young" (ll. 569–70).

63. See Richard Haven, *Patterns of Consciousness,* pp. 29–30, and Paul Magnuson, *Coleridge's Nightmare Poetry,* p. 62.

64. In 1798 the wind "reach'd the ship . . . And dropp'd down, like a stone!"

65. In Sanskrit, Hebrew, Greek, Latin, Japanese, and other languages, the word for "wind" doubles as the word for "spirit." M. H. Abrams discusses the ubiquity of the association and Coleridge's relationship to it in "The Correspondent Breeze: A Romantic Metaphor," in *The Correspondent Breeze: Essays on English Romanticism* (New York: W. W. Norton, 1984), pp. 37–54.

Many critics have seen in the wind of the *Rime* a symbol of the mind or the creative impulse. See, for example, Maud Bodkin, *Archetypal Patterns in Poetry: Psychological Studies of Imagination* (London: Oxford University Press, 1934), pp. 30, 34–35; Richard Harter Fogle, "The Genre of The Ancient Mariner," *Tulane Studies in English* 7 (1957), 123–24; and Robert Penn Warren, "A Poem of Pure Imagination: An Experiment in Reading," in *Selected Essays* (1941; rpt. New York: Random House, 1958), pp. 237–38.

66. Eight years later Coleridge was still playing with the image. Ideas, he wrote, do not recall ideas "any more than Leaves in a forest create each other's motion—The Breeze it is that runs thro' them / it is the Soul, the state of Feeling—." See letter #510, to Robert Southey, 7 August 1803, in *STCL,* II, p. 961.

67. Stripped of its more nightmarish aspects, it might sound like the spiritual commotion Coleridge describes in his notebooks, a flurry in which his soul "courses, drives, and eddies": "A wild activity of thoughts, imaginations, feelings, and impulses of motion, rises up from within me—a sort of *bottom-wind,* that blows to no point of the compass, & comes from I know not whence, but agitates the whole of me" (Letter #484, to Thomas Wedgwood, 17 January 1803, in *STCL,* II, p. 916). This is a "correspondent breeze," a motion of the soul analogous to motions of the air. Though its realm is the spirit, Coleridge does not claim to have created it himself. Though internal, it does not belong to him; it "comes from I know not whence."

68. B. R. McElderry, Jr., shows that Coleridge took his critics' criticisms seriously enough to follow whatever particular changes in diction they recommended and to work on passages that aroused special ire ("Coleridge's Revision of 'The Ancient Mariner,'" p. 71).

69. Robert Southey, quoted in Hayden, p. 4.

70. For example, Lamb, in a letter to Southey intended as a defense of the

poem, deplored a passage about the supernatural behavior of the wind as "fertile in unmeaning miracles." See Jackson, p. 60.

Chapter 3: The Poetry of Property

1. In *Lyrical Ballads, [by Wordsworth and Coleridge,] the text of the 1798 edition with the additional 1800 poems and the Prefaces,* edited by R. L. Brett and A. R. Jones (London: Methuen, 1963), pp. 276–77. I use this edition for the tests of the place-naming poems, the Lucy poems, the Matthew poems, and "Michael."

2. At this period, writes Stephen Gill, Wordsworth was just "beginning . . . to conceive of himself more professionally as a poet. He was thinking about publishing, making money, establishing a reputation, marketing, and accumulating material for future volumes." For Gill's description of Wordsworth's quasi-entrepreneurial activities and pronouncements about the volume, see his *William Wordsworth: A Life* (Oxford: Oxford University Press, 1989), pp. 164–65.

3. Wayne Koestenbaum, who remarks that "a counting house pleasure suffuses the *Lyrical Ballads,* for the book's joys come from accretion," reads the poems as allegories of their collaborative production, which production, as Koestenbaum sees it, is fundamentally homoerotic, obsessed with female fecundity, and involved in sexually and poetically "compensatory strategies of repetition" designed to test the poets' anxiety whether "two men might be as useless for the purposes of poetic generation as they are for sexual reproduction." Though the approach is intriguing, the readings of the poems themselves—which can be found in *Double Talk: The Erotics of Male Literary Collaboration,* (New York: Routledge, 1989), pp. 71–111—are questionable.

4. "I suspect that at some point, many readers have wondered why Wordsworth is so specific in the title about the circumstances of the visit, and so vague in the poem. Why would a writer call attention to a famous ruin and then studiously ignore it, as if repudiating its material and historical facticity?" Thus Marjorie Levinson, who uses the discrepancy as an opening into the historical subtext of the poem. See *Wordsworth's Great Period Poems: Four Essays* (Cambridge: Cambridge University Press, 1986).

5. In "Tintern Abbey" the *Rime* is rewritten. Its waters are domesticated as "inland" waters, its Hermit settled in silence by his fire, its terrible powers of memory made restorative, and its perception of the world as a hall of mirrors revalued as a comforting assurance of spiritual kindness.

6. See Don H. Bialostosky, *Making Tales: The Poetics of Wordsworth's Narrative Experiments* (Chicago: Chicago University Press, 1984), pp. 90–91.

7. So Kenneth R. Johnston, *Wordsworth and 'The Recluse'* (New Haven: Yale University Press, 1984), p. 84.

8. Cf. Tilottama Rajan, who detects in the poems "an anxiously recent quality," at odds perhaps with their unself-consciousness but well justified by their failure to "accomplish their project of carving out a place for themselves in regional literature." For her remarks, see *The Supplement of Reading: Figures of Under-*

standing in Romantic Theory and Practice (Ithaca: Cornell University Press, 1990), pp. 146–47.

9. David Simpson observes that "Wordsworth's protagonists, many of them rural architects of one kind or another, are frequently engaged in an exploration of the tensions between an 'unappropriated earth' and the types and emblems which the human mind seeks to derive from or erect upon it." See *Wordsworth and the Figurings of the Real* (London: Macmillan, 1982), p. 21.

10. *One Foot in Eden: Modes of Pastoral in Romantic Poetry* (Chapel Hill: University of North Carolina Press, 1986), p. 90.

11. It is more than simple oblivion, of course, and the place-naming poems are not its only vehicles. See Alan Liu, *Wordsworth: The Sense of History* (Stanford: Stanford University Press, 1989), pp. 91–115, for an analysis of the picturesque and "imaginary property" in relation to bureaucracy, the construction of the "natural," and the economic circumstances of the Lake Country around 1800. Ann Bermingham analyzes the development of the entire genre of English rustic landscape painting as the aesthetic correlary of enclosure: "Precisely when the countryside—or at least large portions of it—was becoming unrecognizable, and dramatically marked by historical change, it was offered as the image of the homely, the stable, the ahistorical." See *Landscape and Ideology: The English Rustic Tradition, 1740–1860* (Berkeley: University of California Press, 1986), p. 9 and passim.

12. *STCN,* I, p. 579.

13. Brett and Jones, *Lyrical Ballads,* p. 217.

14. John Williams notes the practice of one Thomas Hollis, an eighteenth-century property-owner, who "quite simply named portions of his estate, fields, farms and woods, after prominent political figures, delegating the useless areas to villains, and the fruitful parts to heroes. The names used for fields included New England, Adams, Russell, and John Toland; farms were named after Milton, Sidney, Russell (again), Harrington and Neville." According to Williams, Wordsworth was aware that he had been "living only a few miles away from a landscape transformed into a record of Commonwealthman political history." See *Wordsworth: Romantic Poetry and Revolutionary Politics* (Manchester: Manchester University Press, 1989), p. 17.

15. Heather Glen regards the place-naming poems as "direct attempts to reply to that question which the Goslar lyrics left blankly unanswered: how might the 'rocks and stones and trees' of an indifferent universe be endowed with human meaning?" See her *Vision and Disenchantment: Blake's 'Songs' and Wordsworth's 'Lyrical Ballads'* (Cambridge: Cambridge University Press, 1983).

16. James Averill, *Wordsworth and the Poetry of Human Suffering* (Ithaca: Cornell University Press, 1980), p. 198.

17. Geoffrey Hartman writes, "Wordsworth projects nature as something that speaks 'rememberable things,' as something that textualizes a phantom voice: perhaps the language of dream image and phrase." "Words, Wish, Worth: Wordsworth," in Harold Bloom et al., eds., *Deconstruction and Criticism* (New York: Seabury Press, 1979), p. 194.

18. "In one sense, ancient religion is a form of geography," writes Herbert N. Schneidau in *Sacred Discontent: The Bible and Western Tradition* (Baton Rouge: Louisiana State University Press, 1976), p. 71.

19. Joseph Rykwert, *The Idea of a Town: The Anthropology of Urban Form in Rome, Italy, and the Ancient World* (London: Faber and Faber, 1976), pp. 58–59.

20. Ibid., p. 107. From the stone age through modern times, Gertrude Rachel Levy notes, the "emblematic stones" that were associated with the origins of stone architecture were simultaneously "spirit houses" and "extensions of the Earth's fertility." *The Gate of Horn: A Study of the Religious Conceptions of the Stone Age and Their Influence upon European Thought* (London: Faber and Faber, 1948), p. 123.

21. Rykwert, p. 112.

22. Ibid., p. 116.

23. On romantically and preromantically haunted landscapes, see Geoffrey Hartman, "Romantic Poetry and the Genius Loci," in *Beyond Formalism: Literary Essays 1958–1970* (New Haven: Yale University Press, 1970), pp. 311–36.

24. In these poems "naming is a joyfully spontaneous act that almost escapes elegiac implications." See Geoffrey Hartman, "Wordsworth, Inscriptions, and Romantic Nature Poetry," in *Beyond Formalism,* p. 222n.

25. The poem was composed during the same period as the poems on the naming of places included in the volume but was printed with them under the heading of "Poems on the Naming of Places" only after 1815.

26. For a time it was believed that this piece, published pseudonymously in the *Morning Post* in October of 1800, was one of the place-naming poems Wordsworth mentioned having received from Coleridge for inclusion in the place-naming section of the *Lyrical Ballads*. So Ernest Hartley Coleridge, ed., *CPW,* I, p. 349n. De Selincourt discovered an earlier version of it among Wordsworth's notebooks, however, and it is now believed that Wordsworth remembered it and showed it to Coleridge either when Coleridge discovered a rock-seat in the Grasmere orchard or when Wordsworth and his friends were building the Windy-Brow seat during the period when Wordsworth would have been busy writing place-naming poems. Coleridge revised it somewhat before he sent it off to be printed. See De Selincourt, *WPW,* I, p. 372, and Jane Worthington Smyser, "Coleridge's Use of Wordsworth's Juvenilia," *PMLA* 65, (1950), 425.

27. De Selincourt, *WPW,* I, p. 372.

28. Wordsworth wrote a little piece that seems, like this "Inscription," to be a place-naming poem in reverse. It goes:

Orchard Pathway, to and fro,
Ever with thee, did I go,
Weaving Verses, a huge store!
These, and many hundreds more,
And, in memory of the same,
This little lot shall bear thy name!

[*WPW,* II, p. 488]

29. An inscription, Wordsworth thought, tended toward anonymity, but he assumed the reader would suppose a human consciousness to have been originally behind the inscription and its moral. In this poem the landscape itself embodies and intends a moral reproof, reminding men that they are but travelers through their own lives. See letter #232, 16 November 1811, in *The Letters of William and*

Dorothy Wordsworth: The Middle Years, edited by Ernest De Selincourt, revised by Mary Moormon, 2nd ed. (Oxford: Clarendon Press, 1969), I, p. 516. Hereafter cited as *MY*.

30. "Lines left upon a Seat in a Yew-tree," "The Nightingale," "We are seven," "The Thorn," "Tintern Abbey," "Hart-leap Well," "The Brothers."

31. I cannot agree with Glen, who argues that "it seems to be a growing sense of the otherness of this place, its separation from anything that the speaker can create or control, which leads to the desire to name it." *Vision and Disenchantment,* p. 305.

32. The poem rehearses on a simpler level the same kind of narrative impatience Kenneth Johnston detects in "Home at Grasmere," of which he writes, "If all its linguistic peculiarities were generalized into a single compressed sentence, they would collapse all tenses into one: 'Once upon a time I am living happily ever after.'" See *Wordsworth and 'The Recluse,'* p. 88.

33. Mary Moorman, *William Wordsworth: A Biography. The Early Years, 1770–1803* (Oxford University Press, 1957), p. 463, and John Beer, *Wordsworth in Time* (London: Faber and Faber, 1979), p. 102.

34. Letter from John Wordsworth to Mary Hutchinson, 25 February 1801, in the Wordsworth Letters and Papers at Dove Cottage, Grasmere, as quoted in Mary Moorman, p. 506.

35. John Beer remarks of the echoed laughter, "As it is thrown about the mountain peaks it sounds less and less like human laughter, more and more like voices of infinity. The final succession of images—clear blue sky, speaking-trumpet, the clouds of Glaramara and the misty head of Kirkstone—are, in fact, close to Wordsworth's images of apocalypse. They also may have the final ambiguity of the apocalyse as Wordsworth sees it: it may portend the final revelation of infinity within the natural order, or it may simply prove that the whole human quest for meaning has been no more than a closet-drama played out against a void" (*Wordsworth in Time,* p. 105). Mr. Beer sees more at stake here than I do.

36. *WPW,* II, p. 487.

37. David Simpson, *Irony and Authority in Romantic Poetry* (Totowa, N.J.: Rowman and Littlefield, 1979), p. 76.

38. Ibid.

39. Wallace Jackson remarks, "The real subject of the poem is Wordsworth's experience of Mary to which the form of the poem corresponds. Description is the translation of the disclosed being of Mary Hutchinson, as Wordsworth knows his awareness of her, into the objectifications of landscape" (*The Probable and the Marvelous: Blake, Wordsworth, and the Eighteenth-Century Critical Tradition* [Athens: The University of Georgia Press, 1978], p. 137).

40. Glen, *Vision and Disenchantment,* p. 320.

41. See letter #144, 6 or 7 October 1800, from Wordsworth to Biggs and Cottle, in *EY,* p. 305. Raimonda Modiano discusses Wordsworth's plan to include Coleridgean material in this section of the volume as an invitation to Coleridge "to surrender his sovereign territory and join in a truly communal enterprise" and as a "dangerous challenge" to remodel himself in Wordsworth's image by "[abandoning] the supernatural ideal and [concerning] himself instead with the feelings which grow from 'little Incidents' among 'rural Objects.'" As a result of accepting

this challenge, "Coleridge was forced into an impossible competition on his rival's home ground." For her analysis, see *Coleridge and the Concept of Nature* (Tallahassee: Florida State University Press, 1985), pp. 37–40.

Chapter 4: "Michael," "Christabel," and the Poetry of Possession

1. Stephen Parrish, *The Art of the Lyrical Ballads* (Cambridge: Harvard University Press, 1973), p. 149.

2. *Journals of Dorothy Wordsworth,* edited by E. De Selincourt (London: Macmillan, 1959), I, p. 64.

3. *STCL,* I, p. 643, note #2.

4. See, for example, *STCL,* I, pp. 627 and 631. For a wonderful discussion of Coleridge's relations to literary property, see Jerome Christensen, *Coleridge's Blessed Machine of Language* (Ithaca: Cornell University Press, 1981), especially chaps. 3 and 4.

5. *BL,* II, p. 8.

6. The critics did not know quite what to say about the poem. That in their attempts to locate the source of their uneasiness they fell into improprieties not unlike those from which "Christabel" itself suffers is therefore unsurprising. On this subject see Karen Swann, "Literary Gentlemen and Lovely Ladies: The Debate on the Character of *Christabel,*" *ELH* 52 (1985), 397–418.

7. *Journals of Dorothy Wordsworth,* I, pp. 65–69 passim, 72.

8. See Geoffrey Durrant, "Wordsworth and the Poetry of Objects," *Mosaic* 5:1 (1971), 114, 115. Harold E. Toliver writes, "Wordsworth often in fact progresses from descriptive canvassing and action to an emblematic stillness that freezes vitality, from a pastoral of sensuous observance to a pastoral of immanent glory (reminiscent of Eden and celestial paradise respectively). The interesting moment is the transition from one to the other and the hovering vision that includes them both simultaneously" (*Pastoral Forms and Attitudes* [Berkeley: University of California Press, 1971], p. 238). David B. Pirie's attempt, in *William Wordsworth: The Poetry of Grandeur and of Tenderness* ([New York: Methuen, 1982], pp. 108–25), to show how "Michael" defeats the temptation to symbolize by adhering, somewhat grimly, to realism is interestingly unpersuasive: the pastoral horrors Pirie finds implicit in the poem are not at all apparent to me.

9. All citations of "Michael" are from *Lyrical Ballads: The text of the 1798 edition with the additional 1800 poems and the Prefaces,* edited by R. L. Brett and A. R. Jones (London: Methuen, 1963).

10. Susan J. Wolfson points out an echo of the Advertisement in these words. "Those readers, Wordsworth had cautioned, 'will look round' for something familiar to their notions of poetry 'and will be induced to enquire by what species of courtesy these attempts can be permitted to assume that title.' Readers of *Michael* find themselves in a similarly spare, unpromising circumstance: 'alone / With a few sheep, with rocks and stones, and kites' (10–11)" (*The Questioning Presence: Wordsworth, Keats, and the Interrogative Mode in Romantic Poetry* [Ithaca: Cornell University Press, 1986], p. 86).

11. The economics that matter in "Michael" are primarily literary; the costs it calculates are those of storytelling. The poem's narrative and financial evasiveness suggests that the appropriation of this poetic ground may have been a less innocent business than Wordsworth makes it out to be.

12. But see Marjorie Levinson for a contrary view. In a subtle reading of the poem against Wordsworth's remarks about it to Fox, Levinson finds the poem to be fractured by its simultaneous but incompatible desires to present a defense of property and to show the aesthetic and ethical benefits of losing that property. Levinson's analysis can be found in *Wordsworth's Great Period Poems: Four Essays* (Cambridge: Cambridge University Press, 1986), pp. 58–79.

13. Letter #157, to Thomas Poole, 9 April 1801, in *EY,* p. 322.

14. Letter #152, 14 January 1801, in *EY,* pp. 314–15.

15. Heinzelman goes on to remark the vulnerability of each property, the land and the poem, to disregard. "Wordsworth in fact challenges the reader to help him prove that the *labor* embodied by both of them together in the literary work is abundant recompense for the dispossession of Michael's *land*" (Kurt Heinzelman, *The Economics of the Imagination* [Amherst: University of Massachusetts Press, 1980], p. 221). Marjorie Levinson takes a hard look at the nature and legitimacy of this recompense, finding it questionable. "It is the poets-to-come who are invited to profit by the ruin [Michael experiences]," she notes; Michael himself gains nothing by his ordeal. "When the reader begins to see Michael as a man heroic in his capacity to accept his loss and generous in his semiotic legacy to the poet, the graft [of the aesthetic onto the historical] can be said to have taken. The ideology of the text absorbs us insofar as we forget that Michael is, throughout the first, longest, and best part of the poem, *precisely* he who *cannot* give up, who cannot be other than literal and materialist in his relation to Nature and to Luke" (*Wordsworth's Great Period Poems,* pp. 77, 79).

16. As Don H. Bialostosky remarks, Wordsworth himself stresses the second-hand nature of his material, "completely excluding claims to direct personal experience. . . . He presents his telling of the 'Tale' of Michael as neither occasioned by a specific personal encounter with the ruined sheepfold nor validated by a personal sighting of or meeting with the hero but as told to him by others and confirmed by conversations with them" (*Making Tales: The Poetics of Wordsworth's Narrative Experiments* [Chicago: University of Chicago Press, 1984], p. 99).

17. Geoffrey Hartman, *Wordsworth's Poetry, 1787–1814* (1964; rpt. New Haven: Yale University Press, 1977), p. 266. Sydney Lea observes, "It is sadly relevant that Wordsworth's induction both offers a legacy and prefaces a narrative of *failed legacy*" ("Wordsworth and His 'Michael': The Pastor Passes," *ELH* 45 [1978], 58).

18. Peter J. Manning, who describes the poet's treatment of Luke as "affectless," suggests that Wordsworth seems to be "determinedly deflecting attention from the remorse that his failure might well be thought to have caused in him." Manning sees Luke as the object of the poet's anxieties for different reasons than I do. See " 'Michael,' Luke, and Wordsworth," *Criticism* 19 (1977), 195–211.

19. Lea remarks, "We dare not overspeculate, yet perhaps Luke's ways are evil primarily in Michael's mind—we have, after all, no details about them, only Mi-

chael's responses. It may be that the boy's 'crime' is foremost the breach of the pastoral covenant: he has gone metaphorically as well as literally into foreign parts" ("Wordsworth and His 'Michael,'" p. 59). See also John Jones, *The Egotistical Sublime: A History of Wordsworth's Imagination* (London: Chatto & Windus, 1954), p. 100.

20. I cannot agree with Heinzelman, who regards Luke's sin as having "relinquish[ed] his natural inheritance by seeking private gain" (p. 217). Marjorie Levinson returns the blame to Michael, who, having produced Luke and invested him with the value of his labor, "not only converts a use value to an exchange value, he involves his family in the mechanisms of the market he had thus far avoided." See *Wordsworth's Great Period Poems,* p. 68.

21. What is the nature of the debt that has brought such ruin upon Michael's family? It is no ordinary financial problem the poet has been dealing with. Once Luke is out of the way, the economic threat that entangled and destroyed him disappears. Although no debts seem to have been paid, creditors leave Michael alone, and he remains in control of his land until he dies. John Bushnell points out the inconsistency of the financial motives in the poem: "If Michael was unable to pay the interest on his mortgage earlier . . . how could he pay for it after Luke's disappearance? Wordsworth has allowed his course of events to move from the legally possible to the narratively expedient. . . . once he decides [to send Luke away rather than to sell the land], he fulfills his debt metaphorically and even literally in the narrative, while legally he seems to have fulfilled no debt at all" ("'Where is the Lamb for a Burnt Offering?': Michael's Covenant and Sacrifice," *Wordsworth Circle* 12 [1981], 248). It is as if the equivalence between the heir and the inheritance that Michael relies upon to solve the financial crisis had been validated: the sacrifice of the son seems to have been all that was required. But required by whom? Who profits? Perhaps only Luke's successful rival, the ambivalent heir and opportunistic elegist.

22. Levinson notices a similar effect, that of "a work at odds with itself, a work that tries to say one thing but succeeds in saying another and opposite thing." But for her, the source of strain is the rivalry between the Jewish and the Christian readings of the binding of Isaac, and what is at stake in the rivalry is the relationship between real historical conditions and the possibility of spiritual or aesthetic transcendence of those conditions. See *Wordworth's Great Period Poems,* p. 79.

23. Lea makes the same point in "Wordsworth and His 'Michael,'" p. 60.

24. On the matter of the biblical background, see Hartman, *Wordsworth's Poetry,* p. 265; Manning, "'Michael,' Luke, and Wordsworth," pp. 201–2; Murray Roston, *Poet and Prophet: The Bible and the Growth of Romanticism* (Evanston: Northwestern University Press, 1965), pp. 182–83; Randel Helms, "On the Genesis of Wordsworth's *Michael,*" *English Language Notes* 15:1 (September 1977), 38–43; Levinson, *Wordsworth's Great Period Poems,* pp. 68–79. This would be the first of many substitutions. Genesis is filled with stories of swaps, bargains, and substitutions, several of them—including the stories of Jacob and Esau, and Joseph and his brothers—shadowy presences behind this poem. A number of details here, such as the "mess of pottage" and Isabel's warning to Luke ("do not go away, / For if thou leave thy Father he will die" [307–8]) seem to have no other function

than to remind the reader how many sons and brothers have submitted to exchange and sacrifice in order that the line of inheritance continue unbroken.

25. See R. S. Woof, "John Stoddart, 'Michael' and Lyrical Ballads," *Ariel* 1:2 (April 1970), 7–22; "Mr Woof's Reply to Mr Wordsworth," *Ariel* 3:2 (April 1972), 72–79; Jonathan Wordsworth, "A Note on the Ballad Version of 'Michael,'" *Ariel* 2:2 (April 1971), 66–71; Mark Reed, "On the Development of Wordsworth's 'Michael,'" *Ariel* 3:2 (April 1972), 70–79; and Stephen Parrish, "'Michael," Mr Woof and Mr Wordsworth," *Ariel* 3:2 (April 1972), 80–83.

26. Quoted by Stephen Parrish, "Michael and the Pastoral Ballad," in Jonathan Wordsworth, ed., *Bicentenary Wordsworth Studies in Memory of John Alban Finch* (Ithaca: Cornell University Press, 1970), p. 52.

27. Mark Reed, *Wordsworth: The Chronology of the Early Years 1770–1799* (Cambridge: Harvard University Press, 1967), p. 323.

28. Coleridge himself believed "A Character" described him, but Wordsworth told Isabella Fenwick that he wrote it about Jones. See Woof, "Mr Woof's Reply to Mr Wordsworth;" Reed, "On the Development of Wordsworth's 'Michael'" and Parrish, "'Michael,' Mr Woof and Mr Wordsworth."

29. After "Michael" was published, Wordsworth wrote to Thomas Poole asking his opinion, as "the inheritor of an estate which has long been in possession of your family," of the poem's merit, remarking that "in writing it I had your character often before my eyes, and sometimes thought I was delineating such a man as you yourself would have been under the same circumstances." But he went on to offer for Poole's approval a passage he considered adding to the poem. It includes the following lines, in which Paul Magnuson has suggested to me one can hear what sounds like a description of Coleridge:

—And the Shepherd oft
Would draw out of his heart the obscurities,
And admirations, that were there, of God
And of his works, or, yielding to the bent
Of his peculiar humour, would let loose
His tongue, and give it the mind's freedom, then
Discoursing on remote imaginations, strong
Conceits, devices, day-dreams, thoughts and schemes,
The fancies of a solitary Man!

See letter #157, 9 April 1801, in *EY*, pp. 322, 324.

30. Reading "Christabel" as an allegory of Coleridge's relations with Wordsworth and with his own imaginative powers, Warren Stevenson has worked out a full set of identifications for the poem's characters, with Christabel representing Coleridge "the true poet," Sir Leoline as STC "the mere social being, versifier, family-man, and friend," Geraldine as "the worst element in Wordsworth's Nature: the materialist, the egoist, the unbeliever," "a false aspirant to the title of divinely inspired poet," and Bard Bracy as Charles Lamb. See *Nimbus of Glory: A Study of Coleridge's Three Great Poems* (Salzburg: Institut für Anglistik und Amerikanistik, 1983), pp. 3–24.

31. Geraldine's putative father, Lord Roland de Vaux of Tryermaine, is Sir Leoline's "heart's best brother" (417).

32. For one interpretation of this doubling, see Paul Magnuson, *Coleridge's Nightmare Poetry* (Charlottesville: University Press of Virginia, 1974), pp. 101–4.

33. Camille Paglia sees the damage as even more extensive. For her, "part 1 encompasses the totality of Coleridge's vision and . . . the second part written three years later, as well as the rough plan he projected for three more parts, was born of fear at what he had already created." If Paglia is right, Part II is an attempt to muffle the implications of Part I. See "Christabel," in Harold Bloom, ed., *Samuel Taylor Coleridge* (New York: Chelsea House, 1986), p. 223.

34. Witness the critics' tendency to praise the poem almost as if Wordsworth had succeeded in breaking down the boundary between art and nature. James H. Averill's remark is not atypical: "To some degree, the attempt to present things-as-they-are absolves the poet of responsibility for his story. He can think of himself as a kind of historian, one who hardly invents his plot and therefore is morally bound to hold an honest mirror up to life" (*Wordsworth and the Poetry of Human Suffering* (Ithaca: Cornell University Press, 1980), p. 233).

The antihistorical effect is what Harold Bloom has named "apophrades," "the return of the dead": "the triumph of having so stationed the precursor, in one's own work, that particular passages in *his* work seem to be not presages of one's own advent, but rather to be indebted to one's own achievement, and even (necessarily) to be lessened by one's greater splendor." See *The Anxiety of Influence: A Theory of Poetry* (New York: Oxford University Press, 1973), p. 141.

35. *CPW,* pp. 213–14.

36. Anne K. Mellor, noting the oddity of Coleridge's self-justification, regards the preface as "a voice of conventional morality . . . set beside an imaginative vision that denies the very foundation of that morality (the assumption that right and wrong, good and evil, yours and mine, can be distinguished)." Unlike her, I find the implications of the preface as disquieting as those of the poem itself. Mellor's analysis can be found in *English Romantic Irony* (Cambridge: Harvard University Press, 1980), p. 161.

37. Or, as Paglia notes, "The irony of Geraldine's tale of rape is that she is herself a rapist. What Christabel hears is what is to be done to her" ("Christabel," p. 219).

38. As Richard Rand observes, Geraldine herself "is a kind of poem, and the story of Christabel is the story of one of her readers. In writing the poem, Coleridge tells about the process of reading, the process, indeed, of reading the poem known as *Christabel*" ("Geraldine," *Glyph* 3 (1978), 76.

39. His evasiveness about the particulars of her wickedness anticipates Wordsworth's reluctance to go into the details of Luke's corruption.

40. The clue will reappear for us through Christabel's visionary trance: "Again she saw that bosom old, / Again she felt that bosom cold . . . " (11. 457–58). It comes through indirectly in the Baron's threat to "dislodge their reptile souls" from those who kidnapped Geraldine (11. 442–43) and, of course, in the ladies' partial metamorphoses into snakes.

41. One might even say that Wordsworth, as final censor of the entire poem, acts merely as Geraldine's agent.

42. Rand calls the deformity as "seal," "a hallmark or signature, but one that also 'seals' up or encrypts the fact of its own existence, of its meaning (if it has one), and of its history (which is never revealed). And this seal, by sight and by touch, also seals up Christabel, and so becomes her seal and signature as well" ("Geraldine," p. 76).

Chapter 5: The Haunted Language of the Lucy Poems

1. "As I have had no books I have been obliged to write in self-defence," Wordsworth writes, presenting two Lucy poems and a fragment of *The Prelude* (*EY*, #105, 14 or 21 December 1798, p. 236).

2. "My hope was that I should be able to learn German as I learn'd French, in this I have been woefully deceived. I acquired more french in two months, than I should acquire German in five years living as we have lived. In short sorry am I to say it I do not consider myself as knowing *any* thing of the German language" (*EY*, #110, 27 February 1799, p. 255).

3. To say this is to say more than that the poet seems to be speaking in his own person. Despite the best efforts of the sleuths, we cannot with any certainty identify Lucy with anyone Wordsworth knew or connect these poems with any documentable loss. My point is formal rather than biographical: both individually and as a group (the structure of the group recapitulates the structure of its member poems), the Lucy poems refuse to be contained.

4. This evasion of narrative in the Lucy poems and in the other pieces written at Goslar has led James Averill to comment, "Elegy, particularly as Wordsworth practices it, is suspended between narrative and lyric. It does not choose to tell a story that gives emotional significance to the poem, yet the knowledge of death informs thoughts or incidents that would be trivial without it. . . . [T]hese unremarkable events are part of a larger, sadder tale. Such a consciousness of mortality takes the place of the consecutive plot of tragic romance" (*Wordsworth and the Poetry of Human Suffering* [Ithaca: Cornell University Press, 1980], p. 207).

5. Some readers, however, have taken the poet's stiff-lippedness as an indication that perhaps he is not grieving so wholeheartedly after all. See, for example, Richard Matlack, "Wordsworth's Lucy Poems in Psychobiographical Context," *PMLA* 93 (1978), 46–65, for the argument that Wordsworth's ambivalence toward his sister's presence at Goslar feeds into the ambivalence of the poems.

6. Geoffrey Hartman, "Wordsworth and Goethe in Literary History," in *The Fate of Reading and Other Essays* (Chicago: University of Chicago Press, 1975), p. 186.

7. See Hugh Sykes Davies, "Another New Poem by Wordsworth," *Essays in Criticism* 15 (1965), 135–65.

8. See, for example, Heather Glen's fine reading of the poems in *Vision and Disenchantment: Blake's 'Songs' and Wordsworth's 'Lyrical Ballads'* (Cambridge: Cambridge University Press, 1983), pp. 286–87.

9. Frances Ferguson, *Wordsworth: Language as Counter-Spirit* (New Haven: Yale University Press, 1977), p. 175.

10. Ibid., p. 176, and Douglas H. Thomson, "Wordsworth's Lucy of 'Nutting,'" *Studies in Romanticism* 18 (1978), 287–98.

11. See Hartman, *Wordsworth's Poetry, 1787–1814* (1964; rpt. New Haven: Yale University Press, 1977), pp. 158–60.

12. Sigmund Freud, "Mourning and Melancholia," *The Standard Edition of the Complete Psychological Works of Sigmund Freud,* translated by James Strachey (London: Hogarth Press, 1955), XIV, 244–45.

13. Peter M. Sacks, *The English Elegy: Studies in the Genre from Spenser to Yeats* (Baltimore: The Johns Hopkins University Press, 1985), p. 19.

14. Ibid., p. 16.

15. Sacks compares the traditional elegiac contest to ancient funeral games, where "the winners exemplify and seem to immortalize the qualities of the deceased, or at least those virtues deemed important for the community's survival. . . . [I]n Greece the right to mourn was from earliest times legally connected to the right to inherit" (pp. 16, 17).

16. Ibid., pp. 8–9.

17. *The Prelude,* begun that same winter, is a more complex example of a similar problem, a poem in which most of the poet's life and the deaths of those closest to him go practically unacknowledged. Its posthumous publication brought to life the voice of a still young man speaking to his still living friend Coleridge and his still sane sister Dorothy. The half-century of revision that preceded its publication merely solidified the poet's refusal to acknowledge the facts of time, death, and madness. It is a refusal to mourn spoken from beyond the grave.

18. "The Two April Mornings" offers us the memory of a dead girl, an Emma rather than a Lucy; the man who mourns her is the poet's aged friend rather than the poet himself. "The Fountain" involves no girl at all; its grief is impersonal. Both poems are, nevertheless, members of what John Danby calls the "larger [poetic] complex" that contains the Lucy poems (John Danby, *The Simple Wordsworth: Studies in the Poems 1797–1807* [London: Routledge and Kegan Paul, 1960], p. 88).

19. Sacks, *The English Elegy,* pp. 23, 24.

20. Although by removing the original conclusion to "Strange fits of Passion" Wordsworth established that poem as the beginning of the story whose conclusion the other poems supply, what follows does not amount to a narrative.

21. For a reading of the Lucy poems' triangularity in which the reader occupies the third vertex, see William H. Galperin, *Revision and Authority in Wordsworth: The Interpretation of a Career* (Philadelphia: University of Pennsylvania Press, 1989), pp. 96–102.

22. Hartman, *Wordsworth's Poetry,* p. 159.

23. See René Girard, *Deceit, Desire, and the Novel,* translated by Yvonne Freccero (1961; trans. Baltimore: The Johns Hopkins University Press, 1965). Girard has in mind human doubles and rivals; here in Wordsworth the rival seems to be language itself.

24. Hartman, *Wordsworth's Poetry,* pp. 157–60.

25. There are other instances of the poet's devoting most of a poem to quoting one or more of his characters. "The Brothers," for example, ceases temporarily to be a narrative and behaves like a drama; much of "Hart-leap Well" is in the voices of Sir Walter and the Shepherd; and Matthew's voice occupies much of "The Fountain" and "The Two April Mornings." But in all these poems the autonomy of the quoted voices is qualified to some extent by the poet's voice, which frames them or comments on them in such a way that we are reminded that the poem after all belongs to him. In the Lucy poems our faith in the poet's verbal control is undercut as we see his words turning against his conscious intentions.

26. Ferguson, *Language as Counter-spirit,* p. 189. Individual natural objects sometimes make fanciful speeches ("The Waterfall and the Eglantine," "The Oak and the Broom"), but they do not speak as Nature.

27. Theresa M. Kelley discusses the relationship between the figure of Proteus and attitudes toward traditional allegory in "Proteus and Romantic Allegory," *English Literary History* 49 (1982), 623–52. In the Renaissance, Proteus, whom the Roman poets had known as *ambiguus,* served as a figure for the lawmaker, the lawbreaker, the prophet or artist, the deceitful magus, the maker and destroyer of concord, and the violator of sexual norms (A. Bartlett Giamatti, "Proteus Unbound: Some Versions of the Sea God in the Renaissance," in Peter Demetz, Thomas Greene, and Lowry Nelson, Jr., eds., *The Disciplines of Criticism: Essays in Literary Theory, Interpretation, and History* [New Haven: Yale University Press, 1968], pp. 443–44). He sometimes served as a figure for "mutable nature, specifically the cycle of the seasons, in particular winter which overwhelms beauty" or as "a personification of matter" (A. C. Hamilton, ed., *The Faerie Queene* [London: Longman, 1977], p. 380n. Hamilton is commenting on Proteus's abduction of Florimell in III. viii, an episode resembling the rape of Persephone by Dis). Wordsworth's Nature is nothing if not ambiguous, a maker of fiats, a breaker of human bonds, a prophet, a maker and destroyer of concord, a virgin-violator, a creature of subtle and shifting words—very much like Proteus.

28. *Paradise Lost,* IV, 268–72.

29. See Carl Woodring, *Wordsworth* (Boston: Houghton Mifflin Company, 1965), p. 46, and Irene H. Chayes, "Little Girls Lost: Problems of a Romantic Archetype," in Northrop Frye, ed., *Blake: A Collection of Critical Essays* [Englewood Cliffs, N.J: Prentice-Hall, 1966], p. 76.)

30. Most critics assume that Wordsworth's Nature is female, a queen thinking of adopting a maid-in-waiting or a Demeter-figure who somehow receives her Persephone-figure daughter instead of losing her. (See, for example, James G. Taaffe, "Poet and Lover in Wordsworth's 'Lucy' Poems," *Modern Language Review* 61 [1966], 178; and Chayes, p. 76.) But the voice we hear is not feminine and definitely not maternal. Ferguson describes Nature in this poem as a "child molester" and insists, "It is not a benevolent mother, but rather a Plutonic male" (*Language as Counter-Spirit,* pp. 188, 189). Although it may seem frivolous to argue about the gender of an allegorical figure consisting of nothing more than a voice, it seems important to do so here because of the way it affects our reading of the poet's response to Lucy's death. His response will be different if he believes he is losing Lucy to a sexual rival or to a foster-mother. It may be that his feeling

is itself confused, as it seems to be in "Strange fits of passion," but even in confusion or ambivalence choices may be distinct.

31. Nature here diverges considerably from his Chaucerian and Spenserian forebears, who functioned as judges and regulators of other creatures' passions, who heard pleas and arguments presented, and who engaged in dialogue with other figures.

32. Hartman, *Wordsworth's Poetry,* p. 159.

33. Ferguson, *Language as Counterspirit,* p. 191.

34. Hartman, *Wordsworth's Poetry,* p. 158

35. This convergence, erotic but also semiotic, may explain the ambiguities about the gender of the moon in "Strange fits" and Nature in "Three years she grew."

36. Speaking of "Strange fits of passion," Barbara Johnson remarks, "The strange fit depicted in the poem can in some sense be read . . . as the revenge of personification, the return of a poetic principle that Wordsworth had attempted to exclude. The strangeness of the passion arises from the poem's uncanny encounter with what the theory that produced it had repressed" (*A World of Difference* [Baltimore: The Johns Hopkins University Press, 1987], pp. 96–97).

37. That Coleridge did figure in Wordsworth's imagination at that time as dead is suggested by the fact that, as Reeve Parker remarks of another poem begun in Goslar, "Coleridge heard *The Prelude* as an elegy for himself, an elegy he had helped shape" (*Coleridge's Meditative Art* [Ithaca: Cornell University Press, 1975], p. 221). But see note 17.

38. Lucy Newlyn, *Coleridge, Wordsworth, and the Language of Allusion* (Oxford: Oxford University Press, 1986), pp. 165–94; Paul Magnuson, *Coleridge and Wordsworth: A Lyrical Dialogue* (Princeton: Princeton University Press, 1988), pp. 170–71, 186–99.

Chapter 6: The Heterogeneity of the *Biographia Literaria*

1. Stephen Gill points out, however, that despite Wordsworth's assertion that he had given the *Biographia* little more than a hasty glance, he proceeded to revise his own work in accordance with the *Biographia*'s criticisms (*William Wordsworth: A Life* [Oxford: Oxford University Press, 1989], p. 474, n. 35).

2. Gayatri Chakravorty Spivak sums up its deficiencies nicely when she calls it "un-well-made." See "The Letter as Cutting Edge" in *Yale French Studies* 55/56 (1977), 208–26.

3. George Whalley, "The Integrity of 'Biographia Literaria,'" in *Essays and Studies.* Essays and Studies Collected for the English Association by Geoffrey Bullough, Vol. 6, new series (London: John Murray, 1953), p. 88. Whalley articulates this position in order to repudiate it.

4. Sigmund Freud, *The Interpretation of Dreams,* in *The Standard Edition of the Complete Psychological Works of Sigmund Freud,* translated by James Strachey et al. (1953; rpt. London: The Hogarth Press, 1978), IV, 111n., and V, 525.

5. On the *Biographia* as a response to *The Prelude, The Excursion,* the idea of *The Recluse,* and the 1815 "Essay, Supplementary to the Preface," see Kenneth

Johnston, *Wordsworth and 'The Recluse'* (New Haven: Yale University Press, 1984), pp. 333–62.

6. Attempting to present the work as a coherent whole, George Whalley offers the following rather confusing scheme. The first four chapters trace Coleridge's development as a poet and present his case against bad critics. The next four, devoted to discussion of theories of association, Whalley sees as written with an eye toward correcting Wordsworth, whose own notions on the subject, apparent in *The Excursion* and "Ruth," were "indistinct" and "jejune." Then follows a miscellany: "a chapter on the possibilities of philosophy; he traces some of his more notable discoveries and debts and points out that one cannot always tell the contents of a book by the label on the binding. A long digression . . . offers a rest before entering upon the philosophic hard core of Chapter 12, the bed-rock promised at the start. . . . From this point he moves outward again, diffracting his conclusions into the sphere of poetry by drawing the distinction between Fancy and imagination" ("The Integrity of 'Biographia Literaria,'" pp. 98–100). From all this Whalley derives an impression of unity, though even in his description the final chapters seem not to follow an ordered course.

7. Thus J. A. Appleyard, *Coleridge's Philosophy of Literature: The Development of a Concept of Poetry 1791–1819* (Cambridge: Harvard University Press, 1965), p. 169. Appleyard unkindly describes the work as "primarily a record . . . of the state of [Coleridge's] mind in the summer of 1815" (p. 170).

8. Leslie Stephen, *Hours in a Library* (London: Smith, Elder & Co., 1909), III, p. 331.

9. *BL,* I, pp. 110–111.

10. Ibid., p. 113.

11. Jerome Christensen analyzes the same passage along similar lines. But, preferring to regard her case as an extreme version of the condition that afflicts us all, he is finally unwilling to allow for an altogether alien motivation for the girl's behavior. "Although rational investigation shows that the girl's ravings are wholly mechanical, *we know* that the 'will' and the 'reason' are never entirely suspended—we know because Coleridge has told us so. Somewhere within, the woman desired to be possessed: she cannot be entirely guiltless because the activity of the learned machinery received its blessing somewhere in her mind. The converse implication is also true. The most willed, reasonable action of the woman or the physician is in some way conditioned and cannot be completely to his or her credit. . . . No one can fully possess anything—certainly not language, least of all himself" (*Coleridge's Blessed Machine of Language* [Ithaca: Cornell University Press, 1981], pp. 112–13).

12. *BL,* I, pp. 113, 114.

13. Ibid., p. 114.

14. *Coleridge's Blessed Machine of Language,* p. 111.

15. Ibid., p. 112.

16. The echoes of other writers—not just Plotinus but also Milton—become stronger just when Coleridge turns from secular to sacred questions, as if he were afraid to speak in his own voice on matters of import.

17. *BL,* I, pp. 114–15. Coleridge is translating from Plotinus, *Enneads,* I. 6. 4.

18. We have already seen how Christabel, imitating the look on Geraldine's face, momentarily becomes what she sees. "For Coleridge," writes Michael Cooke, "reading is becoming. The sense of the self symbolically inhering in the things it meets, even to the extent of a quasi-Platonic sense of itself becoming manifest as it meets those things, cannot be separated from the subject matter of Coleridge's reading" ("*Quisque Sui Faber:* Coleridge in the *Biographia Literaria,*" *Philological Quarterly* 50 (1971), 220.

19. The term is Thomas McFarland's adaption of the Greek *diasparaktos,* "torn to pieces." He uses the word to talk about Romantic "incompleteness, fragmentation, and ruin" in *Romanticism and the Forms of Ruin: Wordsworth, Coleridge, and Modalities of Fragmentation* (Princeton: Princeton University Press, 1981).

20. It would be hard to say whether Coleridge feared or desired such a state of affairs. Perhaps during those times when his will seemed paralyzed he may have hoped that memory could supply its place.

Writing to John Thelwall in 1796, before the decline of his poetic abilities, Coleridge includes a self-description that anticipates the later image of the possessed girl: "My face, unless when animated by immediate eloquence, expresses great Sloth, & great, indeed almost ideotic, good nature. 'Tis a mere carcase of a face: fat, flabby, & expressive chiefly of inexpression. Yet, I am told, that my eyes, eyebrows, & forehead are physiognomically good—; but of this the Deponent knoweth not" (Letter #156, to John Thelwall, 19 November 1796, in *STCL,* I, pp. 259–60). Is this a genius peering through the mask of an idiot, an idiot possessed by the spirit of a genius, or an idiot inspired?

21. I. A. Richards, *Coleridge on Imagination* (Bloomington: Indiana University Press, 1960), p. 60.

22. Jean-Pierre Mileur, *Vision and Revision: Coleridge's Art of Immanence* (Berkeley and Los Angeles: University of California Press, 1983), p. ix.

23. *BL,* I, p. 5. An anonymous reviewer despaired at the result: "Of course, a work, which professed to give an account of opinions, that are linked to each other by no other connection than that which arises from their having belonged to the same individual cannot be supposed to be arranged upon any method founded on the nature of things; and consequently to give a systematic criticism of them, would be altogether impracticable" (*Romantic Bards and British Reviewers: A Selected Edition of the Contemporary Reviews of the Works of Wordsworth, Coleridge, Byron, Keats and Shelley,* edited by John O. Hayden [Lincoln: University of Nebraska Press, 1971], pp. 155–56).

24. *STCN,* I, #1515.

25. See Daniel Mark Fogel, "A Compositional History of the *Biographia Literaria,*" in Fredson Bowers, ed., *Studies in Bibliography,* Bibliographical Society of the University of Virginia, 30 (Charlottesville: University Press of Virginia, 1977), and *BL,* I, p. lii, for a contrary view.

26. Anonymous review from the *British Critic,* in Hayden, pp. 164–65.

27. De Quincey notes other, lesser plagiarisms both in the *Biographia* and elsewhere in Coleridge's work, explaining that his motive in discovering the problem

to the public was "to forestall . . . other discoverers who would make a more unfriendly use of the discovery" (*Recollections of the Lakes and the Lake Poets,* edited by David Wright [Harmondsworth, England: Penguin Books, 1970], p. 37).

28. Ibid., p. 41. Although De Quincey does not go so far as to call Coleridge possessed, this fantastical junk-heap recalls the sorts of thing that people bewitched or possessed were occasionally reported to have vomited up. In sixteenth-century Amsterdam, for example, thirty boys "exorcised for possession . . . suffered atrocious pains and convulsions as though insane, and vomited thimbles, rags, bits of pottery, glass, hair, and other rubbish of the devil." A century and a half later your typical victim of possession might be carrying around in his person "wood, needles, knives, glass, hair, eggshells, woolen and linen cloths, *Glufen* [gloves?], nails, balls of thread, yarn, stones, and the like, and . . . these things might come to sight through the various openings of the body or in the sores and ulcers caused by sorcery" (Henry Charles Lea, *Materials Toward a History of Witchcraft,* edited by Arthur C. Howland [New York: Thomas Yoseloff, 1957], III, p. 1046. De Quincey's reading is precisely an exorcism.

29. De Quincey, p. 40.

30. Ibid., p. 40.

31. James Gillman, *The Life of Samuel Taylor Coleridge* (London: William Pickering, 1838; rpt. University Microfilms, 1971), I, p. 245.

32. *BL,* I, p. 147.

33. Ibid., p. 160–61.

34. He dearly loved to point out plagiarisms, some real and some only imagined, especially when he himself had been trying to pass off others' work as his own. The fifth chapter of the *Biographia,* for example, which draws heavily upon J. G. E. Maass's *Versuch uber die Einbildungskraft,* ends with a gratuitous attack upon Hume's honesty. (See *BL,* I, p. 104 and notes 1 and 3.) Even less just is his treatment of Schelling, the source of much of the *Biographia*'s philosophy. In chapter 9 Coleridge takes him to task for failing to acknowledge deeply enough his obligations to Boehme: "The coincidence of SCHELLING'S system with certain general ideas of Behmen, he declares to have been *mere* coincidence; while *my* obligations have been more direct. *He* needs give to Behmen only feelings of sympathy; while I owe him a debt of gratitude" (*BL,* I, p. 161). Thus parading his own virtuous humility, he projects his iniquity onto the victim of his own largely unacknowledged depredations. This behavior indicates neither that unacknowledged translations and paraphrases simply slipped into Coleridge's work by accident as he drew upon inadequately marked passages from his notebooks, nor that he took from the works of others in a spirit of friendly sharing. Had Coleridge been unaware of or indifferent to what was happening, the *Biographia* would undoubtedly have made less fuss about the issues of plagiarism and literary property.

35. According to his plans for establishing a pantisocracy in the Susquehannah Valley he, together with Southey, the Fricker sisters, and a few others, would practice "aspheterism," or unselfishness. Each member of the group would share equally not only in the rights and privileges of the group but also in its material wealth. H. M. Margoliouth paints an idealized portrait of Coleridge as a man of

"complete spiritual and intellectual unselfishness" in both worldly and wordly matters: "On the material side Coleridge would always be the gainer by aspheterism, but it is only just to remember that he practiced it throughout life on the intellectual side: he was none of your scholars who hoard an idea or a discovery for fear someone else should steal the credit" (*Wordsworth and Coleridge 1795–1837* [Oxford: Oxford University Press, 1953; rpt. Archon Books, 1966], p. 78). Nevertheless, given Coleridge's distressing habit of claiming he had been robbed of credit by careless or treacherous acquaintances who published his ideas as their own, it would be a mistake to explain the plagiarisms as a practical application of the aspheterism that had aroused his zeal as a young man.

36. *BL,* I, p. 118.

37. Ibid., p. 43.

38. Ibid., p. 223.

39. For Wellek, the plagiarism is evidence of intellectual weakness, even philosophical incompetence on Coleridge's part. Wellek finds Coleridge guilty of "a fundamental lack of real philosophical individuality," of having "little insight into the incompatibility of different trends of thought. . . . It is not the fact that several central passages in Coleridge are borrowed or paraphrased or influenced by other thinkers; it is rather the circumstance that these adaptations of other thought are heterogeneous, incoherent and even contradictory which makes the study of Coleridge's philosophy ultimately so futile." Insensitive to the nuances of meaning in the material he worked with, Coleridge could hardly understand how concepts might be worked into a real system. "This fundamental inability to think systematically and therefore philosophically drove Coleridge to borrowings, conscious and unconscious, and brought into his structure the feeling of instability and looseness." See *Immanuel Kant in England 1793–1838* (Princeton: Princeton University Press, 1931), pp. 66–68. Fruman blames the plagiarisms, together with what he sees as Coleridge's habitual and unremitting lying, on neurotic self-doubt and an inability to deny himself any immediate gratification—be it opium or the admiration of his audience. His erudition, which Fruman suspects to have been far less magnificent than Coleridge pretended, had its source in caution; he was less likely to be caught stealing if he stole from obscure corners of the library. For Fruman's encyclopedic compilation of Coleridge's attempts to mislead friends and readers, see *Coleridge, the Damaged Archangel* (New York: George Braziller, 1971).

40. Richard Haven, *Patterns of Consciousness: An Essay on Coleridge* (Amherst: University of Massachusetts Press, 1969), pp. 16–20. For Haven, neither the words themselves nor even their sources matter as much as how Coleridge used them. He credits Coleridge with making deeply imaginative use of his philosophical materials. This frees him to stress the importance of looking at the borrowed material in the context Coleridge gave it, but it keeps him from treating the anxiety that Coleridge seems to have felt about the propriety of his behaviour.

41. Thomas McFarland, *Coleridge and the Pantheist Tradition* (Oxford: Oxford University Press, 1969), p. 27. McFarland argues that the charge of plagiarism is invalid "when it is a question of the use of common materials by two or more individuals vitally involved in the culture of a period, but that it has a certain validity when defined as the mere repetition of borrowed materials without the

achievement of reticulated pattern" (pp. 45, 47). Coleridge did more than repeat his sources, McFarland says; he worked out an imaginative synthesis of what he read and what he thought. He took not only from Schelling but from many others; he did not become the disciple of any one philosopher. Turning Wellek's charge back upon itself, McFarland argues that Coleridge brought together various and sometimes irreconcilable philosophical concepts not from any inability to understand how conceptual systems work but because he felt no obligation to remain loyal to any one of his sources. Like Fruman, Bate, and others, however, McFarland agrees that there was a psychological component to the practice, too, and analyzes his literary dependence as a form of masochism. *Romanticism and the Forms of Ruin* stresses this theme. For stout defenses against Fruman's criticisms, see Geoffrey Hartman's review of Fruman's book in *The New York Times Book Review,* 12 March 1972, pp. 1, 36; and McFarland, "Coleridge's Plagiarisms Once More: A Review Essay," *Yale Review* 63 (1974), 252–86.

42. McFarland, *Coleridge and the Pantheist Tradition,* p. 40. Possibly Coleridge was not convinced he was the thief. A notebook entry from the end of 1804 suggests that he may long have regarded these metaphysical wares as rightly his own: "In the Preface to my Metaphys. Works I should say—Once & for all read Tetens, Kant, Fichte, & c—& there you will trace or if you are on the hunt, track me. Why then not acknowledge your obligations step by step? Because, I could not do in a multitude of glaring resemblances without a lie / for they had been mine, formed, & full formed in my own mind, before I had ever heard of these Writers, because to have fixed on the partic. instances in which I have really been indebted to these Writers would have been very hard, if possible, to me who read for truth & self-satisfaction, not to make a book, & who always rejoiced & was jubilant when I found my own ideas well expressed already by others, < & would have looked like a *trick,* to skulk there not quoted, > & lastly, let me say, that the Soul is *Mine.* I fear him not for a Critic who an confound a Fellow-thinker with a Compiler" (*STCN,* II, #2375).

Fundamentally he seems to fear that once he concedes small, particular obligations to other philosophers, his readers may assume obligation in cases where he is in fact being original. Although the eleven-year gap between justification and offense suggests chronic guilt, Coleridge's prediction of how critics would respond to his finagling was canny.

43. "Throughout most of his life the unconfident Coleridge—inhibited when he tried to write directly and formally in his own voice (inhibited, that is, when he was trying to write anything he felt was really important)—became most completely alive and the resources of his mind most open when he could talk or write vicariously: when he could speak on behalf of another, as a champion or defensive critic, or appropriate and embellish arguments from another in order to show what they could lead to, if helped along the way, or could give to another a deeper sense of the aims and supports for which he had been groping" (Bate, *Coleridge* (1968; rpt. Cambridge: Harvard University Press, 1987), p. 37).

44. *Coleridge's Blessed Machine of Language,* pp. 105–6. Coleridge is then like a parasite or guest to the text whose margins he fills. He finds the structure of his argument provided by his source and need take no responsibility for the direction

the argument takes. Christensen's Coleridge bears a certain resemblance to a guerilla or an exiled leader of the opposition: "The resourcefulness of the commentator derives from a tactical freedom to exploit aggressively any source of argument, which, in turn, depends on his fundamental distance from any general premise. . . . The anxiety of the marginalist is owed to the fact that his resourcefulness is always derived, his freedom licensed, as it were, by his host—the authority on which he obsessively relies and which he compulsively disrupts" (pp. 108–9).

45. Although this demonization clearly enough has its terrifying aspects, it provides comfort, too. In the following passage, written late in 1803, Coleridge seems to figure psychological dependence as the sharing of a common spirit: "My nature requires another Nature for its support, & reposes only in another from the necessary Indigence of its Being.—Intensely similar, yet not the same; or may I venture to say, the same indeed, but dissimilar, as the same Breath sent with the same force, the same pauses, & with the same melody pre-imaged in the mind, into the Flute and the Clarion shall be the same Soul diversely incarnate" (*STCN,* I, #1679).

46. "A Compositional History of the *Biographia Literaria,*" p. 232.

47. *The Autobiography of Alice B. Toklas* may be a comparable example, but its confusion of voices is playful in a way that the *Biographia*'s is not.

48. Avrom Fleishman, *Figures of Autobiography: The Language of Self-Writing in Victorian and Modern England* (Berkeley and Los Angeles: University of California Press, 1983), p. 33. The movement of substitution works the other way in this case, id for ego, it (or he) for I. It is doubtful in any case whether Fleishman means to invoke the full implications of the Freudian model.

49. Ibid., p. 33. See also Paul de Man, *The Rhetoric of Romanticism* (New York: Columbia University Press, 1984), pp. 69–72.

50. Letter #390, in *STCL,* II, p. 714. In the context from which Coleridge takes it (Juvenal's eleventh satire) the line is a warning to men that they should know their limits and not overspend themselves:

> From heaven descends the maxim *Know Thyself*—
> To be taken to heart and remembered, whether you're choosing
> A wife, or aiming to win a seat in that august body
> The Senate.
> . . . .
> A man should know his own measure
> In great things and small alike: when you're buying fish
> Don't go hankering after salmon on a herring income.

From Juvenal, *The Sixteen Satires,* translated by Peter Green (Harmondsworth, England: Penguin Books, 1967), p. 228. Self-knowledge is financial common sense.

51. In a notebook entry of 1805 apparently having to do with Wordsworth, Coleridge writes, "O that my Spirit purged by Death of its Weaknesses, which are alas! my *identity* might flow into *thine,* & live and act in thee, & be Thou." The passage has many parallels in Coleridge's writings. See *STCN,* II, #2712.

52. Inconsistently enough, however, he did not back off from Schelling with despair once he found the metaphysician's spot already occupied. Instead of retreating and extolling his predecessor, he denied the precedence and swallowed his words.

53. *BL,* I, p. 252. See also *BL,* II, p. 240n.

54. This is according to the statistical table of the proportions of direct translation, paraphrase, and summary in each chapter provided by Bate and Engell (*BL,* II, p. 254).

55. Leslie Brisman discusses romantic imagination in terms of reorigination in his *Romantic Origins* (Ithaca: Cornell University Press, 1978).

56. Frances Ferguson, "Coleridge and the Deluded Reader: 'The Rime of the Ancient Mariner,'" *Georgia Review* 31 (1977), 634.

57. *BL,* I, pp. 259–60.

58. Ibid., p. 259.

59. Ibid., pp. 264–65.

60. At least this is how Coleridge and Schelling see it. As Paul Fry pointed out to me, the relationship between A and B is not necessarily any more reality-directed than that of A to itself.

61. F. W. J. Schelling, *System of Transcendental Idealism (1800),* translated by Peter Heath (Charlottesville: University Press of Virginia, 1978), p. 22.

62. Schelling, p. 23.

63. *BL,* I, p. 257.

64. Ibid., p. 260.

65. Ibid., p. 272.

66. Ibid., p. 273.

67. Ibid., p. 279.

68. Ibid., pp. 279–80.

69. Schelling, p. 27.

70. Ibid., pp. 36, 37.

71. Ibid., pp. 43–44.

72. Ibid., p. 53.

73. Ibid., pp. 53–54.

74. Ibid., p. 53.

75. Schelling's deconstruction of the self, which turns out to embody the alterity against which it seeks to define itself, was not entirely his own work, either. His immediate predecessor in the deconstruction of identity was Fichte. For a history of the relationship between the writings of these two philosophers on this subject, see Joseph L. Esposito, *Schelling's Idealism and Philosophy of Nature* (Lewisburg: Bucknell University Press, 1977), particularly pp. 24–26, 45–46, and 103.

76. *BL,* I, p. 300.

77. He will do the same thing later in his life as well, when he writes letters to the authorities of his son's college in his son's name. See his letters to the Provost and Fellows of Oriel College and to the Warden of Merton College, #1249A and #1253A, 30 September 1820 and December, 1820, in *STCL,* V, pp. 103–6, 120–23. Coleridge's dishonesty in matters of authorship was not always motivated by a desire to claim undue credit for himself.

78. Leslie Brisman proposes to call the author of this letter "Porlock," the "natural man" in Coleridge and "a serpent in the garden" of his mind. (*Romantic Origins* pp. 31–35.) Gayatri Spivak calls him "obturateur" and relates the letter to the Lacanian symbolic ("The Letter as Cutting Edge," pp. 208–26). More usefully,

Kenneth Johnston, who anticipates much of what I have to say about the letter, identifies the persona behind the letter as a Coleridgean version of Wordsworth. For his analysis, see *Wordsworth and 'The Recluse,'* pp. 355–60.

79. *BL,* I, pp. 301.

80. In the Preface to the 1814 edition of *The Excursion* Wordsworth writes that *The Prelude* and *The Recluse* "have the same kind of relation to each other . . . as the antechapel has to the body of a gothic church." Furthermore, his "minor Pieces . . . when they shall be properly arranged, will be found by the attentive Reader to have such connection with the main Work as may give them claim to be likened to the little cells, oratories, and sepulchral recesses, ordinarily included in those edifices."

81. *The Prelude, 1799, 1805, 1850,* edited by Jonathan Wordsworth, M. H. Abrams, and Stephen Gill (New York: Norton, 1979), I; lines here are from the 1805 edition.

82. "The Wordsworthian text inspires itself before our ears. . . . [I]t adds up to nothing progressive, to nothing but a new, confident, even self-originating textuality. The text is built almost *ex nihilo*" (Geoffrey Hartman, "Words, Wish, Worth: Wordsworth," in Harold Bloom et al., eds., *Deconstruction and Criticism* [New York: Seabury Press, 1979], p. 210).

83. Ferguson writes of Wordsworth's fondness for echoing himself, "Although Wordsworth could evade literary influence no more than any other poet, his internal echoings constitute a covert claim that he has sealed up the necessary parts of the whole, that he has provided the objects for his own allusions. His attempt at freedom from tradition takes the guise of a redoubling of his own work which is so internally reflexive that it may seem (at least to the poet) to have no need for external appeals" (*Language as Counter-Spirit* [New Haven: Yale University Press, 1977], p. 171.

84. Not until 1805 did Wordsworth mark the gap between the first 54 lines and the rest of the poem. Apparently it was the first passage he worked on. But it does not appear in the two-part *Prelude* of 1798–1799. Its appearance at the head of the 1805 and 1850 *Preludes* is a return to a text from the past. For a history of the poem's composition and a reconstruction of its earliest appearance, see *The Prelude, 1798–99,* edited by Stephen Parrish (Ithaca: Cornell University Press, 1977), especially pp. 6, 123.

85. Thomas McFarland, for example, argues that Coleridge introduces the letter and breaks off his line of argument because it is leading him uncomfortably close to pantheism. See "The Origin and Significance of Coleridge's Theory of Secondary Imagination," in *Originality and Imagination* (Baltimore: The Johns Hopkins University Press, 1985), pp. 92–93.

86. *BL,* I, pp. 304–5.

87. Ibid., pp. 253–54.

88. Ibid., p. 255.

89. Ibid., pp. 254–55.

90. Ibid., p. 254. The editors point out that the phrase "of the thought with the thing" is Coleridge's addition; Schelling is not fully responsible for this extra complexity. See p. 252n.

91. Fourteen years earlier Coleridge faulted Locke for the same sloppiness in defining the mind and its contents. See letter #384, to Josiah Wedgwood, February 1801, in *STCL,* II, p. 696.

92. *Langenscheidt's New College German Dictionary,* compiled by Heinz Messinger (Berlin and Munich: Langenscheidt, 1973), p. 541.

93. Ca. 1809–1810 Coleridge wrote, "We understand Nature just as if at a distance we looked at the Image of a Person in a Looking-glass, plainly and fervently discoursing—yet what he uttered, we could decypher only by the motion of the Lips, and the mien, and the expression of the muscles of the Countenance" (*STCN,* III, #3659).

94. *BL,* I, p. 255. But Geoffrey Hartman suggests that Coleridge felt himself to be nevertheless unable to achieve this imaginative coinstantaneity: "He is afflicted by secondariness as by a curse: his relation to writing of all kinds is more embarrassed than that of Keats and more devious than that of Akenside. His imagination sees itself as inherently 'secondary'—not only because it follows great precursors in poetry or philosophy (though that is a factor) but chiefly because of the one precursor, the 'primary Imagination . . . living power and prime agent of all human perception . . . repetition in the finite mind of the eternal act of creation in the infinite I AM.' His religious sensibility, conspiring with a burdened personal situation, makes him feel at a hopeless remove from originality" ("Evening Star and Evening Land," in *The Fate of Reading and Other Essays* [Chicago: University of Chicago Press, 1975], p. 167).

95. Coleridge conflates God's speech in Genesis with His speech in Exodus; to him, "Let there be light" sounds like "I am that I am." That he chooses to overlook the temporal interval and to collapse these distinct episodes and utterances suggests that despite his abhorrence of the pantheism that earlier fascinated him, Coleridge still cannot help interpreting Creation as a revelation or explication of God's nature.

Chapter 7: The Impropriety of the Imagination

1. Such natural self-representation is what the reconciliation of nature and consciousness would amount to. Earl Wasserman discusses the English romantics' attempts at such a reconciliation in their poetry. Although he seems to believe in the success of their attempts, he is somehow never quite able to catch the machinery of the reconciliation at work: "How the object is transformed into the stuff of the mind Wordsworth does not here say"; "it is not readily conceivable how Coleridge's epistemology could be translated into the life of a poem by shaping its matter, imparting a special quality to its imagery, or providing a process for the transformation of images into symbols. In other words, it is difficult to conceive of poetry in which his epistemology and his theories of imagination and symbolism would be recognizable as shaping forces" ("The English Romantics: The Grounds of Knowledge," *Studies in Romanticism* 4 [1964],) 23, 30).

2. M. H. Abrams, *The Mirror and the Lamp: Romantic Theory and the Critical Tradition* (New York: Oxford University Press, 1953; rpt. 1977), p. 171. Abrams

is describing one of the aspects of a plant relevant to Coleridge's purposes. The others are the primacy of the whole over its parts, growth, spontaneous organization, and unity (pp. 171–74).

3. David Sampson contends that "the controversy over the so-called 'new poetry' derived ultimately from a very old debate concerning the nature of pastoral" ("Wordsworth and 'The Deficiencies of Language,'" *English Literary History* 51 (1984), 53–68).

4. Marjorie Barstow develops the history of this impulse from Chaucer onwards and places Wordsworth and Coleridge in its context. See *Wordsworth's Theory of Poetic Diction: A Study of the Historical and Personal Background of the Lyrical Ballads* (New Haven: Yale University Press, 1917).

5. As W. J. B. Owen has pointed out, when Wordsworth calls upon nature his real object may well be permanence. Whereas mountains stand from generation to generation, the face of the city constantly changes (*Wordsworth as Critic* [Toronto: University of Toronto Press, 1969], pp. 3–5).

6. *Prose Works,* I, p. 140.

7. *Wordsworth as Critic,* pp. 112–13.

8. Roger Sharrock, "Wordsworth's Revolt Against Literature," *Essays in Criticism* 3 (1953), 401.

9. *Prose Works,* I, p. 138.

10. Ibid., 149.

11. *The Art of the Lyrical Ballads* (Cambridge: Harvard University Press, 1973), p. 140. The full argument, which occupies chapters 3 and 4, is most densely elaborated on pp. 137–48.

12. *Prose Works,* I, p. 142.

13. Wordsworth is on his way toward a description of the negative capability of chameleon poethood. But the germs of the egotistical sublime are present as well. Humility before the truth of the common man's response to common things shades off into pride in the poet's ability to feel upon provocation so subtle as to be virtually imperceptible, even imaginary.

14. For a discussion of Coleridge's critique of Wordsworth conducted along lines more historically and philosophically informed than mine, see James C. McKusick, *Coleridge's Philosophy of Language* (New Haven: Yale University Press, 1986), pp. 110–18.

15. *BL,* II, pp. 13–14.

16. Ibid., 52.

17. Ibid., 44. See also *STCN,* III, #3415: "It is scarce possible that [anyone who wanted to learn to read and become a poet] might not procure the Bible, & many religious Books, which at all events would give him the best & most natural Language."

18. Ibid., 54.

19. Ibid., 81.

20. "The notion that poetry in general should employ the language of the 'lower and middle classes of society' was never Wordsworth's ideal at any time. It is only his definition of an experiment that he chose to try in thirteen out of nineteen

poems by him in the first edition of the *Lyrical Ballads;* and the famous Preface is little more than a somewhat unwilling and frankly inadequate attempt to explain this same experiment" (Barstow, *Wordsworth's Theory of Poetic Diction,* p. xii).

21. *BL,* II, pp. 121–36.

22. Coleridge's tact may be responsible for confusing the issues: certainly it is less insulting to suggest that a poet's readers may find his sudden shifts in style hard to follow than it is to point out that the poet plumps out lines and stanzas with undistinguished verbiage. But humble verse is always potentially incongruous, being already a deviation from what Coleridge took to be the norms of poetry.

23. *BL,* II, p. 135.

24. See Parrish, *The Art of the Lyrical Ballads,* p. 142.

25. *BL,* II, p. 136.

26. See Paul Hamilton: "Each of the defects which Coleridge describes is not generically distinct from the others, but contributes to their cumulative effect." Hamilton finds Coleridge's central concern to be the incoherence of the principles governing Wordsworth's verse. "Coleridge's adverse criticism of Wordsworth suggests that his poetry conspires against the nature of poetry itself," Hamilton suggests, and finds the heart of the paradox to be in the way that Wordsworth's "egotism, which insists on an eccentric response, combines with his poetic literalism, which submits to things as they are, to strand Wordsworth in a hopelessly paradoxical position. Coleridge will not allow Wordsworthian eccentricity to constitute a defamiliarization of the real" (*Coleridge's Poetics* [Stanford: Stanford University Press, 1983], pp. 160, 161).

27. One class of "characteristic defects" might even be evidence of the sublimest possibility of all: "I have indeed considered the disproportion of human passions to their ordinary objects among the strongest internal evidences of our future destination, and the attempt to restore them to their rightful claimants, the most imperious duty and the noblest task of genius" (*The Friend,* edited by Barbara Rooke [Princeton: Princeton University Press, 1969], I, p. 35).

28. See Steven Knapp's analysis of Coleridge's discomfort, which he interprets in terms of "a refusal to accept Wordsworth's ambiguous naturalization of allegory," in *Personification and the Sublime: Milton to Coleridge* (Cambridge: Harvard University Press, 1985), pp. 100–106.

29. *BL,* II, pp. 138–39.

30. Ibid., p. 139.

31. Ibid., p. 140.

32. Hamilton notes the same pattern but interprets it disapprovingly. "This volte-face on Coleridge's part cries out for explanation. The excellences which he lists are just the reverse of the defects and nothing more. It is with some blandness that Coleridge tells us of the last, culminating defect that it 'is a fault of which none but a man of genius is capable'. . . . He does not feel threatened or puzzled by this surfacing antinomy, and fails to sense the paradoxes and tensions in his own thought. The result is an undeniable cramping of his critical approach, and a revealing distrust of experiment and originality" (*Coleridge's Poetics,* p. 163).

33. "The one sure thing that can be said about the *Biographia* is that Coleridge's

literary life is the story of Wordsworth's genius—a sharp saying that cuts both ways," notes Christensen in *Coleridge's Blessed Machine of Language* (Ithaca: Cornell University Press, 1981), p. 132.

34. *BL,* II, p. 142.

35. Ibid., p. 142.

36. Ibid., pp. 144–45, 148.

37. Ibid., p. 148.

38. Ibid., p.150.

39. Such metonymic valuation would not be out of character for the author of the *Biographia,* whose peculiar critical weightings of Wordsworth and other poets Raimonda Modiano studies in "Coleridge and Wordsworth: The Ethics of Gift Exchange and Literary Ownership," in Christine Gallant, ed., *Coleridge's Theory of Imagination Today,* Georgia State Literary Studies, No. 4 (New York: AMS Press, 1989), pp. 243–56.

40. *BL,* II, pp. 141–42.

41. The very confusion between the man and his work contributes to the suggestion that the work is its own source.

42. It would be interesting to know whether Coleridge was thinking of his own past relationship with Wordsworth when he wrote this. Does the glorification of Wordsworth's genius also indirectly glorify Coleridge's own?

43. *Blessed Machine,* pp. 139, 149, 161.

44. Barbara Hardy argues that Coleridge's distinction between fancy and imagination is the product of an error in logic. Seeing a difference in complexity between one image and another, Coleridge worked backwards from effect to cause to "find" separate origins for the simple and for the complex. There is, however, no reliable criterion for distinguishing between the two faculties; the terms indicate more about the critic's enthusiasm for a passage than anything about the passage itself. See "Distinction Without Difference: Coleridge's Fancy and Imagination," *Essays in Criticism* 1 (1951), 336–44. Frances Ferguson agrees: "He has granted so much [in his definitions] to the primary and secondary imaginations that it is difficult to see how the fancy can exist at all, except as a debased or parodic form of the secondary imagination" ("Coleridge on Language and Delusion," *Genre* 11 [1979], 193–94).

45. Coleridge did recognize the existence of linguistic homogeneity, although he regarded it as native to languages other than English. Entry 3762 in *STCN,* III, for example, discusses puns in Italian, Latin, and German as evidence "that Language itself is formed upon associations of this kind, that possibly the sensus genericus of whole classes of words may be thus decyphered, . . . that words are not mere symbols of things & thoughts but themselves things—and that any harmony in the things symbolized will perforce be presented to us more easily as well as with additional beauty by a correspondent harmony of the Symbols with each other:

"Thus—Heri vidi fragilem frangi, hodie mortalem mori—Gestern sah ich was gebrechliches brechen, heute was sterbliches sterben—compared with the English. This the beauty of homogeneous Languages—So veni, vidi, vici." The virtue of homogeneous language is not simply that its words are related but that their relation reflects the relations between things in the real world; the symbols are related to one another as the things they symbolize are related. Entry 4247, written about the same time as the *Biographia,* makes a similar point.

46. "He seems to take positive delight in finding oppositions to reconcile," observes Alice D. Snyder. "He never tired of calling attention to the fact that extremes meet, but he is very evidently looking to find in nature as many pairs of extremes as possible. . . . It would, I think, be fair to call Coleridge's interest in the principle of the Reconciliation of Opposites a constitutional malady" (*The Critical Principle of the Reconciliation of Opposites as Employed by Coleridge* [1918; rpt. Folcroft, PA: Folcroft Press, 1970), pp. 19, 20.

47. *BL,* II, pp. 16–17.

48. The obvious analogue to such a unit of sameness would once have been the atom; now, depending upon one's leaning toward or away from deconstruction, it would be either the monopole or the quark, a particle with no constituents, no internal structure. Coleridge wants to believe in the semantic monopole and writes as if it existed, but he shows us only dipoles.

49. *BL,* II, p. 72.

50. Cf. Lawrence Buell, who, pointing out that the *Biographia* fails to conform to its own prescription for organic wholeness, says the theory was meant to apply to poetry, not to autobiographical prose ("The Question of Form in Coleridge's *Biographia Literaria,*" *English Literary History* 46 [1979], 399–417).

51. See Jerome Christensen's analysis of the same conceptual tangle in *Coleridge's Blessed Machine of Language,* pp. 137–61.

52. *BL,* II, p. 54.

53. "A man of Genius," wrote Coleridge, "using a rich and expressive Language (the Greek, German, or English) is an excellent instance and illustration of the ever individualizing process and dynamic Being, of Ideas. What a magnificent History of acts of individual minds, sanctioned by the collective Mind of the Country a Language is—" (quoted from an autograph notebook, MS. C, in Ferguson, in "Coleridge on Language and Delusion," p. 195).

54. *BL,* II, p. 122.

55. For a discussion of coins and the significance of what is inscribed upon them, see Marc Shell, *The Economy of Literature* (Baltimore: The Johns Hopkins University Press, 1978), pp. 63–66.

56. Coleridge did not hold the distinction, as commonly understood, to be very important in any case. "It is among the miseries of the present age that it recognizes no medium between *Literal* and *Metaphorical,*" Coleridge wrote in *The Statesman's Manual. Lay Sermons,* edited by R. J. White (Princeton: Princeton University Press, 1972), p. 30.

57. Coleridge may have had trouble remembering what new coins looked like, however. At the time of composition, unworn coins (unless gold, which circulated but little) were rare. There had been no silver coinage since 1787, and that was largely hoarded; the previous silver issue, of 1763, was small. Copper had last been coined in 1805–1807, and it was subject to intensive use. A typical coin circulating during this period might have lost ten to fifteen percent of its mass through attrition. And, of course, since the weight of a coin still mattered, despite the conventionality

of its legal value, bad money drove out good. For this information I am grateful to John Burnham of the Numismatics Collection, Sterling Memorial Library, Yale University.

58. During the first two decades of the nineteenth century, however, English gold coins were worth more than their nominal value; silver coins too, though not pretending to represent the value of their own metal, were undervalued. As a result gold and, to a lesser extent, silver coins were smuggled out of England to the continent, where they were melted down and sold. There was no assurance that an English coin would remain an English coin. See Pierre Vilar, *A History of Gold and Money 1450–1920,* translated by Judith White (1969; London: NLB, 1976), pp. 285, 313.

59. *STCN,* III, #4247 (1815).

60. Compare *Essays on His Times in The Morning Post and The Courier,* edited by David V. Erdman (Princeton: Princeton University Press, 1978), III, p. 120. Hereafter this work will be referred to as *EOT.*

Ferguson finds Coleridge deeply ambivalent about the relationship between signs and what they represent. "On the one hand, Coleridge wishes greater power upon words and desires that language actually constitute the things which it signifies. On the other hand, he fears that the power of words is too great—great enough, at least, to dupe men into believing that language does constitute the things which it signifies." "Coleridge on Language and Delusion," pp. 201–2.

61. *EOT,* II, p. 132.

62. Ibid., p. 239. Marx supplies a fancifully mundane explanation of the difference, figuring the function in the effect: "In the course of its friction against all kinds of hands, pouches, pockets, purses, money-belts, bags, chests and strong-boxes, the coin rubs off, loses one gold atom here and another one there and thus, as it wears off in its wanderings over the world, it loses more and more of its intrinsic substance. By being used it gets used up. . . . The longer a coin remains in circulation . . . the greater the discrepancy between its form as coin and its actual gold or silver substance. What remains is *magni nominis umbra.* The body of the coin becomes but a shadow. . . . While other beings lose their idealism in contact with the outer world, the coin is idealized by practice, becoming gradually transformed into a mere phantom of its golden or silver body" (Karl Marx, *A Contribution to the Critique of Political Economy,* translated by N. I. Stone [Chicago: Charles H. Kerr & Co., 1904], pp. 140–42).

63. See Marx, pp. 162–163.

64. Hans Aarsleff notes its occurrence in Quintilian, Bacon, Hobbes, Locke, Leibniz, and Robert South (*The Study of Language in England 1780–1860* [1967; rpt. Minneapolis: University of Minnesota Press, 1983], p. 233, n. 36). See also Jacques Derrida, "White Mythology: Metaphor in the Text of Philosophy," in *Margins of Philosophy,* translated by Alan Bass (Chicago: University of Chicago Press, 1982), pp. 216–19.

65. *EOT,* II, pp. 124–29, 131–33, 228–30, 238–42, 249–54; *EOT,* III, pp. 116–23. The Bank Restriction Act, issued in May of 1797 and remaining in effect until 1821, suspended the Bank of England's responsibility toward holders of bank notes; the notes could not be redeemed for gold. From 1797 to 1812 this

"forced currency" was not, however, legal tender. The absurdity of the situation threatened disaster in 1811, when Lord King declared he would accept his rents only in gold or bank notes equivalent to the price of the gold. A few months later Parliament recognized officially the function that the bank notes played actually and required all creditors to accept payment in Bank of England notes as legal tender. It was during this period that controversy sprang up over the nature of money, particularly whether the value of money depended upon the amount of gold in the vaults of the Bank of England or whether it depended upon the country's balance of payments and the demand for currency. See Vilar, pp. 281, 310–11, 316–17.

66. *Money, Language, and Thought: Literary and Philosophic Economies from the Medieval to the Modern Era* (Berkeley: University of California Press, 1982), p. 156.

67. "Autobiography . . . is not a genre or a mode, but a figure of reading or understanding that occurs, to some degree, in all texts. . . . [A]ny book with a readable title page is, to some extent, autobiographical" (*The Rhetoric of Romanticism* [New York: Columbia University Press, 1984], p. 70).

68. Marc Shell points out that "what does matter in considering whether a coin is genuine or counterfeit is the issuing authority. A coin as money is counterfeit when the stated place of origin does not correspond to the actual place of origin. A counterfeit coin may claim to have and may actually have the same weight and purity as the legitimate coin of which it is the counterfeit. It is, however, treason for a private citizen to mint coins" (*Money, Language, and Thought,* p. 160).

Chapter 8: Wordsworth and the Reform of Copyright

1. *MY,* II, p. 844.

2. Mary Moorman, *William Wordsworth: A Biography. The Later Years, 1803–1850* (Oxford: Clarendon Press, 1965), p. 555.

3. Talfourd, a writer of some reputation among his contemporaries, wrote essays and plays and edited the papers of some of the Romantics. It was largely for Wordsworth's sake that Talfourd wanted to pass this measure, and in his enthusiasm he sometimes made himself into a mouthpiece for the poet he so admired; at moments his Parliamentary addresses sounded remarkably like the prefaces to Wordsworth's volumes of poetry. It was surely an unintentional irony that this defense of a writer's property in his own words should in its practice undermine the exclusiveness of that property.

4. William Wordsworth, "A Plea for Authors, May 1838" and "A Poet to His Grandchild." The latter is based on the bizarre fantasy of an orphan grandchild whose children will be doomed to a mysterious imbecility—an inability to understand the few Wordsworth poems they can still remember—unless the copyright laws are changed.

5. P. M. Zall, "Wordsworth and the Copyright Act of 1842," *PMLA* 70 (1955), 134.

6. *The Letters of William and Dorothy Wordsworth: The Later Years,* edited

by Ernest De Selincourt, revised by Alan G. Hill (Oxford: Oxford University Press, 1979), II, p. 225. Hereafter cited as *LY*.

7. *MY,* I, p. 266.

8. *LY,* II, p. 265.

9. *LY,* III, p. 576.

10. Moorman, *The Later Years,* p. 260.

11. "My aversion from publication increases every day, so much so, that no motives whatever, nothing but pecuniary necessity, will, I think, ever prevail upon me to commit myself to the press again," he wrote Cottle in 1799, to whom he complained also that Southey ought to have been more lenient toward a volume Wordsworth professed to have published "for money and money alone." See *EY,* p. 267.

12. This amount Cottle paid to Wordsworth and Coleridge jointly. The 1800 edition brought Wordsworth £100. See Harold Cox and John E. Chandler, *The House of Longman, 1724–1924; With a Record of Their Bicentenary Celebrations* (London: Longman, 1925), p. 16.

13. *MY,* II, p. 8.

14. Moorman, *Later Years,* 546.

15. *LY,* III, p. 536.

16. "Petition of Wm. Wordsworth, Esq.," in Thomas Noon Talfourd, *Three Speeches Delivered in the House of Commons in Favour of a Measure for an Extension of Copyright* (London: 1840), p. 112.

17. For a sense of what these sums meant, consider Thomas Moore, who earned £3000 for his *Lalla Rookh,* or Sir Walter Scott, who got £35,000 for *Woodstock* and *Napoleon* and could ask £5000 for the copyright of a work he had not yet begun to write. Perhaps the comparisons are unfair, but they do reveal the comparative moderation of Wordsworth's demands—or at least the moderation of his power to have his demands met. See Lee Erickson, "The Poets' Corner: The Impact of Technological Changes in Printing on English Poetry, 1800–1850," *ELH* 52 (1985), 894–95, and Eric Quayle, *The Ruin of Sir Walter Scott* (London: Rupert Hart-Davis, 1968), pp. 60, 233–34.

18. In a letter to his daughter, Wordsworth appears to admit that he knows his efforts are out of proportion to what he might expect to gain by their success. See *LY,* II, p. 921.

19. See *LY,* III, p. 366. To the objections his opponents raised against the extension of copyright—that it would create monopolies, encourage inventors of mechanical devices to agitate for extensions of their patents, drive up book prices, and impair the availability of certain works—Wordsworth makes only the most cursory responses. The growth of the reading public, he wrote, would ensure that holders of copyright would keep the prices of their books low and the supplies large, "consequently the apprehension of a prolonged privilege being injurious to the people is entitled to little or no regard" (in Talfourd, *Three Speeches,* p. 114.)

20. In Talfourd, *Three Speeches,* p. 112.

21. Ibid., p. 114.

22. A monument served as a supplementary voice or a stone tongue; it was necessary only to him whose life was mute or abbreviated. And Burns had already

a sufficiency of memorials. "Of the pre-Romantic writers, Burns, with thirty-five specimens, is the most prolific epitaphist," notes Ernest Bernhardt-Kabisch ("The Epitaph and the Romantic Poets: A Survey," *Huntington Library Quarterly* 30 (1967), 114).

23. *MY,* II, pp. 535–36. Two decades later Wordsworth denied a similar request for a contribution toward a memorial for Shakespeare in rather different terms, saying it was less necessary to make memorials for the dead than to do justice by the living (*Some Letters of the Wordsworth Family Now First Published With a Few Unpublished Letters of Coleridge and Southey and Others,* edited by Leslie Nathan Broughton [Ithaca: Cornell University Press, 1942], p. 79).

24. Thomas Weiskel, *The Romantic Sublime: Studies in the Structure and Psychology of Transcendence* (Baltimore: The Johns Hopkins University Press, 1976), p. 59.

25. On this problem see J. Hillis Miller, "The Stone and the Shell: The Problem of Poetic Form in Wordsworth's Dream of the Arab," in *Mouvements Premiers: Etudes critiques offertes a Georges Poulet* (Paris: Librairie Jose Corti, 1972), pp. 125–47; Weiskel, pp. 175, 186, 192; Cynthia Chase, *Decomposing Figures: Rhetorical Readings in the Romantic Tradition* (Baltimore: The Johns Hopkins University Press, 1986), esp. "The Accidents of Disfiguration"; and Andrzej Warminski, "Facing Wordsworth's First Poetic Spirits," *Diacritics* 17:4 (1987), 18–31.

26. Geoffrey Hartman has made us aware that Wordsworth's genius is often associated with a *genius loci.* Although Wordsworth had usually no legal title to these *loci,* his poems (such as the place-naming poems) often read like fanciful deeds of title, documents in which the poet claims the land or the land claims the poet. For Hartman's discussion of *genii,* see "Romantic Poetry and the Genius Loci" and "Wordsworth, Inscriptions, and Romantic Nature Poetry" in *Beyond Formalism: Literary Essays 1958–1970* (New Haven: Yale University Press, 1970), esp. pp. 212–213 and 329–30.

27. David Simpson observes, "Poetry was for him a *form* of property indeed, but an especially insecure one in the years before the establishment of comprehensive copyright laws. . . . *Lyrical Ballads* . . . was neither wholly Wordsworth's, nor did it place his name before a potentially validating public. Neither poetry nor the self that produced it were adequately individuated; Wordsworth had no true freehold upon his work, and no sense of a consolidated selfhood from which such 'freehold' might have emanated. The copyright of *Lyrical Ballads* had been sold, first to Cottle and then, for the second edition, to Longman. The 'work' that Wordsworth had done was in this further sense not properly his own, so that it is hardly surprising that his poetry should have concerned itself so forcefully with over-strenuous images of individualism" (*Wordsworth's Historical Imagination: The Poetry of Displacement* [New York: Methuen, 1987], p. 49).

28. *Prose Works,* I, p. 132.

29. As Frances Ferguson has pointed out, Wordsworth seemed to see the epitaph as the original or essential form of poetry. See her *Wordsworth: Language as Counter-Spirit* (New Haven: Yale University Press, 1977), p. 29.

30. Quoted in *Prose Works,* III, p. 317.

31. See, for example, *WPW,* II, p. 513, and *Prose Works,* III, p. 77.

32. On writing as physical labor see, for example, *EY,* pp. 339–40.

33. De Quincey, *Recollections of the Lakes and the Lake Poets,* edited by David Wright (Harmondsworth, England: Penguin Books, 1970), p. 217.

34. Paul de Man, "International Structure of the Romantic Image," in *The Rhetoric of Romanticism* (New York: Columbia University Press, 1984), p. 7.

35. Geoffrey Durrant, "Wordsworth and the Poetry of Objects," *Mosaic* 5:1 (1971), 108; Robert F. Gleckner, "Romanticism and the Self-Annihilation of Language," *Criticism* 18 (1976), 176; Thomas McFarland, "Creative Fantasy and Matter-of-Fact Reality in Wordsworth's Poetry," *JEGP* 75 (1976), 4; Weiskel, *The Romantic Sublime,* p. 185.

36. For Hartman, its matter-of-factness is partly the effect of mournful hallucination; the poetry memorializes not things but "ghostly" words. See Geoffrey H. Hartman, "A Touching Compulsion: Wordsworth and the Problem of Literary Representation," *Georgia Review* 31 (1977), 357, 358, 360, 361.

37. Maurice Blanchot, *The Gaze of Orpheus,* translated by Lydia Davis (Barrytown, NY: Station Hill Press, 1981), p. 47.

38. Hartley Coleridge presented himself rather as an unfortunate orphan than an independent author. Most writers stayed out of the wrangling or, at most, allowed their names to be used in petitions drafted by others. Harriet Martineau, Robert Browning, Leigh Hunt, Charles Dickens, Mary Russell Mitford, Samuel Rogers, and Joanna Baillie were among those who signed petitions on behalf of English authors.

39. Typical was Archibald Alison, who based his plea upon simple arithmetic. Alison calculated that by the time he finished his history of Europe during the French Revolution he would have spent £4000 on research, an expenditure that he expected he would need the full term of copyright to recover. He reckoned the copyright would have to last thirty or forty years before it became "a property of great value" to his family. See Talfourd, *Three Speeches,* pp. 115–17.

40. *Prose Works,* III, p. 313.

41. A helpful discussion of the history of English copyright through the eighteenth century can be found in Lyman Ray Patterson, *Copyright in Historical Perspective* (Nashville: Vanderbilt University Press, 1968). See also Mark Rose, "The Author as Proprietor: *Donaldson v. Becket* and the Genealogy of Modern Authorship," *Representations* 23 (Summer 1988), pp. 51–85.

42. Perhaps coincidentally, about the same time as the longevity of their copyrights was threatened, booksellers took to selling patent medicines. See Marjorie Plant, *The English Book Trade: An Economic History of the Making and Sale of Books* (London: Allen & Unwin, 1939), p. 96.

43. Oddly enough, it was not only the advocates of perpetual copyright who participated in this mythmaking. Alexander Donaldson himself, principal challenger of the London booksellers and their monopolistic claims, allowed himself, in addressing *Some Thoughts on the State of Literary Property* (London: Alexander Donaldson 1764) to the public, to speak of an "author's rights of property" in his work as if those were the root of the controversy, and so did the judges who eventually decided in his favor. In practice, indeed, this particular authorial right still had little meaning except when exercised by a bookseller. Any work whose

copyright the author retained was liable not to be published, the booksellers customarily refusing to publish anything to which they could not secure the copyright and sometimes actively interfering with the sale of works whose copyrights were kept from them. But authors rarely tried to circumvent booksellers. In 1736 the Society for the Encouragement of Learning had been established to provide an alternative to the established booksellers: the society would support the costs of printing and reimburse itself from the profits of selling the book, while the author would retain the copyright. But the best-known authors of the day refused to have anything to do with with such a scheme, and after a few years of unrewarding and unremunerative work, the society disbanded. See A. S. Collins, *Authorship in the Days of Johnson: Being a Study of the Relation Between Author, Patron, Publisher and Public, 1726–1780* (London: Robert Holden & Co., 1927), pp. 20–21, 42–43.

44. "If the decision of the House of Lords had been detrimental to authors," Collins writes, "or had seemed to authors likely to prove so, there would surely have been some stir among them; instead of which, they were mostly silent, and when they spoke, seemed chiefly concerned for the booksellers with whom they were on terms of friendship and intimacy. . . . [T]he silence of writers is very marked in contrast with the vigorous pamphleteering of the booksellers" (Collins, pp. 109, 111).

45. Oliver Goldsmith was one of the few who cared enough to protest against the identification of his interests with the publishers': "The booksellers affect, in their petition, to espouse the interest of authors. Nothing can be more opposite to the interest of modern literature than the tenor of their request." See *Observations of the Late Dr. Goldsmith,* Petitions and Papers Relating to the Bill of the Booksellers, No. 7 (London: 1774; rpt. New York, 1975).

46. Moxon, Wordsworth's own publisher, was unusual in siding with the authors against his fellow publishers in this matter.

47. Wordsworth was no legal scholar. When he began working for copyright reform, he had not even read the law, and it is doubtful that he ever read the proceedings of the decisive 1774 cases. He seems to have acquired a usable knowledge of this, as of many other matters, through cultural osmosis.

48. This was an error those involved in the earlier debates had avoided. Everyone involved in the controversy was aware that in copyright they were dealing with a sort of ontological amphibian, an intangible property whose value lay in the power it gave its owner to produce tangible goods for sale. Because the right of exclusive propagation had to be kept distinct from rights in what was so propagated, because the ownership of a copyright was manifestly different from the ownership of a physical book, copyright came to signify the ownership of the intangible part of the book, its intellectual qualities.

49. "The Claims of Authors to an Extension of Copyright," *The Examiner,* 7 April 1839, No. 1627, p. 214.

50. *LY,* III, p. 572.

51. Ibid., p. 573.

52. *Prose Works,* III, p. 312.

53. J. Douglas Kneale, whose fine study of *The Prelude* is an extended meditation on the materiality of inscription and the dead letter, speaks of the usurpation of

writing upon voice in terms I would apply to Wordsworth's interest in seeing the materiality of his words guaranteed through copyright: "In such strength of usurpation, when voice becomes writing, Wordsworth's text acknowledges the passing from living voice to the dead letter but seeks to outlive this death through the epitaphic permanence of writing that aspires to the phonocentric immediacy of speech. The voice of Wordsworth's poetry is always the voice to be accomplished in writing." See *Monumental Writing: Aspects of Rhetoric in Wordsworth's Poetry* (Lincoln: University of Nebraska Press, 1988), p. 84.

54. What material being meant to Wordsworth is hard to know; the remarks that follow these undo all our certainty about the difference between the corporeal and the immaterial: "With a feeling congenial to this, I was often unable to think of external things as having external existence, and I communed with all that I saw as something not apart from, but inherent in, my own immaterial nature" (*The Prose Works of William Wordsworth,* edited by Alexander B. Grosart, 3 vols. [1876; rpt. New York: AMS Press, 1967], Vol. 3, p. 194.)

55. Talfourd, *Three Speeches,* p. 143.

56. Or second second self, perhaps. One may wonder whether the death of Coleridge in 1834—for so long Wordsworth's primary second self—had anything to do with the magnitude of passion, amounting almost to desperation, that Wordsworth brought to the cause of copyright reform in the later 1830s.

57. In Talfourd, *Three Speeches,* pp. 111–12.

58. Ibid., p. 114.

59. Jacques Derrida, "Living On: Border Lines," in *Deconstruction and Criticism,* edited by Harold Bloom et al. (New York: Seabury Press, 1979), p. 124n.

60. Wordsworth to Richard Sharp, 29 April 1804, in *EY,* p. 470.

61. 6 March 1804, *EY,* p. 454.

62. 29 April 1804, *EY,* p. 470.

63. *LY,* III, p. 680.

64. Letter to Henry Taylor, 29 June 1838, quoted in *William Wordsworth: The Prelude 1799, 1805, 1850,* edited by Jonathan Wordsworth, M. H. Abrams, and Stephen Gill (New York: Norton, 1979), p. 536.

65. So J. Douglas Kneale, who regards *The Prelude,* "the letter [that] kills," as usurping upon Wordsworth's life; in Kneale's view, this usurpation precludes the possibility of immortality. See *Monumental Writing,* p. 146.

66. Quoted in *William Wordsworth: The Prelude,* p. 539.

67. Sigmund Freud, "The Uncanny," *The Standard Edition of the Complete Psychological Works of Sigmund Freud,* edited and translated by James Strachey (London: Hogarth Press, 1955), vol. 17, p. 235.

68. Blanchot, *The Gaze of Orpheus,* p. 83.

69. On Wordsworth and inscription, see Hartman, *Beyond Formalism* pp. 208, 221.

70. *Prose Works,* II, p. 49.

71. Ibid., 76.

72. Ibid., 84.

73. According to Stephen K. Land, Wordsworth uses the analogy in full awareness of what it implies. "Wordsworth often seems to consider language as something

of a necessary evil. . . . [J]ust as the soul is essentially other than the body so thought is essentially independent of language." See "The Silent Poet: An Aspect of Wordsworth's Semantic Theory," *University of Toronto Quarterly* 42 (1973), 163.

74. *Prose Works,* II, p. 53.

75. Wordsworth warned the versemaker to eschew unnecessary details, to present the character of the deceased as through a kindly mist (Grosart, *Prose Works,* Vol. 2, p. 58); the physical conditions of the inscription will ensure the erasure of detail, will ensure that the writing itself will soon blur.

76. Paul H. Fry, "The Absent Dead: Wordsworth, Byron, and the Epitaph," *Studies in Romanticism* 17 (1978), 419. See also Ferguson, *Language as Counter-Spirit,* p. 29.

77. *Prose Works,* III, p. 313.

Conclusion

1. My description of the imagination's resistance to naming follows in ways I hope are evident from what Harold Bloom, Geoffrey Hartman, and Thomas Weiskel have taught us about the tonic effects the Romantics discovered in error, blockage, and misreading.

Index